A Case for Conservatism

A Case for Conservatism

JOHN KEKES

Cornell University Press

ITHACA AND LONDON

First published 1998 by Cornell University Press

Printed in the United States of America

Library of Congress Cataloging-in-Publication Data

Kekes, John.
    A case for conservatism / John Kekes.
      p. cm.
    Companion to the author's Against liberalism.
    Includes bibliographical references and index.
    ISBN 0-8014-3556-0 (alk. paper).
    1. Conservatism. 2. Conservatism—Moral and ethical aspects. I. Kekes, John. Against liberalism. II. Title.
JC573.K44   1998
32.52—dc21   98-8358

Cloth printing   10 9 8 7 6 5 4 3 2 1

for
J.Y.K.
again and always

Contents

Preface

Since the end of the Second World War, popularly elected conservative governments have for many years held office in most of the industrialized democracies. In all such countries, conservatives, whether in office or out of it, have formed one of the major political parties. Elections have often turned on the acceptance or rejection of readily identifiable conservative policies. The same is true of liberal and socialist governments, parties, and policies. The fact is, however, that while reasoned and morally committed defenses of liberal and socialist policies abound, there is a dearth of similar defenses of conservative policies. The resulting impression is that the electoral victories of liberals or socialists were triumphs of reason and morality, but that conservative victories signified the sway of passion over reason and of self-interest over morality.

Part of the explanation of this false impression is that most of those whose business it is to reflect on, rather than engage in, practical politics—academics, authors, journalists, newscasters, and pundits—have been liberals or socialists. But conservatives are also responsible for this false impression, because the voice of reasonable and morally committed conservatives is not much heard. And even when it is heard, it usually takes the form of reacting to liberal or socialist policies, rather than proposing constructive alternatives to them.

The aim of this book is to try to change this state of affairs. There is not a great deal that a single book is likely to accomplish. But perhaps it will show that conservatives need not be silent, unreasonable, or callous, and perhaps conservatives will be encouraged by it to contribute more to reflection on practical politics in the future than they have done in the past. That, in any case, is the hope that has motivated the writing of this book.

ix

Conservatism is like liberalism and socialism in having several different versions. Conservatives disagree with each other about basic questions, just as liberals and socialists do. It is, therefore, especially important to make clear at the beginning that the present work aims to develop and defend a particular version of conservatism. In order to avoid pedantry and verbosity, this version will be referred to throughout the book as "conservatism." The reader should understand, however, that there are other versions and that there are conservatives who do not accept the version that will be put forward here.

This book has a companion in the author's *Against Liberalism,* published by Cornell University Press in 1997. That work was mainly critical of the major contemporary rival of conservatism; the present one is mainly constructive in championing an alternative approach. Although the two works complement each other, they are intended to stand independently.

Portions of the book make use of previously published material. Chapter 2 is based on "What is Conservatism?" *Philosophy,* 72 (1997), pp. 351–374; Chapter 6 incorporates parts of "Moral Conventionalism," *American Philosophical Quarterly,* 22 (1985), pp. 37–46, and "Moral Intuition," *American Philosophical Quarterly,* 23 (1986), pp. 83–93; and Chapter 8 partly overlaps with Chapter 6 of *Against Liberalism* (Ithaca: Cornell University Press, 1997).

James Gouinlock, Wallace Matson, and Evan Simpson read the penultimate version of the manuscript and provided extremely helpful criticisms which led to numerous improvements. Eric Fried and Anthony O'Hear did likewise with portions of the manuscript. Their help is gratefully acknowledged. The transformation of the manuscript into a book was guided by Roger Haydon. His outstanding efficiency, good will, and sympathy for views that are not his own make him come as close to the Platonic ideal of an Editor as the imperfections of the real world allow.

The author welcomes communications from readers regarding the book; they should be sent to: jkekes@csc.albany.edu.

ITHAKA   John Kekes
Charlton,
New York

A Case for Conservatism

Introduction

The aim of this book is to convince reasonable and morally committed people that good lives are more likely to be lived under conservative political arrangements than under any other alternatives currently available. Conservatism is a political morality. It is political because it concerns the political arrangements that make a society good; and it is moral because it holds that the goodness of a society depends on the goodness of the lives of the people who live in it.

Conservatism has different versions because its advocates disagree about what political arrangements would make a society good. There is, however, no disagreement about having to find the right political arrangements by means of reflection on the history of the society whose arrangements they are. Some of these arrangements have proved to be conducive and others detrimental to good lives. Conservatives aim to conserve the former and reform the latter. The conservative attitude, therefore, is not indiscriminate prejudice in favor of traditional arrangements, but a reasonable and reflective defense of traditional arrangements that have stood the test of time.

One distinctive feature of the conservatism defended here is its commitment to four basic beliefs: skepticism, pluralism, traditionalism, and pessimism. These beliefs are not theoretical constructs invented as external standards for evaluating political arrangements. They are constitutive features of the arrangements themselves, features that partly explain why the arrangements have been conducive to good lives. The beliefs are extracted from political arrangements rather than imposed on them as conclusions derived from some philosophical, political, or moral theory.

Another distinctive feature of conservatism is its insistence that any

1

adequate political morality must have three levels: universal, social, and individual. A good society requires the protection of possibilities and limits on each of these levels. The possibilities are conditions necessary for good lives; the limits prohibit the violation of these conditions. Some of these possibilities and limits are universal, because there are some conditions all good lives require, no matter how they are conceived; others are social, because there are some conditions that all good lives require within the context of a particular society, although these conditions usually vary from society to society; and yet others are individual because they are required only by particular conceptions of a good life, and they vary with these conceptions. Each good life, therefore, has universal, social, and individual requirements, and conservatives believe that the aim of political morality is to make political arrangements that protect these requirements on all three levels.

Political moralities must be concerned both with approximating the good and with avoiding evil. The first involves stressing possibilities; the second limits. The first is the constructive contribution of political arrangements that enable individuals to make good lives for themselves. It is on this that all the main contemporary rivals of conservatism concentrate. They differ from each other only because they differ about how the good is to be approximated. It is yet a further distinctive feature of conservatism that it attributes equal importance to avoiding evil by setting limits. A good society must prohibit certain ways of living and acting. What these ways are depends on the universal, social, and individual requirements of good lives as they are historically conceived in the political morality of a particular society. How reasonable these historical conceptions are partly depends on the extent to which they reflect the fundamental importance of the basic conservatives beliefs of skepticism, pluralism, traditionalism, and pessimism.

It has been said by both defenders and critics of conservatism that it is not a position that lends itself to a systematic statement and defense. Some main reasons adduced in support of this view have been that conservatism is not theoretical but practical, and a practical activity cannot be fully systematized; that conservatism is merely opposition to ill-conceived changes in political arrangements, so it has no substantive content that could be systematized; and that conservatism is a reaction to ideological politics, thus it would be inconsistent to systematize it, since that would make conservatism just another instance of that very ideological approach that it is meant to oppose. There is something to be said for each of these claims. On balance, however, they are all mistaken because conservatism can be systematically stated and defended. The best argument in support of this view is to state and defend it systematically, and that is what will be done in the chapters that follow.

These introductory remarks about the structure of the argument are intended to make evident that the present work differs from most others about conservatism. It is not about the history of conservatism;[1] it is not a description of the thought of various contemporary conservatives;[2] it is not centrally concerned with practical conservative politics,[3] although of course it has significant implications for it; it is not an attempt to present a certain temperament that inclines people to adopt a conservative position;[4] it is not a mere survey of some central conservative values, ideals, doctrines, or principles;[5] and it is not a critical reflection on the present state of society from a conservative point of view.[6] It is rather an attempt to articulate the basic beliefs of conservatism, show that they are true, and defend them against criticism. Past and present conservative thought, various psychological dispositions, and the exigencies of the prevailing political situation all have a bearing on the case to be made. But their bearing is secondary and derivative. The primary concern of the argument is with making a case for conservatism.[7] That case has been deeply influenced by the political ideas of Aristotle, David Hume, and Michael Oakeshott, but the book is not a study of their thoughts. Indeed, these illustrious figures are rarely mentioned.

Many readers of a book on political morality expect to be given a number of specific policies, which, if adopted, would, in the author's opinion, make the readers' society better. This expectation will not be met by the present work. Before reasonable policies could be proposed it is necessary to formulate and defend the basic beliefs from which they could follow. And that is the aim of the present work. This is not to say that the proposal of specific policies is of secondary importance. On the contrary, adequate political moralities must be centrally concerned with making policy recommendations. But not everything can be done at once. This book is about the presuppositions of policies; the policies themselves will be the subject of a future work.

It is a characteristically conservative belief that in moral and political thought there is not much scope for novelty and originality. The fundamental nature of good and evil are well known because they are established by enduring features of the world, societies, and human beings. There is little need for research here and the prospects for new discoveries are dim. Most personal and political experiments in living are re-arrangements and re-adjustments of familiar elements. If political arrangements are detrimental to good lives, it is not because of ignorance of good and evil. It is because knowledge of them is obscured by other considerations, or because there is disagreement about how that knowledge bears on changing historical circumstances, or because people prefer evil to good.

The case to be made for conservatism does not therefore consist in proposing a new theory. It rather has the form of reminding readers of what they already know, but perhaps tend to forget under the endlessly repeated liberal and socialist rhetoric that echoes the prevailing political orthodoxy. These reminders point to the conclusion that if conservatism is rightly understood, it will be seen as the best approach to a good society, one that protects the political arrangements under which good lives can be lived.

The Conservative Attitude

> If we take the widest and wisest view of a Cause, there is no such thing as a Lost Cause because there is no such thing as a Gained Cause . . . we fight rather to keep something alive than in the the expectation that anything will triumph.
>
> —T.S. ELIOT, *"Francis Herbert Bradley"*

The source of conservatism is a natural attitude that combines the enjoyment of something valued with the fear of losing it. If there were beings who did not enjoy having what they valued and were not afraid of losing it, they would not be recognizably human. And if there were human beings like that, it would have to be explained what special circumstances (such as low intelligence or trauma) are responsible for their indifference. The attitude then is basic to human psychology, but it need not be conscious or articulate. If the enjoyment is smooth and unhampered and if nothing immediate seems to threaten it, there is no reason why people should be aware of having it. Their attitude will then be like their attitude to using their limbs or speaking their mother tongue. Conservatives can appeal to this basic attitude—to natural conservatism—and realistically hope to be understood. Natural conservatism values and aims to protect the tried and true; both together, because the tried alone may have little in its favor and much against it and because the true needs to be tried, and tried again, to be shown to be indeed true.

Natural conservatism, of course, is only one basic attitude that people have. Curiosity, love of adventure, the challenge of limits are some of many others. Societies or individuals may reasonably give prominence in different circumstances to one or another of these, as well as numerous other, basic attitudes. It is reasonable to give prominence to the conservative one if the tried and true conditions of good lives are threatened. For then they have to be protected. That requires, however, recognizing the threat, understanding its nature, finding ways to fend it off, and choosing the best way. Natural conservatism must become reflective in the face of such threats.

Natural conservatism, then, has its source in the unreflective enjoyment of conditions necessary for living a good life and in the desire to protect them if threatened. If the threat is present, then natural conservatism must be transformed into a reflective one that can meet it. To understand conservatism, it is necessary therefore to understand the nature of the enjoyment, fear, and reflection that create the underlying attitude.[1]

NATURAL CONSERVATISM

That being alive is on balance both good and difficult will be generally conceded. There were times and places in history when and where the good was quite good and coping with the difficulties left enough energy for more than a few especially fortunate people to enjoy their lives. Periclean Athens, Augustan Rome, Renaissance Florence, Elizabethan England, France of Louis XIV, England again as she emerged from the Napoleonic wars, and, dare one say, America after World War Two were such times and places. It was good to be alive not just for a privileged few, but also for a substantial number of ordinary people living ordinary lives. There was order, security, prosperity, and a not baseless hope that the future will be better than the past. The rulers did not rule too badly, especially in comparison with those of neighboring societies, and the ruled could get on with their lives without too much interference. There was, of course, the timeless fabric of human existence, birth, copulation, and death, to which may be added, less euphonically, maturing and aging, work and leisure, fortune and misfortune, duty and pleasure, necessity and luxury, and so on. The times were quite good because this unavoidable substratum was civilized by the existence of traditional ways of responding to the human condition. These ways provided time-honored forms of enjoying life if it was going well, accommodating misfortune if it befell one, coping with private or public crises if they occurred, and answering questions if they were asked about the meaning and value of all the hustle and bustle that living unavoidably involves. These traditional ways did not make everybody's life good, but they made it clear what would make a life good and they made it possible for many people to achieve it.

Consider now the position of people living at such a time and enjoying its benefits. One salient fact about them is that they have something to lose, something they want very much to keep. They want their lives to continue without substantial changes. They like the familiar and prefer it to the strange and the experimental, not because they lack wholeheartedness or verve, but because they enjoy what they have. They find the familiar good for the best of all reasons: it makes their lives good. Why should they take risks if winning would bring only meager rewards and losing would endanger what they have excellent reasons for valuing? People in this position will have one of the two motives for being natural conservatives.

Michael Oakeshott describes this motivation as the "propensity to use and enjoy what is available rather than wish for or to look for something else; to delight in what is present rather than what was or what may be. Reflection may bring to light an appropriate gratefulness for what is available, and consequently the acknowledgment of a gift or an inheritance from the past; but there is no mere idolizing of what is past and gone. What is esteemed is the present. . . . [I]t is a disposition appropriate to a man who is acutely aware of having something to lose which he has learned to care for; a man in some degree rich in opportunities for enjoyment, but not so much that he can be indifferent to loss. . . . To be conservative, then, is to prefer the familiar to the unknown, to prefer the tried to the untried, fact to mystery, the actual to the possible, the limited to the unbounded, the near to the distant, the sufficient to the superabundant, the convenient to the perfect, present laughter to utopian bliss."[2]

It must be added at once that the good times in history in which such a motivation is appropriate are rare and when they happen a substantial number of people do not enjoy its benefits. Even if natural conservatism were an understandable, and perhaps reasonable, attitude for those who are fortunate enough to live at such times and to benefit from them, many people would still have good reasons for wanting to change some of the prevailing conditions. These reasons, however, need not make it unreasonable for them to be natural conservatives.

To begin with, while good times in history are certainly rare, not-so-bad times are less so. There are and have been numerous stable societies in which there was adequate, although flawed, order, security, prosperity, and hope of a better future to enable a considerable segment of the population to live tolerably well. It is true that some of the prevailing conditions presented real obstacles, but it was not out of the question to circumvent them, and many people have succeeded in doing so. This was the case in Victorian England, nineteenth-century America, Wilhelmine Germany, fin-de-siecle France, and throughout much of the recent history of most prosperous Western industrialized countries, such as Canada, Denmark, Italy, Sweden, and Switzerland to mention only some of the smaller examples. To be sure, there were and are many conditions in all of these not-so-bad societies that reasonable people would want to change. But they exist alongside conditions that it is reasonable to want to protect. Natural conservatism is not an indiscriminate endorsement of all the prevailing conditions in one's society, but only of those that make lives better.

Moreover, it is reasonable to want to protect the conditions of good lives not only for those who benefit from them, but also for those who do not. For how else could lives that are bad be changed for the better if not by extending the favorable conditions to those who hitherto have not benefited from them? That, however, requires the protection of those conditions. Natural conservatism is a reasonable attitude, therefore, not only for those who enjoy their lives, but also for those who hope to enjoy them in the future. Natural conservatives, furthermore, will be motivated not merely to protect the conditions that make their enjoyment of life possible, but also to extend them to others in their society. For the more people there are with little to lose, the more they will threaten the very conditions on which present and future good lives depend.

This attitude will seem to be callously sanguine to all those critics who are outraged by the misfortunes of the people in their society who have not benefited from the prevailing arrangements. These critics point at poverty, discrimination, and injustice, and they blame their society for accepting them. In this, the critics show bad judgment. They are right, of course, in there being ills in their society. They are wrong, however, in not seeing also that the ills affect, in contemporary Western societies, perhaps 10 to 20 percent of the population, and that the other 80 to 90 percent are enabled by the prevailing arrangements to live good lives. It is a great and historically rare achievement to guarantee this possibility for such a large proportion of the people in a society. Naturally, it would be better still if everyone could benefit from it, and naturally again a society ought to aim at diminishing misfortune and increasing the ranks of the fortunate. But to judge a society on the basis of the minority who have not benefited from its arrangements, while ignoring the large majority who have benefited from them, is to be guilty of an unreasonable prejudice. This prejudice leads to denigrating great achievements just because they are not greater still.

Is there then no context in which natural conservatism would be an inappropriate attitude? Of course there is: the bad times in history. These are the times in which the prevailing conditions are so wretched, the enjoyment of life is restricted to so few, and the prospects of a better future are so poor for so many people that drastic change is called for. At these times, it is reasonable to take risks, as it was in Nazi Germany and Stalinist Russia. As the history of revolutions shows, however, taking risks can lead to loss. Drastic changes can make a bad state of affairs even worse, as they have done in Russia in 1917 and in Iran in 1979.

How to apportion history among the quite good, not-so-bad, and outright bad times is a difficult question that need not be discussed here. But it is the simple truth that even at the best of times there are serious threats that endanger the conditions of good lives; that in not-so-bad times some of these conditions are being compromised; and that in bad times their defense has failed and the conditions have been or are being destroyed. At all times, therefore, it is reasonable to fear these threats. This fear is the second component of natural conservatism. As its first component, the enjoyment of these conditions, concentrates on the bright side of life, and motivates reasonable people by focusing on what is good, so its second component, the fear of what threatens these conditions, calls attention to the darker side of existence, and prompts reasonable people to resist evil.

It is not an exaggeration to speak of evil here. Evil is the most severe condemnation that our moral vocabulary affords, and it should not be used lightly. But it is appropriate to use it to condemn the violation of the conditions of good lives. For what is at stake are not luxuries that add spice to life—chamber music, golf, and air conditioning—but necessities without which no life can be good. The conditions are of a civilized existence in which there are rules that prohibit destructive conduct, provide ways of adjudicating conflicts, assign responsibility for the production of basic goods, and maintain the means to their own enforcement. Such rules are essential to order, security, prosperity, and hope, and they are conditions of good lives, no matter how differently they are conceived. When the rules hold, civilized life is possible; when they do not, barbarism looms—a state in which anything goes because nothing is prohibited or required.

One need not go farther than recent history to find occasions when the conditions of civilized life were crumbling. Stalin's murderous campaign against the kulaks, Hitler's against the Jews, the Red Guards that Mao unleashed on China, the mass murders inflicted by Pol Pot on Cambodia, the ethnic cleansing in what used to be Yugoslavia, the transformation of Iran into a Shiite state, the Uganda of Idi Amin, the countless left and right-wing regimes maintained through systematic, large-scale torture and the destruction of people deemed undesirable, the civil wars in Afghanistan, Algeria, Angola, Lebanon, Northern Ireland, Rwanda, and elsewhere are all vivid reminders that it is accurate to speak of evil in describing them.

Czeslaw Milosz's depiction of this state of affairs is but one of many harrowing accounts. "Man tends to regard the order he lives in as natural. . . . His first stroll along a street littered with glass from bomb-scarred windows shakes his faith in the "naturalness" of his world. The wind scatters papers from hastily evacuated offices, papers labeled "Confidential" or "Top Secret" that evoke visions of safes, keys, conferences, couriers, and secretaries. Now the wind blows them through the street for anyone to read; yet no one does, for each man is urgently concerned with finding a loaf of bread. Strangely enough, the world goes on even though the offices and secrets have lost all meaning. Farther down the street, he stops before a house split in half by a bomb, the privacy of people's homes—the family smells, the warmth of the beehive life, the furniture preserving the memory of loves and hatreds—cut open to the public view . . . on the third floor a solitary white bathtub, rain-rinsed of all recollection of those who once bathed in it. Its formerly influential and respected owners, now destitute, walk the fields in search of stray potatoes. Thus overnight money loses its value and becomes a meaning-less mass of printed paper. His walk takes him past a little boy poking a stick into a heap of smoking ruins whistling a song about a great leader who will preserve the nation against all enemies. The song remains, but the leader of yesterday is already part of an extinct past. He finds that he acquires habits quickly. Once, if he had stumbled upon a corpse on the street, he would have called the police. A crowd would have gathered, and much talk and comment would have ensued. Now he knows that he must avoid the dark body lying in the gutter, and refrain from asking un-necessary questions. . . . A man passing that corner meets a leveled rifle, raises his hand, is pushed into a van, and from that moment is lost to his family and friends. He may be sent to a concentration camp, or he may face a firing squad, his lips sealed with plaster lest he cry out against the state; but, in any case, he serves as a warning to his fellow-men. Perhaps one might escape such a fate by remaining at home. But the father of the family must go out in order to provide bread and soup for his wife and children; and every night they worry about whether or not he will return. Since these conditions last for years, everyone gradually comes to look upon the city as a jungle, and upon the faith of twentieth-century man as identical with that of a cave man living in the midst of powerful monsters."[3]

The effects of all this are not merely physical. Evil corrupts even those who are neither victims nor persecutors. Although advances in technol-ogy have made murder, torture, and terror much more efficient than they were in the clumsy days of the Crusades, Inquisition, witch hunts, slavery, and the brutal colonization of many peoples, still the millions that have fallen victims in modern times were but a minority in the soci-ety in which they were made to suffer. For large numbers of people, life goes on even in the midst of evil. But it is not to be supposed that these people are left unaffected by what is happening in their midst. They need to protect themselves, and since the rules are crumbling, it be-comes unclear how they can do so. If persecution is not for crimes, in-nocence is no protection. They cannot trust others because the traditional patterns have broken down. Neighbors, colleagues, acquain-tances, and even friends and family members grow suspicious of one an-other, suspicion breeds reciprocal suspicion, hostility increases, and it becomes impossible even for decent, well-intentioned people who have not done evil to live an ordinary life in the company of other ordinary people. The corrosive effects of the large-scale violation of the conditions of civilized life spread, leaving no acceptable choices to the vast majority of non-victims.

Olga Friedenberg in a letter to Boris Pasternak describes life in these circumstances. "Wherever you looked, in all our institutions, in all our homes, *skloka* was brewing. *Skloka* is a phenomenon born of our social order, an entirely new term and concept, not to be translated into any language of the civilized world. It is hard to define. It stands for base, trivial hostility, unconscionable spite breeding petty intrigues, the vicious pitting of one clique against another. It thrives on calumny, informing, spying, scheming, slander, the igniting of base passions. Taut nerves and weakening morals allow one individual or group rabidly to hate another individual or group. *Skloka* is natural for people who have been incited to attack one another, who have been made bestial by desperation, who have been driven to the wall." [4]

Natural conservatism then is a basic attitude that combines enjoyment and fear. The enjoyment is of the conditions that make life good and the fear is of the evil that threatens these conditions. It is a reasonable attitude for those whose lives are good and for those who hope to make their lives better, provided their society is not so bad as to systematically violate or fail to protect very many of the conditions of good lives.

The foregoing description of natural conservatism is no more than a reminder of what any thoughtful person knows anyway. That however is significant in itself because it strengthens the point that conservatism has a natural basis. Having made this point, it must now be said that the work of explaining and making a case for conservatism has barely begun. Even if natural conservatism is a reasonable and basic attitude for many people in many contexts, it is by no means the only one. Reasonable basic attitudes often conflict, and nothing has been said yet about why natural conservatism should prevail over those that are incompatible with it. Moreover, although there are also many reasonable basic attitudes that do not conflict with one another, the economy of life still requires imposing a hierarchy of importance on them. It must be explained why natural conservatism should be ranked high in importance among basic attitudes.

A further problem is that it is one thing to have an attitude and quite another to express it effectively. Enjoyment and fear may be appropriate, but making the enjoyment last and coping with the threat that is rightly feared inevitably take one beyond the basic attitude. And enjoyment and fear may be inappropriate. Perhaps what is enjoyed should not be because it is a mistake to regard it as a condition of a good life. Or, if it is a condition, that kind of life ought not to be regarded as good. Perhaps the fear is too much or too little because the threat to which it is a response is misjudged. Natural attitudes are unreflective, uninformed, and liable to go wrong in countless ways. That is why they need to be controlled by reflection. And that is why natural conservatism must be transformed and made reflective.

Of the multitude of conditions of good lives, reflective conservatism concentrates on those that can be best secured by political arrangements. Not all conditions can be so secured, and not all that can be ought to be, because there are areas of life that should be left to the discretion of individuals. Reflective conservatism, therefore, is not an ambitious view about the nature of good lives, but a much more modest view about the political conditions that make good lives possible. Its aim is to identify, maintain, and protect the arrangements that secure these conditions. All decent and reasonable political moralities share this aim and acknowledge reflection as an indispensable means to it. What distinguishes reflective conservatism from them is the starting point, the mode, and the aim of the reflection it favors.

THE STARTING POINT OF CONSERVATIVE REFLECTION

Unlike enjoyment and fear, reflection does not occur spontaneously. Conservatives see no need to reflect on political arrangements if they are agreed to be in good order. It is best then to leave them alone. Reflection is needed if some the political arrangements are thought to have gone awry. Among the signs of this are that it is widely suspected that the arrangements fail to serve their purpose, that many people are dissatisfied with them, that they chafe under the requirements for maintaining them, and that they actively resist or passively resent their enforcement. These doubts lead to conflicts between the arrangements and the people who are subject to them. The reflection of conservatives is prompted by these conflicts.

Its origin makes the subsequent reflection concrete and practical, rather than abstract and theoretical, because its aim is to cope with the conflict that prompted it; local, rather than global, because the conflict concerns the political arrangements of the conservative's own society; and corrective, rather than innovative, because the object of the reflection is to correct either the arrangements or the perception of them that give rise to the conflict. This is not to say that conservatives cannot avail themselves of the resources of theorizing, that their views never have implications beyond the context of their society, or that they must always eschew innovation. The proper understanding of conservative reflection is that it begins with a concrete, practical, local, and corrective approach to coping with specific conflicts, and it requires persuasive reasons to turn to abstract theory, global concerns, and innovation.

As Karl Popper put it: these arrangements "have the important double function of not only creating a certain order . . . but also giving us something . . . that we can criticize and change. . . . Too many social reformers have an idea that they would like to clean the canvas . . . of the social world, wiping off everything and starting from scratch. . . . This idea is nonsense and impossible to realize. . . . If we wipe out the social world in which we live, wipe out its traditions and create a new world on the basis of blue-prints, then we shall very soon have to alter the new world, making little changes and adjustments. But if we are to make these little changes and adjustments, which will be needed in any case, why not start from here and now in the social world we have? It does not matter what you have and where you start. You always have to make little adjustments. Since you always have to make them, it is very much more sensible and reasonable to start with what happens to exist at the moment, because of these things we at least know where the shoe pinches. We at least know of certain things that they are bad and that we want them changed."[5]

This starting point is not so obvious as to be not worth mentioning. One's starting point affects one's destination and much political reflection starts quite differently. Some liberals start with a contract that rational and self-interested agents would supposedly arrive at in a hypothetical situation, and evaluate political arrangements on the basis of how closely they conform to the terms of the supposed contract. Utilitarian liberals start with some ideal of individual or collective welfare, and aim to change political arrangements so as to be better means to the achievement of their ideal. Socialists start with the desirability of a classless or egalitarian society, and criticize the prevailing arrangements for failing to conform to what they regard as most worth having. Revolutionaries and terrorists start with the goal of destroying the existing arrangements because they regard them as evil. Romantics and reactionaries start with some idyllic Golden Age in the past, and they see the present as a corrupt falling away from it. In starting thus, all these opponents of conservatism begin with a presumption against the existing political arrangements. And they will take themselves to have arrived at their destination if they succeed in transforming these arrangements into what they think they ought to be. Conservatives differ from them because they start with a presumption in favor of the existing political arrangements, unless they are incorrigibly evil, and they aim to correct them only to the extent that coping with the conflicts makes necessary.

Conservatives start with this presumption because they take the endurance of the traditional arrangements of quite good and not-so-bad societies to be a strong initial reason for supporting them, and because they think that the arrangements are unlikely to have endured unless they helped those subject to them to live good lives. This initial reason may be overridden if it is found on further reflection that the arrangements contributed to good lives only negligibly or that there are stronger reasons in favor of other ways of trying to make lives better. It is also true, of course, that the traditional arrangements of bad societies are so wretched as to exclude any presumption in their favor. In which case, conservatives will not be even initially disposed to support them.

The widespread rejection of the conservative starting point creates a climate of opinion that plays a significant role in the prevailing hostility toward conservatism. There is all the difference between starting with a presumption in favor of the existing political arrangements and starting with a presumption against them. The arrangements are often faulty, hard and costly to maintain, and interfere with people's doing as they please. Conservatives see, however, that it is in the nature of political arrangements that they make people feel put upon and that this feeling is not a sufficient reason against having them. Good reasons for some of them can be found, the hardships involved in maintaining some of them need to be borne, and their imperfections may be made tolerable by the alternatives' being much worse. In the minds of their opponents, the hardships and the imperfections are uppermost because their political vision is colored by some ideal compared to which they find the existing arrangements grossly defective.

There are some thoroughly bad societies in which this anti-conservative attitude may be reasonable. But those who start political reflection with a presumption against their own society do not restrict their attitude to bad societies. They hold it generally. By doing so, they fail to see that it is the allegiance of large numbers of their fellow citizens to the arrangements of their society that makes these arrangements traditional, and that their allegiance may not be a mark of indoctrination, cynicism, or indifference, but an indication that they favor the traditional arrangements because they help them to live good lives. As Edmund Burke memorably remarked: "Because half a dozen grasshoppers under a fern make the field ring with their importunate chink, while thousands of great cattle . . . chew the cud and are silent, pray do not imagine that those who make the noise are the only inhabitants of the field . . . or that, after all, they are other than the little shrivelled, meagre, hopping, though troublesome insects of the hour." [6]

THE MODE OF CONSERVATIVE REFLECTION

The ultimate test of any political arrangement is its contribution to good lives. But ascertaining what that contribution is depends on a mode of reflection that is historical. For the reflection must discover the reasons for the arrangement in question: its past contribution to good lives, the alternatives that have been available to it, and how and why it came about that the arrangement has become traditional. The reflection of opponents of conservatism pretends to proceed differently. They focus on some past or future, actual or hypothetical arrangement, which they take to provide the standard of evaluation for existing arrangements. In doing so, however, they actually presuppose that very historical mode of reflection to which they suppose themselves to present an alternative. For any attempt at the reasonable evaluation of an existing arrangement must rest on a prior understanding of the arrangement that is being evaluated. How could a political arrangement be deemed deficient if the reasons for its endurance have not been understood? And how else but historically could those reasons be understood?

Furthermore, opponents of conservatism need not only propose some ideal arrangement and evaluate existing arrangements by comparing them to it, they must also explain why the proposed arrangement is ideal. The ideal cannot be supposed to be its own warrant because that would transform even the most pernicious ideal into an authoritative standard. The proposed ideal must be supported therefore by reasons independent of it. But what could such reasons be if not that the ideal arrangement is more conducive to good lives than the existing arrangements? That reason, however, presupposes having the historical understanding that conservative reflection aims to have. For it presupposes understanding how good lives could have been and have been in the past under the existing arrangements.

This mode of reflection is a necessity, not a luxury. It is not an academic specialty, nor the predilection of a few people given more to thought than to action. It is an activity necessary to maintaining political arrangements that are conducive to good lives, and it is indispensable for their reasonable justification or criticism. What makes it such a requirement is the ubiquity of conflicts about what the arrangements ought to be.

It is crucial to understanding the mode of reflection that conservatives favor that it cannot be guided merely by the pragmatic need to resolve the conflicts that disrupt the prevailing arrangements. If that were all, conflicts could be resolved without much reflection either by arbitrarily favoring one of the conflicting sides over the other or by balancing in some expedient manner their competing claims. This is the normal strategy of opportunistic or unreflective politicians, and it is unsatisfactory because it does not take into account the reasons for and against the conflicting claims.

To illustrate this point, consider the conflict in contemporary America about gun control. If reasonable people take a side in this vexing conflict, they will not be motivated simply by wishing the conflict to cease. They will favor that resolution of the conflict for which they think a stronger case can be made. Nor will they favor just any compromise that may be reached, say banning automatic weapons and permitting others, because their interest will not be merely in resolving the conflict, but in resolving it in the right way. After all, they live in the society and they will be affected by the outcome of the issue. The need for reflection arises because it is reasonable to ask *which* of the conflicting sides ought to be favored or *how* their competing claims ought to be balanced.

The answer cannot just rely on a future-oriented reflection because that will merely dictate that the conflict should be resolved so as to produce the best arrangements. It is necessary to know also what arrangements are the best and what makes them so. It would betray a basic misunderstanding of what is at stake in the conflict if, for instance, it was argued merely that banning guns would save lives, and so they should be banned; or that banning guns would extend even further the government's interference with individual freedom, so guns should not be banned. That banning or permitting guns will have one or the other of these effects is probably true. The question is, however, which is the better effect to aim at in this situation and why it is better.

It may be thought that if this future-oriented answer is supplemented by the commitment to arrangements that protect the political conditions of good lives, then it will make it possible to identify the best arrangement and explain why it is so. But this is still not good enough because the political conditions of good lives may themselves be subject to disagreement between the conflicting sides. Advocates and opponents of gun control are likely to agree that arrangements that protect life and freedom are among the political conditions of good lives, but disagree about whether banning or permitting guns is too high a price to pay for protecting them. To be sure, if agreement on this point could be secured, then the agreed upon conditions would permit the selection of the best arrangement and the resolution of the conflict should aim at it. But could this be done? Could agreement be reached among reasonable people about the political conditions of good lives?

It is the crucial task of the reflection of conservatives to come as close to agreement on this point as possible. To this task, the historical dimension of reflection is central, for it is by its means that the reasons for the arrangements are found. The reflection will provide an explanation of why it was thought that the particular arrangements which are now conflicting with each other were thought to be protecting conditions of good lives. It will thus be explained that the reasons for the constitutional guarantee of the right to bear arms were that at that time guns were required for the protection of both life and freedom, as well as for obtaining food. Times have changed, of course, and these reasons now apply, if at all, only to a vastly reduced number of people. But historical reflection will also lead to understanding that guns have remained important to the good lives of many people. Their use and lore have bonded fathers and sons, as well as friends; brought people closer to nature; fostered various traditions, such as sporting clubs and hunting lodges; skill in their use has contributed to a sense of self-sufficiency, responsibility, and independence; guns have been one means whereby a large number of people have related to each other, established solidarity, common interests, fellowship, and thereby perpetuated a tradition. Historical reflection will also lead to understanding that crimes involving guns have become increasingly frequent, that there is a great difference between the significance of gun ownership in rural and urban settings, that many of the freely available weapons are not guns but sophisticated and potent military equipment with great firepower that can have no legitimate civilian use.

This kind of unbiased historical understanding suggests several reasons that help to explain the mode of reflection conservatives favor and why they favor it. First, it does not presuppose agreement about conceptions of a good life. It explains why people who do have a certain conception find some feature of it important. That, however, can be understood and respected by others as reasons regardless of whether they share that conception. Second, it helps to explain conflicts by understanding what reasons lead each side to feel strongly about the point at issue. This will help them avoid demonizing each other, lowering the tone of their disagreement, and thus exacerbating it. Third, if the reflection is carried far enough, many conflicts will ultimately be found to hinge on the question of whether or not a particular arrangement is required for protecting the conditions of good lives. Fourth, the reason for being optimistic about the possibility of resolving such conflicts is that both parties to it, insofar as they are reasonable and morally committed, want to identify these conditions and protect them whatever they turn out to be, since they are conditions of good lives, including their own.

Given this understanding that reflection helps to achieve in the relevant sort of conflicts, there are two possibilities. One is that the two sides can be brought to an agreement about the arrangements in contention. The agreement, if it is reasonable, is unlikely to be a simple preference for one or the other of the conflicting alternatives: ban or permit the private ownership of all weapons. A reasonable agreement is far more likely to require careful distinctions and compromise, which take into account the complexities of the issue. Such distinctions, for instance, as between different types of weapons, different categories of prospective owners, different likely uses of the weapons, and so forth. And the compromise is likely to permit the ownership of some weapons under some conditions. What makes this compromise possible is that the contending sides want to protect the conditions of all reasonable and morally acceptable conceptions of a good life. If it happens that in the context of a particular society both gun ownership and the reduction of the crime rate involving guns figure among these conditions, then reasonable people will do what is possible to secure both conditions to as great an extent as possible.

The other possibility is that the two sides continue to disagree about the conditions. If their disagreement is reasonable, it will often not be about the necessity or the dispensability of a particular arrangement. It would be very hard to make a reasonable case for the reduction of the crime rate or the freedom to live as one pleases being dispensable. Reasonable people will acknowledge the necessity of both of the conflicting arrangements, but they may disagree about what compromise would best reconcile them because they may disagree about their respective importance. They will argue that the crime rate should be reduced by means other than those that jeopardize freedom or that protecting potential crime victims is more important than some diminution in freedom.

The great significance of the conflict's taking this form is that it is being defused. It is no longer a conflict about conceptions of a good life, but a conflict about how to answer the factual question of how agreed upon conditions can be best realized. The conflict is transformed by reflection from being about ends to being about means. The questions of what are the most effective ways of reducing violent crime and how a way of life will be affected by gun control are factual, and so are the answers to them. Reasonable people can be brought to agree about factual answers to factual questions.

The mode of reflection conservatives favor helps to reach this kind of agreement. If successfully pursued, the reflection will result in certain recommendations about how the prevailing arrangements should be changed so as to resolve the particular conflict to which they have given rise. Reasonable people may agree about what is the best way of changing them because they will be open to the reasons that can be adduced for or against various candidates for change.

The reasons are, in the first instance, historical because they are the reasons that have been given in the past for the prevailing arrangements. But the conflict shows that the reasons no longer hold because circumstances have changed. The arrangements consequently must be adjusted to reflect the changes. The reasons, then, in the second instance, will favor changes that will contribute more to the achievement of the unchanging aim of all reasonable and morally acceptable political arrangements: protecting the conditions of the good lives of those who live under the arrangements.

THE AIM OF CONSERVATIVE REFLECTION

The aim of conservative reflection follows from its starting point and mode, but not without further explanation. The aim is to resolve conflicts about the arrangements that maintain and protect the political conditions of good lives. Conflicts endanger these conditions, and that is why it is important to resolve them. But not just any resolution will do. Conservative reflection aims to find that resolution which, in the existing circumstances, is most conducive to good lives. Finding that depends on a historical understanding of the arrangement in question, which includes understanding the reasons why it has become traditional. More needs to be said about the aim of conservative reflection because the political arrangements and the conditions of good lives they identify, maintain, and protect do not exist in isolation from one another. They are interdependent, and changes in one are bound to affect others. The aim of conservative reflection therefore is not just to resolve conflicts about particular arrangements, but to resolve them in a way that would affect as little as possible other arrangements that are conducive to good lives. Conservative reflection, therefore, must take into account the whole system of prevailing arrangements, and its ultimate aim is not to resolve particular conflicts, but to safeguard the system of arrangements that maintain and protect all the political conditions of good lives.

The explanation of the conservative attitude hitherto has not been specific about what the actual political conditions of good lives are supposed to be. The argument now requires some specificity. This is fortunately not difficult to provide because there is a surprising degree of agreement among conservatives and their various opponents about what political conditions are actually conducive to good lives. It would be foolhardy to attempt to provide a complete list of these conditions, but it is not hard to draw up a representative list that would command general assent among reasonable and morally committed political thinkers who strongly disagree in other respects.

These conditions, in alphabetical order, are: civility (reciprocal good will among citizens), equality (in the legal and political status of mature and responsible citizens), freedom (from interference and to live according to one's conception of a good life), healthy environment (the absence of pollution), justice (criminal and distributive), order (maintained through the rule of law), peace (domestic and international), prosperity (high enough living standard to provide citizens with the means to live according to their conceptions of a good life), rights (guaranteed by a written Bill of Rights, precedent, or unwritten tradition), security (from physical violence and social coercion), toleration (non-interference with unpopular ways of life and conduct), and welfare (a decent level of education, employment, health care, housing, and nutrition).

Several things need to be said about this list. First, the items on it are political conditions of good lives. There is no reason why the list could not be expanded to include additional items. But for any proposed addition a case must be made that would show that what is proposed is a *political* condition and that it is a condition of *all* good lives, not just of a few of them. Second, all the items on the list are conditions that obtain, if they do, to different degrees. It is desirable to have each to as high a degree as possible, but it is most unlikely that any of them could obtain fully. The reason for this is that they conflict both with each other and with non-political conditions of good lives, and that circumstances beyond human control, such as the unavoidable scarcity of resources, present obstacles to their full realization. Third, the political arrangements of quite good and not-so-bad societies are designed to secure these conditions as fully as possible. But this can be done by means of quite different arrangements, and reasonable people committed to securing these conditions can and often do form conflicting views about what the arrangements ought to be. Fourth, even if there is agreement that each item on the list is a necessary political condition of good lives, there are going to be conflicts about their respective importance. These conflicts become especially acute when the conditions conflict with each other. Fifth, these conflicts about the realization of the conditions, about the political arrangements that would secure them, and about their comparative importance are just the conflicts that are the starting point of the reflection of conservatives. Conservatives, of course, will not be alone in reflecting on these conflicts. But they will reflect on them differently than their opponents do. The difference is not just in the starting point and historical mode of the reflection of conservatives, but also in its aim. This last difference can now be made clear with the help of what has been said about the list of conditions and its significance.

The consensus about what political conditions are necessary for all good lives comes to a rapid end when the question of how to resolve conflicts among them has to be answered. To this question conservatives give one kind of answer, and their opponents another. Their opponents choose a small number of conditions from those on the list, impose a particular interpretation on them, and claim that the conditions they have chosen and interpreted are the most important ones. Different opponents choose different conditions and interpretations, but they all agree in choosing some small number of them. This provides the key to how they propose to resolve the conflicts concerning the conditions. If those they regard as important conflict with others, then they think that important ones should override the less important ones. If the conflict is among less important conditions, then they should be resolved in favor of the condition that makes a greater contribution to the realization of the important conditions. The shared strategy of all the opponents of conservatism, therefore, is to attribute overriding importance to some conditions and to make them prevail over conflicting ones.

Take liberalism, for instance, which, in this respect, is typical of all the others. Liberals tend to think that the most important conditions are freedom, interpreted as the capacity for autonomy; equality, interpreted as equal respect for all conceptions of a good life; justice, interpreted by and large as John Rawls does in *A Theory of Justice* and *Political Liberalism;* and rights, as the Bill of Rights was interpreted by the Warren Court. Liberals then contend that these conditions should override whatever conditions conflict with them.

It is crucial to understand that this way of proceeding is essential not just to liberalism, but to all opponents of conservatism. For if they did not attribute overriding status to some conditions of good lives, they would lose their identity. If liberals did not think that freedom, equality, justice, and rights are more important than, say, order, prosperity, security, and peace, they would cease to be liberals. And if other opponents of conservatism did not regard some other conditions as overriding, they too would thereby abandon their political outlook. An essential feature shared by all opponents of conservatism, therefore, is the aim of resolving conflicts always in favor of some small number of specific conditions of good lives at the expense of others.

An essential feature of conservatism is the rejection of this aim. The conservative aim is to identify, maintain, and protect the system formed of all the political conditions of good lives. This aim requires resolving conflicts concerning these conditions and attributing overriding status to some of them. But the great difference between conservatives and their opponents is that conservatives believe that it cannot be specified in advance which condition should be overriding and that any condition can be only temporarily overriding, whereas their opponents believe the contrary.

Conservatives have a standard for resolving conflicts, just as their opponents do. But the conservative standard is not theoretical, a priori, or global, but the concrete, practical, and local one of always resolving conflicts concerning the political conditions of good lives so as to protect the whole system of conditions. What the resolution comes to in particular contexts cannot be specified in advance because it always depends on contingent historically changing considerations. But this does not make the standard arbitrary. For the standard reflects the ultimate aim of conservatism, which is to protect the political conditions of good lives. Their protection sometimes requires that freedom, equality, justice, and rights should override order, prosperity, security, and peace, and it sometimes requires the reverse.

The present objection conservatives raise against their opponents, therefore, is not on account of their opponents' being mistaken about the condition they favor, but on account of being committed always to favor the same specific conditions regardless of what effect that has on the other conditions that are necessary for good lives. Conservatives, therefore, will not think that it is always unjustified to place security over the rights of criminals, prosperity over the equal distribution of resources, peace over the freedom to advocate the violent overthrow of the government, or civility over the toleration of sado-masochistic pornography. This gives the reflection of conservatives a flexibility that their opponents lack.

This flexibility is the result of two features of the reflection that is characteristically conservative. The first is that, unlike their opponents, conservatives have no preconceived ideas about the arrangements and the conditions that should override others in cases of conflict. What should be overriding always depends in all conflicts and in all contexts on what is most likely to contribute to the joint realization of all the conditions required by good lives. The second is that, unlike their opponents, conservatives look to the history of their own society to decide what arrangements are likely to lead to the joint realization of the conditions that are necessary for good lives. And what they will gain from reflection on their history are the arrangements that have stood the test of time and continued to command the allegiance of the people who have lived in their society. The reflection is conservative, therefore, because it interprets the general commitment to protecting the conditions of good lives in terms of the particular, concrete, and local arrangements that have been traditionally made in the interpreters' society.

It is essential to understanding conservatism, however, that the decisive consideration in favor of the conditions that conservatives aim to protect is *not* that they have become traditional, but that they actually *are* conditions of good lives. Conservatives acknowledge, indeed they insist, that the particular interpretations of them that have been favored in their society may or may not be reasonable, that they stand in need of justification, and that they may be criticized and revised or abandoned. What is crucial to the conservative position is that the activities of adducing reasons pro or con and offering justifications or criticisms *must* be done in terms of the historical arrangements and conceptions of a good life that exist in that society. This necessity is logical, not psychological, moral, or political. For nothing could be recognized as having a justificatory or critical force, unless it appeals to the pre-existing commitments of the people in question. These commitments must reflect their history. This is as true of justifications or criticisms that derive from some political theory as it is of those based on the political arrangements of some other, real or ideal, society. For whether these justifications or criticisms count as such will always depend on historical commitments that have already been made.

REFLECTIVE CONSERVATISM

The conservative attitude is that of reflective conservatism. Reflective conservatism adds reflection to the enjoyment of the conditions of good lives and the fear of their loss that motivate natural conservatism. The addition is necessary because these conditions need to be guaranteed by political arrangements and reflection is required for identifying, maintaining, and protecting the arrangements that are likely to do so. Reflection is conservative if at its starting point there are local and concrete conflicts concerning the conditions and the arrangements of a particular society; if its mode is historical, in that it involves seeking an understanding of the reasons for the arrangements in the past of the society in which they prevail; and if its aim is to safeguard a society's whole system of arrangements that guarantee the political conditions of good lives.

CHAPTER 2

What Is Conservatism?

The purpose of the inquiry is not to define a word, but to detect
the secret of what we enjoy, to recognize what is hostile to it, and
to discern how it may be enjoyed more fully.

—MICHAEL OAKESHOTT, *"The Political Economy of Freedom"*

The conservative attitude is a psychological disposition to reflect on the political arrangements of one's society in the manner described in the preceding chapter. If the attitude is expressed and the
reflection results in a policy of action, as they must be if they are to be
more than idle meanderings, then they turn into the political morality of
conservatism. It is political because it is a view about the political arrangements that make one's society good. And it is moral because it takes the
justification of these arrangements to be that they foster good lives.

The nature of good lives is a complicated matter about which a great
deal will be said in subsequent chapters. For the moment, good lives
may be understood as being both satisfying and beneficial. The perti-
nent satisfactions are derived from the enjoyment the agents find in the
important activities of their lives. The appropriate benefits are those
that the agents confer on others. Lives are good if the balance between
the satisfactions enjoyed and the benefits conferred, on the one hand,
and the dissatisfactions suffered and the harms inflicted, on the other, is
strongly in favor of the former. The fundamental aim of the political
morality of conservatism is to conserve the political arrangements that
have historically shown themselves to be conducive to good lives thus
understood.

Conservatism is not alone in being a political morality, aiming at good lives, and judging the goodness of a society by its contribution to the goodness of the lives of the people who live in it. Liberalism and socialism are the most widely favored current alternatives to it. The disagreements among these, and other, political moralities turn on the specific political arrangements that their defenders think a good society ought to have. The case for conservatism is that the political arrangements it favors are more likely than any others to lead to good lives.

The political morality of conservatism rests on four basic beliefs. These beliefs will emerge by considering four distinctions, each of which holds between two extreme beliefs. It will be found that in each case there is a belief intermediate between the extremes, and that is the one which is basic to conservatism. The four basic beliefs jointly constitute the strongest version of conservatism and distinguish it both from other versions of conservatism and from other non-conservative political moralities.[1] The purpose of this chapter is merely to begin the process of articulating and giving reasons for the basic beliefs of conservatism. The process will be completed only in the last chapter. The argument of the book may be understood then as the gradual deepening of the description and justification of these basic beliefs.

RATIONALISM OR FIDEISM

The first distinction poses the question of whether or not conservatives should look beyond their history for the reasons that determine what political arrangements they ought to favor. Some conservatives think so, others do not. To be sure, all conservatives agree that history is the appropriate starting point for their reflection, but some of them believe that it is not a contingent fact that certain political arrangements have historically fostered good lives, while others have been detrimental to them. Conservatives who believe this think that there is a deeper explanation for the historical success or failure of various political arrangements. They believe that there is a rational and moral order in reality. Political arrangements that conform to this order foster good lives, those that conflict with it are bound to make lives worse.

These conservatives are committed to a "belief about the nature and scope of rational understanding, which, on the one hand, confines it to the promulgation of abstract general propositions and, on the other hand, extends its relevance to the whole of human life— a doctrine which may be called 'rationalism'. And there is as much difference between rational enquiry and 'rationalism' as there is between scientific enquiry and 'scientism', and it is a difference of the same kind. Moreover, it is important that a writer who wishes to contest the excessive claims of 'rationalism' should observe the difference, because if he fails to do so he will not only be liable to self-contradiction (for his argument will itself be nothing if it is not rational), but also he will make himself appear the advocate of irrationality, which is going further than he either needs or intends to go."[2]

These rationalistically inclined conservatives are willing to learn from history, but only because history points beyond itself toward more fundamental considerations. That these considerations center on a rational and moral order is agreed to by all of them. But they nevertheless disagree whether the order is providential, as it is held to be by various religions; or a Platonic chain of being at whose pinnacle is the Form of the Good; or the Hegelian unfolding of the dialectic of clashing forces culminating in the final unity of reason and action; or the one reflected by natural law, which, if adhered to, would remove all obstacles from the path of realizing the purpose inherent in human nature; or some further possibility.

Such disagreements notwithstanding, conservatives of this persuasion are convinced that the ultimate reasons for or against specific political arrangements are to be found by understanding the nature and implications of the order in reality. They attribute disagreements to insufficient rationality, and they believe that there is an absolute and eternal truth about these matters. The problem is finding out what it is, or, if it has already been revealed, finding out how the canonical text ought to be interpreted.[3]

The belief that rationalism holds the key to dicovering what political arrangements foster good lives is held not only by some conservatives, but also by some left and right-wing radicals who otherwise disagree with these conservatives. These radicals believe that the laws that govern human affairs have been discovered. Some say that the laws are those of history, others that they are of sociology, psychology, sociobiology, or ethology. Their shared view is, however, that a good society is possible only if its political arrangements reflect the relevant laws. Human misery is a consequence of ignorance or wickedness, which leads people to favor arrangements contrary to the laws. History, as they see it, is the painful story of societies banging their collective heads against the wall. They have found the key, however, the door is now open, history has reached its final phase, and from here on all manner of things would be well, if only their prescriptions were followed.

The historical record of societies whose political arrangements were inspired by rationalistic schemes is most alarming. They tended to impose their certainties on unwilling or indoctrinated people, and often made their lives miserable, all the while promising great improvements just after the present crisis, which usually turned out to be permanent. If the present century has a moral achievement, it is the realization that proceeding in this way is morally and politically dangerous.

Opposed to these rationalistically inclined conservatives and nonconservative Utopians are skeptical conservatives. Their skepticism, however, may take either an extreme or a moderate form. The extreme form of skepticism is fideism. It involves reliance on faith and the repudiation of reason. Fideistic conservatives reject reason as a guide to the political arrangements that a good society ought to have. It makes no difference to them whether the reasons are metaphysical, scientific, or merely empirical. They are opposed to relying on reason whatever form it may take. Their opposition is based on their belief that all forms of reasoning are ultimately based on assumptions that must be accepted on faith and that it is possible to juxtapose to any chain of reasoning another chain that is equally plausible and yet incompatible with it.

Their rejection of the guidance of reason, however, leaves fideistic conservatives with the problem of how to decide what political arrangements they ought to favor. The solution they have historically offered is to be guided by faith or to perpetuate the existing arrangements simply because they are familiar. The dangers of either solution have been as evident in the historical record as the dangers of the preceding approach. Faith breeds dogmatism, the persecution of those who reject it or who hold other faiths, and it provides no ground for regarding the political arrangements it favors as better than contrary ones. Whereas the perpetuation of the status quo on account of its familiarity makes it impossible to improve the existing political arrangements.

A *via media* between the dangerous extremes of rationalistic politics and the fideistic repudiation of reason is skepticism that takes a moderate form. Conservatives who hold this view need not deny that there is a rational and moral order in reality. They are committed only to denying that reliable knowledge of it can be had. Skeptical conservatives are far more impressed by human fallibility than by the success of efforts to overcome it. They think that the claims that some truths are revealed, that some texts are canonical, that some knowledge embodies eternal verities stand in need of persuasive evidence. They regard these claims only as credible as the evidence that is available to support them. But the evidence is as questionable as the claims are that it is adduced to support. According to skeptical conservatives, it is therefore far more reasonable to look to the historical record of various political arrangements than to endeavor to justify or criticize them by appealing to metaphysical or utopian considerations that are bound to be less reliable than the historical record.[4]

Skepticism, however, does not lead conservatives to deny that it is possible to evaluate political arrangements by adducing reasons for or against them. What they deny is that good reasons must be absolute and eternal. The skepticism of these conservatives is, therefore, not a global doubt about it being possible and desirable to be reasonable, to base beliefs on the evidence available in support of them, and to make the strength of beliefs commensurate with the strength of the evidence. Their skepticism is about deducing political conclusions from metaphysical or utopian premises. They want political arrangements to be firmly rooted in the experiences of the people who are subject to them. Since these experiences are unavoidably historical, it is to history that skeptical conservatives look for supporting evidence. They will not try to deduce from metaphysical premises which orifices of the body are suitable for sexual pleasure or evaluate people's desires on the basis of their conformity to some utopian ideal that the people do not share. Skepticism thus avoids the absurdity of basing political arrangements on speculation about what lies beyond experience or of being equally suspicious of all political arrangements because of a global distrust of reason.

ABSOLUTISM OR RELATIVISM

Good lives are good because they are satisfying to the agents and beneficial to others. Satisfactions that contribute to the goodness of the agents' lives and benefits that contribute to the goodness of other people's lives represent values. Lives are made good by these values, and they are made bad by their lack or by being filled with dissatisfactions suffered and harms inflicted on others. Values, however, are diverse. There are countless satisfactions and benefits, there are countless ways of combining them and evaluating their respective importance, and so there are countless ways in which lives can be good. If conservatives are committed to political arrangements that foster good lives, then they must have a view about what lives are good, what satisfactions and benefits are worth valuing. They must have a view, that is, about the values that make lives good. The second distinction that poses questions for conservatives is between two views about the diversity of values. These views have a fundamental influence on the kinds of reasons that their defenders offer for or against particular political arrangements.

Absolutists believe that the diversity of values is apparent, not real. They concede that there are many values, but they think that there is a universal and objective standard that can be appealed to in evaluating the respective importance of all these values. This standard may be a highest value, and all other values then can be ranked on the basis of their contribution to its realization. The highest value may be happiness, duty, God's will, a life of virtue, and so forth. Or the standard may be a principle, such as, for instance, the categorical imperative, the greatest happiness for the greatest number, the Ten Commandments, or the Golden Rule. If a choice needs to be made between different values, then the principle will determine which value ought to take precedence. Absolutists, then, give as their reason for preferring some political arrangements over others that the preferred ones conform more closely to the universal and objective standard than the alternatives to it.[5]

Absolutism, of course, often has a rationalistic basis. For the most frequently offered reason in favor of the universality and objectivity of the standard that absolutists regard as the highest is that it reflects the rational and moral order of reality. This is the inspiration behind the attempts to establish ecclesiastical polities, on the right, and egalitarian, utopian, or millenial ones, on the left. Nevertheless, the connection between absolutism and rationalism is not a necessary one. Standards can be regarded as universal and objective even if they are not metaphysically sanctioned. If, however, their advocates eschew metaphysics, then they must provide some other reason for regarding some particular standard as universal and objective. One such reason will be discussed shortly.

It is a considerable embarrassment to absolutists that the candidates for universal and objective standards are also diverse, and thus face the same problems as the values whose diversity is supposed to be diminished by them. Absolutists acknowledge this, and explain it in terms of human shortcomings that prevent people from recognizing the one and true standard. The history of religious wars, revolutions, left and right-wing tyrannies, and persecutions of countless unbelievers, all aiming to rectify human shortcomings, testifies to the dangers inherent in this explanation.

Opposed to absolutism is relativism. Relativists regard the diversity of values as real: there are many values and there are many ways of combining and ranking them. There is no universal and objective standard that could be appealed to in resolving disagreements about the identity and importance of the satisfactions and benefits that form the substance of values. A good society, however, requires some consensus about what is accepted as a possibility and what is placed beyond limits. The political arrangements of a good society reflect this consensus, and the arrangements change as the consensus does. What counts as a value and how seriously it counts depends, then, according to relativists, on the consensus of a society. A value is what is valued in a particular context; all values, therefore, are context-dependent.

This is not to say that values and the political arrangements that reflect them cannot be rationally justified or criticized. They can be, but the reasons that are given for or against them count as reasons only within the context of the society whose values and political arrangements they are. The reasons appeal to the prevailing consensus, and they will not and are not meant to persuade those who are not part of the consensus. The ultimate appeal of relativists is to point at their arrangements and say: this is what we do here. If relativism takes a conservative form, it often results in the romantic celebration of national identity, of the spirit of a people and an age, of the shared landscape, historical milestones, ceremonies, stylistic conventions, manners, and rituals that unite a society.[6]

Just as absolutism is naturally allied to a rationalistic orientation, so relativism is readily combined with fideism. If there is no discernible rational and moral order in reality, then the best guide to good lives and to the political arrangements that foster them is the historical faith that prevails in a society. But the faith of one society is different from the faith of another. It is only to be expected therefore that good lives and favored political arrangements will correspondingly differ.

Relativists appear to have the advantage of avoiding the dangers of dogmatism and repression that so often engulf absolutism. This appearance, however, is deceptive. Relativism is no less prone to dogmatism and repression than absolutism. From the fact that the political arrangements of the relativist's society are not thought to be binding outside of it, nothing follows about the manner in which they are held within it. In fact, if the world is full of people and societies whose values are often hostile to the values and political arrangements of the relativist's society, then there is much the more reason to guard jealously those values and political arrangements. If the justification of the political arrangements of a society is the consensus that prevails in it, then any value and any political arrangement becomes justifiable just so long as sufficiently large number of people in the society support the consensus favoring them. Thus slavery, female circumcision, the maltreatment of minorities, child prostitution, the mutilation of criminals, blood feuds, bribery, and a lot of other political arrangements may become sanctioned on the grounds that that is what happens to be valued here.

These pitfalls of the rationalistic aspirations of absolutism and the fideistic orientation of relativism make them unreliable sources of reasons for evaluating political arrangements. It is with some relief then that conservatives may turn to pluralism as an intermediate position between these dangerous extremes. Pluralists are in partial agreement and disagreement with both absolutists and relativists. According to pluralists, there is a universal and objective standard, but it is applicable only to some values. The standard is universal and objective enough to apply to *some* values that must be recognized by all political arrangements that foster good lives, but it is not sufficiently universal and objective to apply to *all* the many diverse values that may contribute to good lives. The standard, in other words, is a minimal one.[7]

It is possible to establish with reference to it some universal and objective values required by all good lives, but the standard does not specify all the values that good lives require. It underdetermines the nature of good lives. It regards some political arrangements as necessary for good lives, and it allows for a generous plurality of possible political arrangements beyond the necessary minimum. The standard operates in the realm of moral necessity, and it leaves open what happens in the realm of moral possibility. The standard thus accommodates part of the universalistic aspiration of absolutism and part of the historicist orientation of relativism. Absolutism prevails in the realm of moral necessity; relativism prevails in the realm of moral possibility.

The source of this standard is human nature.[8] To understand human nature sufficiently for the purposes of this standard does not require plumbing the depths of the soul, unraveling the obscure springs of human motivation, or conducting scientific research. It does not call for any metaphysical commitment and it can be held without subscribing to the existence of a natural law. It is enough for it to concentrate on normal people in a commonsensical way. It will then become obvious that good lives depend on the satisfaction of basic physiological, psychological, and social needs: for nutrition, shelter, and rest; for companionship, self-respect, and the hope for a good or better life; for the division of labor, justice, and predictability in human affairs; and so forth. The satisfaction of these needs is a universal and objective requirement of all good lives, whatever the social context may be in which they are lived. If the political arrangements of a society foster their satisfaction, that is a reason for having and conserving them; if the political arrangements hinder their satisfaction, that is a reason for reforming them.

If absolutists merely asserted this, and if relativists merely denied it, then the former would be right and the latter wrong. But both go beyond the mere assertion and denial of this point. Satisfying these minimum requirements of human nature is necessary but not sufficient for good lives. Absolutists go beyond the minimum and think that their universal and objective standard applies all the way up to the achievement of good lives. Relativists deny that there is such a standard. And in this respect, pluralists side with relativists and oppose absolutists. Pluralists think that beyond the minimum level there is a plurality of values, a plurality of ways of ranking them, and a plurality of conceptions of a good life embodying these values and rankings. This is why they think that human nature underdetermines the content of good lives. According to pluralists, then, the political arrangements of a society ought to protect the minimum requirements of good lives and ought to foster a plurality of good lives beyond the minimum.

If pluralism takes a conservative form, it provides two important possibilities for its defenders. In the first place, it provides a universal and objective reason in favor of those political arrangements of the conservative's society that protect the minimum requirements and against those political arrangements that violate them. It motivates, gives direction to, and sets the goal of intended reforms. Pluralism makes it possible to draw reasonable comparisons among different societies on the basis of how well or badly they protect the conditions all good lives need. Pluralistic conservatism thus avoids the objection to relativism that it sanctions any political arrangement that is supported by a wide enough consensus.

In the second place, pluralistic conservatism is most receptive to the view that the best guide to the political arrangements that a society ought to have beyond the minimum level is reflection on the history of the society. It is that history, rather than any metaphysical or utopian consideration, that is most likely to provide the relevant considerations for or against the political arrangements that present themselves as possibilities in that society. It is thus that pluralistic conservatism avoids the dangers of dogmatism and repression that beset absolutism.

INDIVIDUAL OR SOCIETY

The question posed by the third distinction is about the relationship that ought to hold between individuals and the society in which they live. This has a strong claim to being the central question which all political thought aims to answer. It is common ground among all the various political moralities that human beings are essentially social in their nature. In good lives, therefore, the individual and social constituents are essentially and inextricably connected. That, however, still leaves the question of which constituent should be dominant. The answer has far-reaching political consequences. If it is said that the individual constituent should dominate over the social one, then the desirable political arrangements will be those that foster individual autonomy at the expense of social authority. If, on the other hand, the social constituent is thought to be ultimately more important, then the favored political arrangements will have the strengthening of social authority as their primary purpose.

The answer that favors individual autonomy over social authority is typically given by many liberals, especially those under the influence of

Kant. The one that holds that social authority is more important than individual autonomy is characteristically championed by metaphysically oriented absolutist conservatives, on the right, and by communitarians, socialists, and Marxists, on the left. This leaves room for yet another—better—answer, to be considered shortly, offered by conservatives who are skeptics and pluralists.

Putting individual autonomy before social authority raises two very serious problems. First, it assumes that good lives must be autonomous and cannot involve the systematic domination of their individual constituents by some form of social authority. If this were so, no military or devoutly religious life, no life in static, traditional, hierarchical societies, no life, that is, that involves the subordination of the individual's will and judgment to what is regarded as a higher purpose, could be good. This assumption entails thinking of the vast majority of lives lived outside of prosperous Western societies as bad. The mistake is to slide from the reasonable view that autonomous lives may be good to the unreasonable view that a life cannot be good unless it is autonomous. This way of thinking is not only mistaken in its own right, but it is also incompatible with the pluralism to which liberals who think this way claim themselves to be committed.

Second, if a good society is one that fosters the good lives of the individuals who live in it, then giving precedence to autonomy over authority cannot be right, since autonomous lives may be bad. That the will and judgment of individuals take precedence over the pronouncements of social authority leaves it open whether the resulting lives will be satisfying and beneficial enough to be good. Autonomous lives may be frustrating and harmful. The most casual reflection on history shows that social authority often has to prevail over the individual autonomy of fanatics, criminals, fools, and crazies, if a society is indeed dedicated to fostering good lives.

The problems of letting social authority override individual autonomy are no less serious. What is the reason for thinking that if social authority prevails over individual autonomy, then the resulting lives will be good? Lives cannot be good just because some social authority pronounces them to be such. They must actually be satisfying and beneficial, and whether they are must ultimately be judged by the individuals whose will is unavoidably engaged in causing and enjoying the satisfactions and the benefits. Their will and judgment may of course be influenced by the prescriptions of a social authority. But no matter how strong that influence is, it cannot override the ultimate autonomy of individuals in finding what is satisfying or beneficial for them. As the lamentable historical record shows, however, the importance of autonomy has not prevented countless religious and ideological authorities from stigmatizing individuals who reject their prescriptions as heretics, infidels, class enemies, maladjusted, or living with false consciousness, in bad faith or in a state of sin. The result is a repressive society whose dogmatism is reinforced by specious moralizing.

How then is the question to be answered? Which constituent of good lives should be regarded as the decisive one? The answer, as before, is to eschew the extremes and look for an intermediate assumption that accommodates the salvageable portions of both. There is no need to insist that either individual autonomy or social authority should systematically prevail over the other. Both are necessary for good lives. Instead of engaging in futile arguments about their comparative importance, it is far more illuminating to try to understand the connection between them. In fact, they are parts of two interdependent aspects of the same underlying activity. One aspect is as indispensable as the other. The activity is that of individuals trying to make good lives for themselves. Its two aspects are the individual and the social; autonomy and authority are their respective parts; and the connecting link between them is tradition. The intermediate belief that is reasonably favored by conservatives may therefore be called traditionalism.[9]

A tradition is a set of customary beliefs, practices, and actions that has endured from the past to the present and attracted the allegiance of people so that they wish to perpetuate it. A tradition may be reflective and designed, like the deliberations of the Supreme Court, or unreflective and spontaneous, like sports fans rooting for their teams; it may have a formal institutional framework, like the Catholic Church, or it may be unstructured, like mountain-climbing; it may be competitive, like the Olympics; largely passive, like going to the opera; humanitarian, like the Red Cross; self-centered, like jogging; honorific, like the Nobel Prize; or punitive, like criminal proceedings. Traditions may be religious, horticultural, scientific, athletic, political, stylistic, moral, aesthetic, commercial, medical, legal, military, educational, architectural, and so on and on. They permeate human lives.[10]

When individuals gradually and experimentally form their conceptions of a good life what they are to a very large extent doing is deciding which traditions they should participate in. This decision may be taken from the inside of the traditions into which they were born or in which they were raised, or from the outside of traditions that attract, repel, bore, or interest them. The decisions may be conscious, deliberate, clear-cut yes-or-no choices, they may be ways of unconsciously, unreflectively falling in with familiar patterns, or they may be at various points in between. The bulk of the activities of individuals concerned with living in ways that strike them as good is composed of participation in the various traditions of their society.

As individual participate in these activities, they of course exercise their autonomy. They make choices and judgments; their wills are engaged; they learn from the past and plan for the future. But they do so in the frameworks of various traditions which authoritatively provide them with the relevant choices, with the matters that are left to their judgments, and with standards that within a tradition determine what choices and judgments are good or bad, reasonable or unreasonable. Their exercise of autonomy is the individual aspect of their conformity to their tradition's authority, which is the social aspect of what they are doing. They act autonomously *by* following the authoritative patterns of the traditions to which they feel allegiance. When a Catholic goes to confession, a violinist gives a concert, a football player scores a touchdown, a student graduates, a judge sentences a criminal, then the individual and the social, the autonomous and the authoritative, the traditional pattern of doing it and a particular agent's doing of it are inextricably mixed. To understand what is going on in terms of individual autonomy is as one-sided as it is to do so in terms of social authority. Each plays an essential role, and understanding what is going on requires understanding both the roles they play and what makes them essential.

Traditionalism rests on this understanding, and is a political response to it. The response is to have and maintain political arrangements that foster the participation of individuals in the various traditions that have historically endured in their society. The reason for fostering them is that good lives depend on participation in a variety of traditions.

Traditions do not stand independently of each other. They overlap, form parts of each other, and problems or questions occurring in one are often resolved in terms of another. Most traditions have legal, moral, political, aesthetic, stylistic, managerial, and a multitude of other aspects. Furthermore, people participating in one tradition necessarily bring with them the beliefs, values, and practices of many of the other traditions in which they also participate. Changes in one tradition, therefore, are most likely to produce changes in others. Traditions are, as it were, organically connected. That is why changes in one tradition are like waves that reverberate throughout the other traditions of a society.

Some of these changes are for the better, others for the worse. Most of them, however, are complex, have consequences that become less predictable the more distant they are, and thus tend to escape from human control. Since these changes are changes in the traditions upon which good lives depend, the attitude to them of conservative traditionalists will be one of extreme caution. They will want to control the changes insofar as it is possible. They will want them to be no greater than what is necessary for remedying some specific defect. They will be opposed to experimental, general, or large changes because of their uncertain effects on good lives.

Changes, of course, are often necessary because traditions may be vicious, destructive, stultifying, nay-saying, and thus not conducive to good lives. It is part of the purpose of the prevailing political arrangements to draw distinctions among traditions that are unacceptable, suspect but tolerable, and worthy of encouragement—for example, slavery, pornography, and university education. Traditions that violate the minimum requirements of human nature are prohibited. Traditions that have historically shown themselves to make questionable contributions to good lives may be tolerated but not encouraged. Traditions whose historical record testifies to their importance for good lives are cherished.

The obvious question is *who* should decide which tradition is which and *how* that decision should be made. The answer conservatives give is that the decision should be made by those who are legitimately empowered to do so through the political process of their society and they should make the decisions by reflecting on the historical record of the tradition in question. From this answer three corollaries follow. First, the people who are empowered to make the decisions ought to be those who can reflect well on the historical record. The political process works well if it ends up empowering these people. They are unlikely to be ill-educated, passionate about some single issue, inexperienced, or have qualifications that lie in some other field of endeavor. Conservatives, in a word, will not favor populist politics. Second, a society that proceeds in the manner just indicated will be pluralistic because it fosters a plurality of traditions. It will do so because it sees as the justification of its political arrangements that they foster good lives, and fostering them depends on fostering the traditions participation in which may make lives good. Third, the society will be tolerant because it is committed to having as many traditions as possible. This means that its political arrangements will place the burden of proof on those who wish to proscribe a tradition. If a tradition has endured, if it has the allegiance of enough people to perpetuate it, then there is a prima facie case for it. That case may be, and often is, defeated, but the initial presumption is in its favor.

A conservative society that is skeptical, pluralistic, and traditionalist will be in favor of limited government. The purpose of its political arrangements will not be to bring heaven on earth by imposing on people some conception of a good life. No government has a mandate from heaven. The political arrangements of a limited government will interfere as little as possible with the many indigenous traditions that flourish among people subject to it. The purpose of its arrangements will be to enable people to live as they please, rather than to force them to live in a particular way. One of the most important ways of accomplishing this is to have a wide plurality of traditions as a bulwark between individuals and the government that has power over them.

PERFECTIBILITY OR CORRUPTION

One of the safest generalizations about conservatism is that conservatives tend to be pessimists. In some conservative writings—Montaigne's, Hume's, and Oakeshott's—cheerfulness does keep breaking through, in spite of their doubts about the possibility of a significant improvement in the human condition. Conservatives take a dim view of progress. They are not so foolish as to deny that great advances have been made in science, technology, medicine, communication, management, education, and so forth, and that they have changed human lives for the better. But they have also changed human lives for the worse. Advances have been both beneficial and harmful. The stock of human possibilities is enlarged, but the possibilities are for both good and evil, and new possibilities are seldom without new evils. Conservatives tend to be pessimistic because they doubt that more possibilities will make lives on the whole better. Their doubt is based on what they believe are permanent conditions that stand in the way of a significant improvement in the human condition.

Conservatism has been called the politics of imperfection.[11] This characterization is apt in some ways, but it is misleading in others. It rightly suggests that conservatives reject the idea of human perfectibility. Yet it is too sanguine because it conveys the idea that, apart from some imperfections, the human condition is by and large all right. But it is worse than a bad joke to call world wars, the genocide of numerous peoples, tyrannies, systematic torture, and other horrors imperfections. Conservatives are much more impressed by the prevalence of evil than this label implies. They think that its prevalence is a permanent condition that cannot be significantly altered.

Another respect in which the politics of imperfection is a misleading label is its suggestion that the imperfection is in human beings. Now conservatives certainly think that human beings are responsible for much evil, but to think only that is shallow. The prevalence of evil reflects not just a human propensity for evil, but also a contingency that influences what propensities human beings have and develop, and thus influences human affairs independently of human intentions. The human propensity for evil is itself a manifestation of this deeper and more pervasive contingency, which operates through genetic inheritance, environmental factors, the confluence of events that places people at certain places at certain times, the crimes, accidents, pieces of fortune and misfortune that happen or do not happen to them, the historical period, society, and family into which they are born, and so forth. The same contingency also affects people because others, whom they love and depend on, and with whom their lives are intertwined in other ways, are as subject to it as they are themselves.

The view of thoughtful conservatives is not one of hopeless pessimism, according to which contingency makes human nature evil rather than good. Their view is rather a realistic pessimism that holds that whether the balance of good and evil propensities and their realization in people tilts one way or another is a contingent matter over which human beings and the political arrangements they make have insufficient control.[12] This point needs to be stressed. Conservatives do not think that the human condition is devoid of hope. They are, however, realistic about the limited control a society has over its future. Their view is *not* that human beings are corrupt and that their evil propensities are uncontrollable. Their view is rather that human beings have both good and evil propensities and neither they nor their societies can exercise sufficient control to make the realization of good propensities reliably prevail over the realization of evil ones. The right sort of political arrangements will help, of course; just as the wrong sort will make matters worse. But even under the best conceivable political arrangements a great deal of contingency will remain, and it will place beyond human control much good and evil. The chief reason for this is that the human efforts to control contingency are themselves subject to the very contingency they aim to control. And that, of course, is the fundamental reason why conservatives are pessimistic and skeptical about the possibility of significant improvement in the human condition. It is thus that the skepticism and pessimism of conservatives reinforce one another.

It does not follow from this, and conservatives do not believe, that it is a matter of indifference what political arrangements are made. It is true that no political arrangements can guarantee the victory of good over evil, but they can nevertheless influence how things go. Whether that will prove sufficient at a certain time and place is itself a contingent matter insufficiently within human control. The attitude that will result from the realization that this is so will have a negative and positive component. The negative one is acceptance of the fact that not even political arrangements that best reflect the requirements of reason and morality guarantee good lives. The positive one is to strive nevertheless to make the political arrangements as good as possible. The impetus behind the latter is the realization that bad political arrangements worsen the already uncertain human condition.

If the choice of political arrangements is governed by this conservative attitude, it will result in arrangements that look in two directions: toward fostering what is taken to be good and toward hindering what is regarded as evil. Conservative political arrangements that aim to foster the good are committed to the conditions of good lives listed in the preceding chapter: civility, equality, freedom, healthy environment, justice, order, peace, prosperity, rights, security, toleration, and welfare. There need be no significant difference between the items on the conservative list and the ones that liberals, socialists, or others may draw up. There will still be two significant differences, however, between conservative politics and the politics of liberals, socialists, and a great many others.

The first of these differences has already been noted: conservative politics is genuinely pluralistic, whereas the alternative approaches are not. Liberals, socialists, and others are committed to regarding some few conditions of good lives on the list as always having an overriding importance. It is their essential claim, the claim that makes them liberals, socialists, or whatever, that when the conditions they favor conflict with the less favored ones on the list, then the ones they favor should prevail. Conservatives reject this approach. Their commitment is to all the conditions on the list taken jointly and their essential claim is that what is important is the conservation of the whole system of conditions. Its conservation sometimes requires favoring one condition over another, sometimes the reverse. And they hold this to be true for each of the items on the list. Conservatives thus differ from liberals, socialists, and others in refusing to make an a priori commitment to the overriding importance of any particular condition or small number of conditions among all those necessary for good lives.

The second significant difference between conservative politics and most current alternatives to it is the insistence of conservatives on the importance of political arrangements whose purpose is to hinder evil. This difference is a direct result of the pessimism of conservatives and the optimistic belief of others in human perfectibility. Their belief is revealed by the assumption that the prevalence of evil is due to bad political arrangements. If people were not poor, oppressed, exploited, discriminated against, and so forth, they optimistically suppose, then they would be naturally inclined to live good lives. The prevalence of evil, they assume, is due to the political corruption of human nature. If political arrangements were good, there would be no corruption. What is needed, therefore, is to make political arrangements that foster the good. The arrangements that hinder evil are unfortunate and temporary measures needed only until the effects of the good arrangements are generally felt.

Conservatives reject this optimism. They do not think that evil is prevalent merely because of bad political arrangements. They think, to the contrary, that one reason why political arrangements are bad is that those who make them have evil propensities. Political arrangements, after all, are made by people, and they are bound to reflect the propensities of their makers. Since the propensities are subject to contingencies over which human control is insufficient, there is no guarantee whatsoever that political arrangements can be made good. Nor that, if they were made good, they would be sufficient to hinder evil.

Conservatives will insist, therefore, on the necessity and importance of political arrangements that hinder evil. They will stress moral education, the enforcement of morality, the treatment of people according to their moral merit or demerit, the importance of swift and severe punishment for serious crimes, and so on. They will oppose the prevailing attitudes that lead to agonizing over the criminal and forgetting the crime, to perpetuating the absurd fiction of a fundamental moral equality between habitual evil-doers and their victims, to guaranteeing the same freedom and welfare-rights to good and evil people, and so forth.

Political arrangements that are meant to hinder evil are liable to abuse. Conservatives know and care about the historical record that testifies to the dreadful things that have been done to people on the many occasions when such arrangements have gone wrong. The remedy, however, cannot be to refuse to make the arrangements; it must be to make them, learn from history, and try hard to avoid their abuse. Conservatives know that in this respect, as in all others, contingency will cause complete success to elude them. But this is precisely the reason why political arrangements are necessary for hindering evil. Their pessimism will lead conservatives to face the worst and try to deny scope to it, rather than endeavor to erect the City of Man on a far from quiescent volcano.

CONSERVATISM: A FIRST APPROXIMATION

The central concern of conservatism is with the political arrangements that make a society good. Since conservatism takes the goodness of a society to depend on the goodness of the lives of the people who live in it, it is a moral view. Good lives, of course, require much more than what political arrangements can secure. The right political arrangements, however, do secure some of the conditions necessary for them. These arrangements, according to conservatives, are to be discovered by reflecting on the history of the actual political arrangements that prevail in one's society. This reflection will disclose that one's society is partly constituted of various enduring traditions in which individuals participate because they conceive of good lives in terms of the beliefs, values, and practices that these traditions embody. The reasons for or against particular political arrangements are then to be found by reflection on their success or failure in fostering the traditions and the participation of individuals in them. This makes it evident that conservatism is a moral and a historically reflective position.

Conservatism therefore is not a mindless defense of whatever happen to be the prevailing political arrangements by those who benefit from them. Political arrangements must be good to merit conservation, and what makes them good is that they enable the people of a society to make good lives for themselves. Because the defense of such arrangements is in everyone's interest in a society, conservatives are committed to the good of everyone in their society, not just to their own. Nor are conservatives led to defend the prevailing political arrangements by instinct, natural affection, habit, custom, or a priori commitments. They defend them because they work; that they work is shown by their history; and it is through reflection on their history that the reasons for them are found. This understanding of conservatism is deepened by adding to it an explanation of the basic conservative beliefs concerning skepticism, pluralism, traditionalism, and pessimism that form its basis.

Skepticism combines the acknowledgment that political arrangements must be based on reason and the recognition that the process of finding reasons is fallible. This leads conservatives to be cautious in accepting reasons, to want reasons to be concrete, tried and true, attested to by experience, without pretending to a quixotic pose of the wholesale rejection of the effort to be as reasonable as possible. Conservatives will thus distrust both forms that the nightmare of reason may take: the horrors of making political arrangements the expression of the latest metaphysical or utopian certainties and of irrational visions inspired by some form of faith, revelation, instinct, passion, glory, or sentimentalism.

The pluralism of conservatives strengthens their skepticism. There is a plurality of political arrangements, traditions, and conceptions of a good life that may be conducive to good lives. Human nature provides a universal and objective standard by which reasons for or against specific political arrangements, traditions, and conceptions of a good life can be evaluated. But the appeal to this standard yields only reasons that fall far short of determining the nature of good lives. For these reasons provide only their minimum requirements, and beyond this level good lives may take a plurality of forms. The minimum, however, is sufficient to justify skepticism regarding the absolutistic attempt to identify the one good form that all lives must strive to approximate and the relativistic attempt to leave good lives merely at the mercy of the conventions that happen to hold in particular societies. At the same time, the minimum established by human nature is an insufficient source of reasons for or against political arrangements, traditions, and conceptions of a good life that conform to and go beyond it.

The traditionalism of conservatives excludes both the view that political arrangements that foster individual autonomy should take precedence over those that foster social authority and the reverse view that favors arrangements that promote social authority at the expense of individual autonomy. Traditionalists acknowledge the importance of both autonomy and authority, but they regard them as inseparable, interdependent, and equally necessary. The legitimate claims of both may be satisfied by the participation of individuals in the various traditions of their society. Good political arrangements protect these traditions and the freedom to participate in them by limiting the government's authority to interfere with either. Their protection will involve making necessary changes in them, but it will aim to keep these changes as small and specific as possible.

Their pessimism leads conservatives to reject both the optimistic belief that good political arrangements and human perfectibility would jointly guarantee good lives and the belief in human corruption that dooms whatever political arrangements are made. Pessimists recognize that the contingency of life renders human control insufficient, that reason and morality do not guarantee good lives, and that the prevalence of evil is an ineliminable feature of the human condition. Pessimists, however, think that although human control is bound to be insufficient, it is also necessary to have as much control as possible, since more can make the human condition better and less can make it worse. Pessimists are committed to making the human condition better without the false hope that they will succeed in making it good.

The strongest version of conservatism begins then with the conservative attitude that combines enjoyment of the political conditions of good lives, fear of their loss, and historical reflection on how best to identify, maintain, and protect them. This conservative attitude is expressed in a political morality that is based on skepticism, pluralism, traditionalism, and pessimism.

CHAPTER 3

Approximating the Good

My hope is to write a book that will be useful, at least to those who read it intelligently, and so I thought it sensible to go straight to a discussion of how things are in real life and not waste time with a discussion of an imaginary world. For many authors have constructed imaginary republics . . . that have never existed and never could; for the gap between how people actually behave and how they ought to behave is so great that anyone who ignores everyday life . . . soon discovers he has been taught to destroy himself.

—NICCOLO MACHIAVELLI, *The Prince*

It is common ground among those who are committed to morality and think about its nature that its ultimate purpose and justification is to make human lives better. This requires promoting the good and preventing the evil that affect human lives. Morality thus has a good-approximating and an evil-avoiding aspect. Both are necessary and neither is sufficient. For approximating the good requires avoiding the evil that stands in the way and the reason for avoiding evil is to remove obstacles that prevent the approximation of the good.

There are, of course, serious moral disagreements about what good and evil are, how they ought to be promoted or prevented, and what would make lives better or worse. These disagreements, however, are moral only if the parties to them are committed to making human lives better. Conservatives are so committed. Conservatism, however, is not an ambitious view about the betterment of human lives in general, but only about the political arrangements that would be conducive to the approximation of the good and the avoidance of evil in the context of a particular society. Conservatism is a morality, but it is a political one.

Conservatism, of course, is not the only political morality there is. Its most popular contemporary competitors are liberalism and socialism. Conservatism differs from them, as well as from other less popular views, partly because of its conception of what ought to be the basic beliefs that a political morality contains. Conservatives think that the basic beliefs ought to be skepticism, pluralism, traditionalism, and pessimism, the beliefs that were introduced in the preceding chapter. The purpose of this chapter and the next one is to deepen the understanding of these beliefs. This chapter will deal with the good-approximating aspect of the political morality of conservatism and with the first three of the beliefs basic to it. The next chapter will concentrate on its evil avoiding aspect and the fourth basic belief.

HUMAN NATURE AND PRIMARY VALUES

As conservatives see it, the aim of the good-approximating aspect of political morality is the betterment of the lives of the people who live together in a society. Their betterment requires, among other things, political arrangements that protect the conditions on which good lives depend. This aspect of the conservative conception of political morality, therefore, has everything to do with good lives, and it must now be explained how conservatives conceive of them.[1]

Lives are good if they are both satisfying to the agents and beneficial for others. Either component alone would not be sufficient, for satisfaction may be obtained at the cost of causing much evil, benefiting others may frequently lead to a loss of satisfaction, and it would be unreasonable to regard either evil or frustrated lives as good. The signs of good lives are that their agents are satisfied with them, do not look to change them in fundamental ways, do not regret the major decisions that have shaped their lives, do not feel lastingly unfulfilled, and would be content to let their lives continue in the direction that has been given to them. But it is equally important for the goodness of lives that the balance between the benefits and the harms that the agents have caused to others be preponderantly in favor of the benefits.

Thinking of good lives in this way requires understanding the relation between their good-making components. One possibility is that the satisfactions enjoyed and the benefits conferred are unrelated aspects of good lives. But this is implausible, because it is not morally indifferent what satisfactions agents seek, because benefiting others is often also satisfying, and because good lives normally exclude the inconsistency of motives and actions that the existence of unrelated good-making aspects is likely to produce. Another possibility is that in good lives enjoying satisfactions and conferring benefits coincide because what the agents find satisfying is the same as what benefits others. One difficulty with this possibility is that the coincidence of the two good-making components can only be partial at best because reasonable agents often derive satisfaction from experiences and activities that do not directly affect the welfare of others. Aesthetic pleasure, peak physical condition, a sense of humor, creative problem-solving, the cultivation of style are often satisfying without causing either benefit or harm to others. It should be recognized therefore that satisfactions may derive from both moral and non-moral values. Consequently good lives are not entirely devoted to seeking what is morally good and avoiding what is morally evil. Living a good life, therefore, is not the same as living a moral life, for good lives have both moral and non-moral components, and satisfaction is often derived from both. Conceptions of a good life are broader, more inclusive than conceptions of a moral life. Good lives require a coherent ordering of both moral and non-moral values.

Values in general are benefits, whose possession makes a life better than it would be without them, and harms, whose infliction makes a life worse than it would otherwise be. Something may be mistakenly regarded as a value because having it would not be beneficial, nor would exposure to it be harmful. There is a difference, therefore, between something being a value and something being valued. The essential point about values is that they are connected with benefits and harms. The reason why it may be mistaken to value something is that it may be a mistake to regard it as beneficial or harmful. The key to values, therefore, is understanding the benefits and harms upon which they depend.

The first step toward that understanding is to distinguish between *primary* and *secondary* values. Primary values are based on benefits and harms that must count as such in all good lives, whereas secondary values derive from benefits and harms that vary with social and individual forms of good lives. The idea behind primary values is that human nature dictates that some things will normally benefit all human beings and, similarly, that some things will normally harm everyone. These universally human benefits and harms are primary goods and evils. Correspondingly, secondary goods and evils are benefits and harms that derive their status from socially and individually variable aspects of good lives.

The distinction between primary and secondary values is drawn by appealing to human nature.[2] The following account merely repeats what everybody knows anyway. But the repetition has a point because the moral significance of these commonplaces tends to be overlooked. Human nature, then, is composed of universally human, socially invariant, and historically constant characteristics. The obvious place to start looking for them is the body. Physiology imposes requirements on all human beings: nutrition, oxygen, protection from the elements are necessary for survival; rest and motion, maturing and aging, pleasure and pain, consumption and elimination, sleep and wakefulness form the rhythm of all human lives; uninjured members of the species perceive the world in the same sense modalities, and, within a narrow range, they are capable of the same motor responses. Part of human nature is that all healthy members of the species have many of the same physiological needs and capacities.

These truisms may be enlarged by noticing that there are also psychological similarities shared by all human beings. They do not merely want to satisfy their physiological needs by employing their capacities; they want to do so in particular ways. These ways differ, of course, from person to person, society to society, age to age. But there is no difference in the psychological aspiration to go beyond the primitive state of necessity and enjoy the luxury of satisfying needs in whatever ways happen to count as civilized. The primitive state is characterized by doing what is necessary for survival, whereas in a civilized one leisure, choices, and the security to go beyond necessity are available. And of course everyone prefers the civilized state to the primitive one. Furthermore, people are alike in their capacity to learn from the past and plan for the future; in having a view, perhaps never clearly articulated, about what they want to make of their lives; they have likes and dislikes, and they try to have much of the former and little of the latter; they have the capacity to think, remember, and imagine, to have feelings, emotions, moods, and ambitions, to make efforts, to go after what they want, or to restrain themselves.

These truisms concern only human beings considered individually. It is possible to go still further in describing obvious features of human nature because contact with others is also an inevitable part of human lives. People are born into small groups, usually families, and they depend on them for the first few years of their lives. They live in a network of close relationships with parents or guardians, other children, and later with sexual partners; and they extend their relationships when they enter the larger community of which the small one is a part. They acquire friends and enemies, they cooperate, compete, look up to, patronize, teach, learn from, imitate, admire, fear, envy, and get angry at people they come to know. They share the grief and joy of those close to them; they have various positions in life which others recognize; they love and hate others; and they are made happy and sad by them.

Beyond these are the facts of human vulnerability, scarce resources, limited strength, intelligence, energy, and skill, which force cooperation on human beings. Social life exists because only within it can they satisfy their physiological and psychological needs in the ways they want and establish close relationships. The forms social life takes is the establishment of some authority, the emergence of institutions and conventional practices, the slow development and the deliberate formulation of rules. These various forms of social life are traditions. Reasonable members of a society conform to traditions because they help them to achieve the satisfactions they seek. Through their authority, institutions, conventions, and rules, traditions impose restrictions on what their adherents can do and provide forms for doing what they want and society allows. Traditions thus establish moral possibilities and moral limits. Different societies have different traditions, but no society can do without them and human beings cannot do without some participation in the traditions of their society, provided they seek the satisfaction of their physiological and psychological needs.

This list of truisms is the evidence that supports the conclusion that there is a universal and unchanging human nature, composed of the commonplaces just enumerated. If human nature is understood in this way, then it makes possible the identification of many benefits and harms that will be the same for everyone, always, everywhere, in normal circumstances.

Primary goods are the satisfactions of the needs by exercising the capacities included in the description of the facts of human nature. They are universally good because it is good for all human beings to have the capacity to satisfy and actually to satisfy the physiological and psychological needs just enumerated. These may be called the goods of the self. It is also good for everyone to be able to and actually to establish close personal relationships with some other people, and thereby enjoy the goods of intimacy. And it is similarly good to live in the kind of society in which the enjoyment of these goods is not only possible, but welcome, thus to have the goods of social order. It is obviously and clearly true that any human life is better if it possesses the goods of the self, intimacy, and social order, and worse if it does not. The primary goods of the self, intimacy, and social order define some of the necessary requirements of all good lives. They are necessary, however good lives are conceived, because they are required for the satisfaction of needs that all human beings have due to a shared nature. Primary evils, then, are the frustration of those needs and the injury of the capacities required for satisfying them.

This account provides some understanding of human nature and through it of the values on which good lives depend, but it does not go very far. It is possible to derive from human nature primary values, but not all values required by good lives are primary. Different societies, traditions, and conceptions of a good life aim at values produced by the particular historical, cultural, and psychological conditions which prevail in some contexts but not in others. Furthermore, while human nature makes it a universal and unchanging truth that the goods of the self, intimacy, and social order are reasonably sought, and the accompanying evils are reasonably avoided, these primary values may take different forms in different contexts. There certainly are obvious variations in these matters.

There are no variations, however, in the desirability of primary goods and in the undesirability of primary evils. This is one universal element present in all societies. Variations concern, among other things, the traditionally recognized *forms* of primary values. But the variations among these traditional forms, great as they are, do not extend so far as to call into question the truism that some of the necessary requirements of all good lives are set by primary values. One aim of these variable traditional forms is indeed to safeguard those requirements. Murder, social ostracism, and anarchy, for instance, are recognized in all societies as violations of primary values. Variations concern such questions as what sort of killing is murder, what kind of exclusion is ostracism, and what sort of tearing of the social fabric is anarchy. The existence of these variations, however, is symptomatic of deeper similarities. The differences merely betoken different ways of interpreting the same primary values. If the primary goods of self, intimacy, and social order were not appropriately recognized in the contexts of different societies, then there would be no need to interpret them, and there would be no scope for differences in their interpretations.

PRIMARY VALUES AND SKEPTICISM

The primary values derived from human nature provide only the minimum requirements of good lives. They set necessary conditions that all good lives must meet, but these conditions, even if taken jointly, are not sufficient to make good the lives of those who conform to them. There is more to good lives than the enjoyment of the goods of the self, intimacy, and social order. The more that there is has to do with secondary values, which will be discussed shortly. What has already been said, however, makes it possible to deepen the explanation of the first conservative assumption: skepticism. Skepticism has emerged as a favored intermediate between the inflation of reason derived from metaphysics and distrust of reason prompted by fideism. One implication of the list of truisms about human nature and primary values that has just been given is that there are strong reasons against either seeking a metaphysical account of good lives or rejecting the possibility that a reasoned account may be found. Another implication is that there are strong reasons for the skepticism of conservatives.

Fideism is mistaken because it is possible to derive from human nature the beginning of an account of good lives that everyone has reasons to accept. The minimum requirements based on primary values are requirements of all good lives, no matter how radically such lives differ about the secondary values they are supposed to embody above the minimum. This is not to say that people may not have reasons to act contrary to primary values. They may, and they sometimes do. It is to say, however, that all lives are made better by the enjoyment of the goods of the self, intimacy, and social order, and that they are made worse by their lack.

Religious convictions may lead people to deprive themselves of the goods of the self; a creative aesthetic life may oblige some to sacrifice the goods of intimacy; and a political cause may lead others to pit themselves systematically against the goods of social order. But there can be no doubt in anyone's mind that however close to good these lives may manage to become, they would be better still if the people in question could have the primary goods that their religious, aesthetic, or political beliefs lead them to do without. Thus, even if people have reasons to put up with, or even to seek, deprivation from primary goods, these reasons must be strong enough to override the pre-existing strong reasons for seeking the primary goods and avoiding the primary evils. These strong reasons pre-exist in everyone because they are created by the physiological, psychological, and social needs inherent in human nature. Fideists are committed to denying that such reasons, or indeed any reasons, have any force, and that is why they are mistaken.

Fideists underestimate the efficacy of reason, but seeing this error should not encourage the opposite mistake made by rationalists of overestimating it. That mistake is to suppose that reason can provide an authoritative account of what *the* good life is for all human beings, always, everywhere, and that only poor reasoning prevents people from formulating and living according to that account. Such an account of the nature of the good life tends to be metaphysical because it goes beyond publicly observable facts and testable generalizations based on them and treats the facts and generalizations as signs that point toward a realm that transcends human experience. What reason is taken to reveal about that realm is the existence of a rational and moral order that permeates reality. Facts experienced and generalizations based on them are no more than imperfect signs of this order that can be understood only by going beyond the facts and generalizations. The kind of reasoning that makes this possible necessarily supersedes human experience, for it aims to understand its significance. And part of its significance is that the key to living a good life is to be found by living according to the rational and moral order discovered by means of this metaphysical reasoning.

It is a serious problem for rationalists that they reach incompatible conclusions about what the rational and moral order is and what its implications are for the good life for human beings. They explain this lack of consensus by attributing it to defective reasoning. That explanation, however, is equally available to each defender of each of the incompatible conclusions. As a result, provided that a rationalistic view is internally consistent and does not ignore the relevant facts and generalizations derived from human experience, there does not appear to be any reasoned ground for preferring one to another. The history of philosophy and religion seems to support this skepticism regarding metaphysics. For each of the major religions and metaphysical systems provides a consistent account of human experience and yet proposes an interpretation of the rational and moral order and the nature of a good life that is radically at odds with interpretations proposed by the others.

Some defenders of these rationalistic accounts concede that reason can yield only conformity to logic and an explanation consistent with human experience, but they think that faith can and should take up the slack created by the insufficiency of reason. The problem with that, once again, is that each account can be and has been supported by faith. Faiths are just as varied and incompatible as reasons are, and when they concern the supposed rational and moral order that lies beyond human experience, the deliverances of one are as open to doubt as the deliverances of another. Neither fideism nor rationalism, therefore, provides a way of choosing between the numerous metaphysical accounts of the nature of a good life. In that case, however, the reasonable attitude toward them does appear to be that of skepticism.

The skepticism about metaphysical accounts of a good life, however, is not directed against reason, but against forcing reason to go beyond the available evidence. That evidence is provided by common human experience. It is available to anyone who wishes to consider it. And what it indicates is that, human nature being what it is, the primary goods of the self, intimacy, and social order are necessary, but not sufficient, for all good lives, however they are conceived. It will become apparent shortly that reason permits one to go further than this. But it does not permit going as far as rationalistic accounts require.

There is yet a further point in favor of skepticism and against metaphysical accounts of a good life. Lives are good to the extent to which they are satisfying to the agents and beneficial for others. The final authority on whether a life is satisfying lies of course with the agent whose life it is. The satisfactions of a life are personal, and if the agent does not have them, the life is not satisfying, and, consequently, not good, regardless of what any metaphysical account may claim. A metaphysical account, therefore, cannot reasonably aim to tell agents what they find satisfying. It may, of course, aim to tell them what they would find satisfying. But an account can be a reliable indication of what agents *would* find satisfying only by being based on what agents actually find satisfying. Nothing short of the actual satisfactions experienced by actual agents could make such an account reliable.

This is the point made by the passage in the epigraph to this chapter that it is "sensible to go straight to the discussion of how things are in real life and not waste time with a discussion of an imaginary world." The skepticism of conservatives leads them to distrust conclusions about good lives derived from a discussion of a world that there is no reason to suppose to be anything but imaginary. Such discussions may concern an imaginary classless society; a state of nature in which there is natural equality and freedom uncorrupted by political arrangements; a society ruled by the Elect, be they philosopher kings, priests, Uebermenschen, patriarchs or matriarchs, the Party, utility maximizers, or those who have been touched by Grace; or a society designed by self-interested rational agents in the original position behind the veil of ignorance. The imaginary world may prompt politics that is left or right-wing, utopian or reactionary, Nazi or Communist, religious or secular, egalitarian or elitist—it makes no difference. Conservatives distrust them all, not because they doubt that reason can make lives better, but because deriving reasons from an imaginary world is a misuse of reason.

The steps that lead to this misuse of reason are understandable and familiar. People survey their society and the lives of those around them, and they see that there is much that could be better. They fasten on to some ideal of how life should be, and they criticize their society and propose improvements on the basis of their ideal. What could be more natural and understandable than that? This question is not rhetorical. The answer to it depends on how good the reasons are for the ideal in the background.

There must be good reasons because without them the ideal would not be a reliable basis for criticism and improvement. But if the ideal is based on an imaginary world, then the good reasons will be lacking. There will then be no reason to suppose that making the existing political arrangements conform more closely to the ideal would be an improvement. On the other hand, the ideal may be a reliable basis for making lives better. But the only kind of reason that could make the ideal reliable is that the ideal reflects better the values to which people in the society are already committed than any alternative available to it. If that commitment is made, however, then the values already held do everything that needs to be done, and the appeal to the ideal is unnecessary.

SECONDARY VALUES AND TRADITION

Skepticism prevents conservatives from supposing that an account of good lives could be rationalistic. It also prevents them from endorsing fideism about the claims of reason. Human nature and primary values provide minimum requirements that everyone has good reasons to accept. The question to be considered now is whether there are good reasons that go beyond this minimum. There are such reasons, and they have to with secondary values and traditions. Good lives depend on both primary and secondary values. Calling them primary and secondary is not intended to imply that the latter are dispensable. The implication is rather that secondary values depend on the primary ones, and that the latter are the same for everyone, whereas the former vary with societies and conceptions of a good life.

One way in which secondary values depend on primary ones is that some secondary values are the particular traditional forms in which primary values are interpreted in some context. For instance, the primary value of the self requires an interpretation to specify some traditional forms that pleasure, the satisfaction of physiological needs, and the employment of capacities may take; the primary value of intimacy must similarly involve the specification of what kinds of sexual practices, child rearing arrangements, and friendship are traditionally regarded as appropriate; and so also the primary value of social order must be spelled out in terms of concrete laws, institutions, and policies which are traditional in particular contexts.

Another way secondary values depend on primary ones is that some secondary values enrich life by representing possibilities beyond the requirements set by primary values. Such secondary values are desirable professions, prized talents, the acceptable balance between political involvement and private life, work and leisure, competition and solidarity, the value attributed to independence, creativity, honor, comfort, success, privacy, and so on. These secondary values also depend on primary ones because their realization is possible only if the necessary requirements set by primary values are first satisfied. If people are hunted or starving, if they are deprived of companionship, affection, or the concern and appreciation of others, if they live in a lawless anarchic society, then they must concentrate on escaping death or lasting injury, and they will have little time or energy left to seek the enjoyments derivable from leisure, privacy, or the creative participation in art or science.

It is a consequence of the dependency of secondary values upon primary ones that the two kinds of value play different roles in morality in general, in particular societies, and in individual conceptions of a good life. One of the chief aims of morality is to define a framework within which individuals could live in accordance with primary and secondary values. Particular societies go beyond general moral requirements by developing and maintaining a framework of traditions that safeguards both the primary and the secondary values recognized in that context. Morality normally appears through the mediation of the traditions of a particular society. A society usually has a much richer inventory of secondary values available than any individual belonging to it could reasonably pursue in a lifetime. Individuals have the task, therefore, of constructing out of the available secondary values some conception of a good life for themselves. This conception will aim to combine in a coherent framework the primary values with such secondary values as they favor. These secondary values will translate into individual terms some of the traditional secondary values society makes available: a way of earning a living, political allegiance, aesthetic sensibility, attitude to sex, raising children, social life, and so on. Such a coherent individually constructed framework is a conception of a good life.

The movement from the generalities embodied in human nature to the concrete values of individual conceptions of a good life, brings with it a shift of emphasis from universal primary values to variable social and individual secondary values. The former define a grid within which human beings must endeavor to make a good life for themselves; the latter provide the ways in which societies, traditions, and individuals fill in the grid. Both are necessary for living a good life, but the first must be in place before the second could be. The resulting conception of good lives is a complex mixture within which the universality and plurality of values, the limits and the possibilities which define the boundaries of human lives, the requirements of one's society, traditions, and individuality, in short, the area of moral necessity and the area of moral possibility are recognized and are given appropriate weight. It is a moral conception because it represents to individual agents how they should proceed, given their nature, society, and individual circumstances, if they want to make a good life for themselves. Since no reasonable person will fail to want that, the conception is bound to appeal to all who understand it and are in the position to pursue it.

Its actual pursuit involves living according to primary and secondary values. In a sense, both are given, and the moral task for individuals is to find out what they are and to conduct themselves according to them. Primary values are discovered by attending to universal human needs; while secondary values are formed by the reciprocal adjustments of the limits and possibilities of one's society, traditions, and individuality. Society presents through its traditions a plurality of secondary values, and part of the process whereby individuals find secondary values to enrich their lives is to grow in their appreciation of these traditional possibilities. This involves coming to see them as possibilities that they may seek to make actual in their lives. But another part of finding secondary values is to evaluate the possibilities they represent in the light of what individual agents take their characters to be and how they would like to transform them. That forward-looking evaluation, however, already involves a choice of some secondary values in terms of which they assess their characters as they presently are and as they want them to become. At the same time, the choice of secondary values depends on such evaluations of their suitability to their character and circumstances as are already in place. In this way, by a process of reciprocal adjustments, increasingly finer assessments of their characters, interdependent interpretations and reinterpretations of the nature and suitability of their traditional possibilities, they make what they believe are good lives for themselves. The making and the living of a good life, however, are not two processes, but one. Good lives are made by living well, and living well means making one's life good.

PLURALISM AND TRADITIONALISM

Pluralism and traditionalism are the second and third basic beliefs of the political morality of conservatism, the first being skepticism. The preceding account of primary and secondary values makes it possible to strengthen the reasons that have already been given for these two beliefs. Pluralism, it will be remembered, is an alternative to the absolutist and relativist approaches to resolving conflicts among values. Ab-

solutists believe that there is a universal and objective standard for resolving these conflicts; relativists deny it. Absolutists attribute the persistence of conflicts to defects in reasoning that prevent people from
recognizing or applying the standard. Relativists attribute their persistence to the lack of such a standard. Both recognize the necessity of resolving conflicts, but one goes about it by invoking the putative
universal and objective standard, whereas the other does so by invoking
the particular standard that happens to prevail in the context in which
the conflict occurs. Both are committed to resolving conflicts by ranking the comparative importance of the conflicting values. But absolutists
think that there is only one right ranking, which is made right by the
universal and objective standard, whereas relativists think that rankings
vary with contexts, and that what makes a particular ranking right is that
it embodies the preferences of the people in that context.

Pluralists proceed differently. They agree that conflicts must be resolved and that resolving them requires the comparative ranking of the
conflicting values. But they deny both that there is one right ranking
that ought to be recognized in all contexts and that the ranking that
ought to prevail depends on the preferences that people in a context
happen to have. Pluralists think that there is one right ranking in each
context, but what that is varies with contexts; and they think that what
makes the ranking right is not determined by subjective preferences, but
by objective, albeit local, not universal, considerations. The account of
primary and secondary values makes it now possible to explain the pluralistic view of why there are conflicts among values and what the objective considerations are that make it possible to cope with these conflicts.

The pluralistic explanation of why values conflict with each other begins with the plurality of values. Values are plural because they are
moral and non-moral; primary and secondary; primary values are of the
self, intimacy, and social order; secondary values have to do with earning
a living, patriotism, friendship, marriage, political activism, creativity, religious belief, raising children, breadth and depth of understanding,
and so on. The plurality of values does not by itself explain why conflicts
occur, for that, it needs to be added that many of the plural values are
incompatible with each other.

It is a common occurrence in everyday life that people must choose
between two values, and if they choose one, they cannot have the other.
An independent, unencumbered, self-reliant life in which people are ac-

countable only to themselves cannot be combined with having a large family and a close marriage; commitment to and success in some discipline or profession cannot coexist with the bemused, distant, uninvolved perspective of an observer; life in politics does not go with a life of contemplation; breadth and depth, freedom and equality, solitude and public-spiritedness, good judgment and passionate involvement, love of comfort and love of achievement, ambition and humility, exist in a state of tension, and the more there is of one, the less there can be of the other. The ubiquitous conflicts of everyday experience, however, are not only between good but also between bad possibilities. Life often requires choosing the lesser of two evils when the choice forces a normally immoral course of action on reasonable and morally committed people. They may rightly claim that they have done the best under the wretched circumstances, yet the burden of having violated their moral convictions has still to be borne, even if it is lightened somewhat by the violation having been forced on them.

The incompatibility of values, therefore, is the result of the intrinsic qualities of the values in question. Because of these qualities, some values are so related as to make them totally or proportionally exclude each other. Habitual gourmandizing and asceticism are totally incompatible, lifelong political activism and solitude are proportionally so. This is an objective fact about values, not something dependent on people's preferences. For having a preference for both of two values whose intrinsic qualities completely or partially exclude each other cannot make them compatible.

Values, then, conflict with each other because they are plural and incompatible. The conflicts force a choice on those who are committed to the incompatible values. The choice involves ranking the values in the order of their comparative importance. And the question is whether that ranking can be objectively based or whether it is merely a matter of the subjective preferences of the people who have to make the choice. Pluralists agree with absolutists and disagree with relativists about there being an objective basis for the ranking. But pluralists also agree with relativists and disagree with absolutists about the basis of the ranking being context-dependent and local, rather than universal. The question pluralists must answer, therefore, is what kind of basis for ranking the comparative importance of conflicting values could there be that combines objectivity and context-dependence?

Pluralists answer that question by appealing to traditions. Traditions unite some secondary values as they apply to some particular area of human life, such as religion, politics, sports, medicine, raising children, celebrating holidays, decorating houses, and so forth. The secondary values are either the particular forms in which some primary values are expressed or the prized possibilities of life that go beyond the basic necessities that primary values embody. In the first case, secondary values will be local customs about universal aspects of life: facing death, using power, preparing food, treating illness, understanding the meaning of life, and the like. In the second case, secondary values will express civilized possibilities having to do with enjoying leisure, doing research, reflecting on the past, making money, competing athletically, rewarding achievement, and so on. Traditions endure through time, they become customary, they combine conventional beliefs and practices, and they come to represent a local way of organizing and responding to some aspect of life. In any society, there is a plurality of traditions, and each person living in a society participates in many of the prevailing traditions. As parents, citizens, patients, litigators, theater-goers, sports fans, professionals, employees, hosts or guests at parties, competitors, and so on and on, they follow in their conduct the conventions of the relevant traditions.

One of the many advantages derivable from participation in a particular tradition is that each tradition provides a way of ranking the comparative importance of the values in its domain. Traditions have a purpose—to raise children, learn from the past, become rich, treat illness—and the comparative importance of the relevant values depends on their respective contribution to the achievement of that purpose. The evaluation of that contribution is or can be perfectly objective, even though it is local and context-dependent. It is the latter because it is contingent on participation in the tradition and on the tradition's having developed in the particular way that it has. An individual need not participate in a tradition, a society need not have that tradition, and the same kind of tradition may develop in different ways in different societies. But given that there is a particular tradition that has developed in a particular way and that an individual participates in it, there is one and only one true answer to the question of which of two conflicting values in its domain is more important in a particular situation.

It may be acknowledged that objectivity in this sense is possible and yet doubts may persist. It may be said that even if conflicts among values can be objectively resolved within a tradition, there is still a plurality of traditions and they may resolve conflicts among the same values differently. People participating in different traditions may know very well what is regarded as important in each tradition and still be at a loss about resolving a particular conflict because different traditions may prompt incompatible resolutions. In the case of such conflicts—between traditions, not between values within the same tradition—what is the objective basis on which their resolution could be based?

The answer depends on understanding that traditions have both an immediate and an ultimate purpose. Their immediate purpose is to guide conduct so as to enable participants to succeed in whatever the relevant activity is: raise children, get rich, select the best rulers, and so forth. Their ultimate purpose is to help people live good lives. Traditions may resolve conflicts among the same values differently because the conflicting values may have different importance for the achievement of their immediate purpose. If solitude and public-spiritedness conflict, then a religious or aesthetic tradition may well resolve their conflict one way and a political or commercial tradition in another. But this does not remove the objective basis from under conflict-resolutions because participation in a tradition is not merely a matter of subjective preferences. That it is not is made obvious by traditions' having not only an intermediate but also an ultimate purpose.

People participate in traditions because they conceive of good lives partly in terms of the values, beliefs, and activities of particular traditions. Reasonable conceptions of a good life involve commitment both to primary values, without which no life can be good, and to a selection of secondary values, which are provided by various traditions. If traditions resolve conflicts among values differently, then an objective choice can still be made by considering which tradition is more important from the point of view of the conception of a good life of the person who has to make the choice. People in such situations have to ask and answer such questions as whether, when the chips are down, their ultimate allegiance lies with religion or politics, with security or beauty, with independence or love, and so on. These are hard questions and there is an understandable reluctance to face them. For all that, however, they have an answer, and the actual answer that people give will be either right or wrong.

The answers, however, will not be universally right or wrong. In reaching a right decision of this kind, people are not legislating for humanity. It is not that one of, say, religion and politics is always, for everyone, and in all contexts ought to be more important than the other. Everything depends on the details. What is the religion? what are its demands? what does it rule out? what is the state of the prevailing politics? is the society quite good, not-so-bad, or awful? what difference would choosing one or the other make to those who face the choice, given their characters and circumstances? can the choice be avoided by opting for something else? Different people in different contexts may answer these questions differently. That is why the right answer will not be universally right. But there will still be right—objectively right—answers because the ultimate test is whether or not the answer will make the chooser's life better. And "better" means, it will be remembered, more satisfying to the agent and more beneficial for others.

APPROXIMATING THE GOOD

The argument of this chapter was intended to describe the good-approximating aspect of conservative political morality, deepen the understanding of three of the four basic beliefs on which that conception rests, and show how these beliefs—skepticism, pluralism, and traditionalism—mutually strengthen one another.

The aim of conservative political morality is to protect the political conditions in which people in a society can make good lives for themselves. Lives are made good partly by the possession of primary goods and the avoidance of primary evils, which are the same for everyone, and partly by the possession of some secondary goods and the avoidance of some secondary evils, which vary with societies, traditions, and individual conceptions of a good life. If political morality is conceived of in this way, then the question must be answered of how to arrive at a reasonable view of what a good life is. Conservatives begin to answer it in terms of skepticism. Stated negatively, skepticism rejects both the attempt to give a rationalistic account of the nature of a good life and the attempt by fideists to deny that a reasonable account can be given. Stated positively, skepticism claims that an account of the nature of a good life will be an account of the nature of good lives.

According to skepticism, an account of good lives must be pluralistic because good lives take many different forms. These forms, however, are not unlimited. Not all forms lives can take will be good, not even if they satisfy the preferences of the people whose lives they are. All accounts of the nature of good lives must recognize the importance of the primary values, as well as of some secondary values, and they must all recognize the necessity to resolve conflicts among the values that would make the lives good. If people have preferences contrary to these requirements, then reason dictates that their satisfaction should be excluded by all good lives. Pluralists, therefore, reject both absolutist accounts according to which there is only one form good lives can take and relativist accounts that suppose that good lives depend solely on the satisfaction of the preferences that people happen to have been conditioned by their society to have.

Primary values derive from human nature. Everyone has a nature, so it is unlikely that any normal adult is going to be without knowledge of what the primary goods and evils are. Secondary values, however, are less obvious for two reasons. First, they are socially, historically, culturally, and individually variable; they fall into desuetude and new ones come into being; and even if they persist, they keep changing, often substantially. Second, there are very many of them, many more than people could reasonably try to make their own in a lifetime. Good lives require secondary values, but not any specific secondary value. People, therefore, must choose among them. Secondary values are embedded in the traditions of a society, and choosing among secondary values involves choosing to participate in the traditions whose secondary values people want to make their own. Good lives thus require the existence of many traditions in a society. Traditionalism leads conservatives to value the plurality of traditions in their society because they see that traditions make good lives possible.

Traditions, however, are not only repositories of secondary values, but also one important means whereby conflicts among values can be resolved. If skepticism and pluralism are right, then values will conflict with each other and reason will not supply a method that would make it possible to establish once and for all a hierarchy among the conflicting values and thereby provide a blueprint for resolving all conflicts. Conflicts among values need to be resolved, but not always in the same way. Conflicts of values are conflicts for people with their particular characters and circumstances. How they resolve the conflicts depends on fol-

lowing the historical practices of the traditions in which they participate. These practices are not arbitrary; they reflect the tried and true
means whereby people participating in that tradition have historically
succeeded in pursuing the particular secondary values that the tradition
aims at and which justify its existence.

It is in this way that three of the four basic beliefs of the political
morality of conservatism are interdependent, reciprocally support each
other, and explain why the reflection of conservatives has a historical
starting point. Furthermore, the three beliefs, taken together, also explain why the conservative approach to conflict-resolution will not aim
at identifying some values that should always be privileged over conflicting ones, but rather at resolving conflicts in such a way as to protect the
whole system of values. For the protection of the whole system of values
is protection of the political conditions of all good lives, and that is the
aim of the political morality of conservatism.

CHAPTER 4

Avoiding Evil

It is one of the commonest beliefs of the day that the human race collectively has before it splendid destinies of various kinds, and that the road to them is to be found in the removal of all restraint on human conduct, in the recognition of a substantial equality between all human creatures, and in the fraternity of general love. These doctrines . . . are regarded not merely as truths, but as truths for which those who believe in them are ready to do battle, and for the establishment of which they are prepared to sacrifice all merely personal ends. Such, stated in the most general terms, is the religion of which I take "Liberty, Equality, Fraternity" to be the creed. I do not believe it.

—JAMES FITZJAMES STEPHEN, *Liberty, Equality, Fraternity*

If the political morality of conservatism concentrated exclusively on approximating the good, it would be seriously incomplete. An adequate political morality must also recognize the central importance of avoiding evil. The good-approximating aspect of morality is sunny, life-affirming, yea-saying, and it proceeds on the assumption that human beings are naturally predisposed toward the good. But political morality also has to have an evil-avoiding aspect, and it is bound to be concerned with the dark, life-denying, nay-saying side of life. It must consider the possibility that human beings are naturally predisposed also toward evil. Both aspects aim to make lives better. Doing so, however, requires not just the pursuit of possibilities whose realization would make lives better, but also the imposition of limits that prohibit the pursuit of evil possibilities. The evil-avoiding aspect of political morality would not be as important as the good-approximating one if evil were not a significant

68

threat to the betterment of human lives. But evil is such a threat, and a conception of political morality that fails to recognize this involves a sentimental falsification that substitutes wishful thinking for facing the hard facts of life.

What these hard facts testify to is the prevalence of evil. As Hegel put it: "When we see . . . the evil, the vice, the ruin that has befallen the most flourishing kingdoms which the mind of man created, we can hardly avoid being filled with . . . a moral sadness, a revolt of good will—if indeed it has any place within us. Without rhetorical exaggeration, a simple truthful account of the miseries that have overwhelmed the noblest nations and finest exemplars of virtue forms a most fearful picture and excites emotions of the profoundest and most hopeless sadness."[1] This observation pre-dates twentieth-century mass murders, unjust wars, vicious dictatorships, concentration camps, large-scale preventable starvation and disease, rampant crime, systematic torture, and an easily expandable list of further evils. The pattern Hegel describes is merely strengthened by these and similar events. But evil need not take such monumental and historic proportions. Ordinary life is full of cruel, hostile, greedy, envious, jealous, aggressive, selfish, cowardly, and devious actions that are undoubtedly evil, even if they affect only a few people.

These are the hard facts, both large and small-scale, that must lead reasonable people to acknowledge the prevalence of evil. And it is because evil is prevalent that an adequate political morality must be centrally concerned with the question of how it can be made less prevalent. The aim of this chapter is to introduce the conservative answer to it that will be further developed in subsequent chapters.

EVIL AND ITS PRODUCTS

Evil will be understood as serious and morally unjustified harm that human beings inflict on other human beings. Harm is serious if it causes damage that prevents people from living as full-fledged agents. The damage may be physiological, psychological, or social; lasting or temporary; painful or incapacitating without pain; but whatever it is, it injures its victims so as to prevent them from functioning as normal human beings normally do. The simplest cases of evil involve the infliction of what has been called in the preceding chapter "primary evils." In such cases, people are injured either by damaging their capacities to obtain or enjoy the minimum requirements of all good lives, or by depriving them of these requirements. Being murdered, maimed, blinded, tortured, enslaved, or starved are some obvious examples. But primary evils may also involve being humiliated, persecuted, terrorized, falsely convicted of crimes, or forced to witness such harm being done to loved ones. All of these evils are primary because they affect universal requirements of all good lives. Evil, however, may also be secondary because its infliction makes it impossible for some people to live a good life, although others would not be seriously affected. Betrayal, solitary confinement, lack of deserved recognition, ridicule, loss of a limb, or disfigurement affect some people far more seriously than others. This need not be because some are more sensitive or weaker than others, but because such secondary evils may have a more devastating effect on some conceptions of a good life than on others.

The infliction of serious harm is not by itself necessarily evil because it may not be morally unjustified. It may be deserved punishment, the only means of preventing even more serious harm to the victim, or the predictable consequence of risks that its victims have knowingly taken. Causing serious harm is morally unjustified, and thus evil, only if there is no morally acceptable reason for it. There is, of course, much room for disagreement about what reasons are morally acceptable, but they need not be settled in order to understand what evil is. No reasonable and morally committed person will dispute that torturing political dissenters for their opinions, killing or maiming people because they belong to a religious, racial, or ethnic group, spreading poverty and disease by stealing the money for alleviating them, and prostituting young children are evil because they inflict serious morally unjustified harm.

Serious morally unjustified harm may be the result of natural causes, such as accidents, epidemics, volcanic eruptions, inclement weather, and so forth. These are regrettable events, but they are outside of the scope of political morality, insofar as they are beyond human control. Evil has to do with what human beings do. And it has chiefly to do with what they do to other human beings. People may cause serious morally unjustified harm to themselves or to non-human victims, such as animals, plants, the landscape, or the planet. But the main concern of the evil-avoiding aspect of morality is with serious and morally unjustified harm that human beings cause to other human beings. It is because many people suffer such harm that evil is prevalent.

When people habitually and predictably perform particular kinds of evil actions, they can be said to have a disposition to act in that manner. Such dispositions are vices. Cruelty, fanaticism, selfishness, greed, envy, are some typical vices. A vice then is a disposition to act in some particular manner that causes serious and morally unjustified harm to other human beings. A vice is a character trait, and people's characters are constituted of many different traits, among which are their virtues and vices. In some people's characters the balance between virtues and vices is tilted overwhelmingly toward vices. The characteristic actions of these people are then evil. They habitually and predictably cause various kinds of serious and morally unjustified harm to others, and their evil actions are not counterbalanced by good actions. Such people are wicked. Wickedness is to have a character that is dominated by vices, one that is the source mainly of evil actions, a character that is unredeemed by virtues and good actions.

In this account of evil, vice, and wickedness not much has been said about how people come to merit these moral condemnations. This is a crucial question, and it will be discussed shortly. For the moment, consider people who are not only wicked, but know it about themselves that they are, they want to be that way, they cultivate their vices, and they perform their evil actions knowingly and deliberately. They intend to cause the evil they habitually and predictably cause. Such people are moral monsters.

Each of these moral condemnations permits of degrees: actions can be more or less evil; character traits can be more or less vicious; and people can be more or less wicked, more or less monstrous. It is often very difficult to say how strong a condemnation is warranted of an action, character trait, or person because, although the evil effects that result from them may be clear, the psychological causes of these effects may remain obscure. The extent of an evil-doer's knowledge, deliberation, and intention are often hard to gauge, and it is just as hard to form an accurate estimate of how much knowledge and deliberation, and how clear an intention a person in a particular context can be expected to possess.

The upshot of this account of evil and its products is that, although it is not difficult to be clear about the meaning of "evil," "vice," "wickedness," and "moral monstrosity," it is nevertheless often difficult to know the extent to which the ascription of some of these terms is justified.

This difficulty is not the result of there being room for doubt about whether and how much serious and morally unjustified harm has been inflicted. There is no serious obstacle to answering the question of whether evil has been done. The difficulty is the result of the obscurity of the psychological processes that have led to the evil-doers' actions. What is difficult is to judge how the evil that people have caused should be taken to reflect on them, on their character traits, on their characters, and on them as moral agents. This difficulty, however, must not be allowed to interfere with the judgment that, for whatever reason, led by whatever motives, evil has been done. It is the occurrence of evil that is of central importance to political morality because that is what presents an obstacle to the betterment of human lives. That people may be vicious, wicked, or moral monsters matters because being in these ways results in evil actions that inflict serious and morally unjustified harm on others.

WHY EVIL IS PREVALENT

That evil, in the sense that has just been explained, is prevalent will be acknowledged by all reasonable people. Because it is prevalent, it is a threat to good lives. Commitment to morality is commitment to making evil less prevalent, but that requires understanding why it is prevalent. As a step toward that understanding, it is necessary to consider the psychological processes that go on in people who cause evil. These processes may result in autonomous or non-autonomous evil actions. Actions are autonomous if (a) their agents choose to perform them, (b) their choices are not forced on them, (c) they understand the significance of their choices and actions, (d) they evaluate the choices and actions available to them, and (e) they make the choices and perform the actions they have favorably evaluated in comparison with the other available choices and actions. Actions of which any one or more of (a) through (e) is not true are non-autonomous.

This is a minimalist account of autonomy. The subject is complex and there is much more to be said about it. The argument, however, is unaffected by these complexities, so they will be ignored.[2] Two points, however, need to be mentioned. The first is that autonomous actions do not require their agents to have consciously gone through and articulated to themselves these steps. It is sufficient for actions' being autonomous that these steps could be inferred from their performance. People who take for granted conventional understanding and evaluations, and who are not articulate about the judgments that go into their choices and actions could thus act autonomously. The second point is that autonomy should not be confused with freedom. Actions are free if they are chosen and the choices are not forced on the agents. Autonomous actions require more; they require agents also at least tacitly to understand and evaluate the significance of their choices and actions. Autonomous actions thus have a freedom and a judgment component, both of which are necessary, and neither alone is sufficient. Conditions (a) and (b) express its freedom component, conditions (c) through (e) express its judgment component.

In order to understand why evil is prevalent, it must now be asked whether its prevalence is the result of autonomous or non-autonomous actions. It would be simple-minded to assume that responsibility for evil lies entirely with one or the other type of action. Both contribute to making evil prevalent. It is fortunately unnecessary to try to answer the extremely complicated question about the extent of their respective contributions. What is important is to understand the psychological processes that lead to both kinds of actions because doing so has significant implications for avoiding evil.

Let us begin with the contribution that autonomous actions make to the prevalence of evil. There are many people who often make unforced choices among alternative courses of action, they perform the actions they have favorably evaluated and whose significance they have understood, and their habitual actions cause serious and morally unjustified harm to other people. Such people knowingly, intentionally, and frequently act in evil ways. What would lead people to act in this manner? One possibility is that they are moral monsters who take satisfaction in the serious harm they cause to others. They may be murderers, torturers, dictators, enforcers, thieves who doom their victims to starvation and disease, and similar wicked specimens. They make it a policy for themselves to acquire knowledge of how to cause evil and they intentionally act on it. The psychological sources of this policy may be violent hatred, passionate indignation, thirst for power, self-loathing projected outward, cynicism, destructiveness, and so forth. Behind these forms of misanthropy may be real or imagined injustice, keenly felt personal superiority or inferiority, lifelong brutalization, or extreme selfishness.

Moral monsters cannot account for much of the prevalent evil. In the first place, moral monsters are bound to be rare because it is exceptionally difficult to be one. Monsters must have a clear vision, great strength of character, an extremely powerful sense of purpose, and they must impose an iron control on such softer emotions as they may have. But they must have more still: they must be consummate actors in order to disguise from others their true nature. Such disguise is necessary because public opinion, at least on the surface, is disposed to favor the good and deplore the evil these people cause. These requirements are unlikely to be met by many people, and that is why moral monsters are bound to be rare. In the second place, such moral monsters as there are cannot by themselves be responsible for the prevalence of evil. The Hitlers, Stalins, and Maos of this world require the participation of numerous accomplices to carry out their evil designs. Without such people, the amount of evil that moral monsters could cause would be severely limited.

Another possibility is that much of the evil that makes it prevalent is the result of the autonomous actions of amoral people who subordinate moral to other considerations. These other considerations may derive from personal, political, religious, or aesthetic projects. Their projects frequently require them to do evil, and they knowingly and intentionally do it. In their judgment, their projects are more important than avoiding evil. They are self-centered or fanatical, they see themselves as instruments of their gods, or they are aesthetes who have grown cruel in their indifference to humanity. In one way, amoralists are like moral monsters because they do evil autonomously. In another way, however, they are unlike them because moral monsters do evil because it is evil, whereas amoralists do it for personal, political, religious, aesthetic, or other reasons. Amoralists may be more or less wicked, depending on what virtues they have in addition to their vices, how their virtues and vices are balanced, and on how much evil they actually cause.

Once again, there obviously are amoralists, but not enough of them to account for the prevalence of evil. The moral education of most people is strong and unavoidable enough not to allow them knowingly, intentionally, and systematically to embrace evil in preference to the good. To be sure, people often prefer evil to good, but they take great pains to hide that fact from themselves, and certainly from others. Moral education and public opinion exert a sufficient force on most people to prompt them to try to give a morally acceptable account of their conduct. The account may be grotesquely mistaken, but there is a commonly felt psychological need to place one's actions in a morally favorable light. Amoralists who habitually and autonomously subordinate good to evil do not have, or allow themselves to feel, that need. This is possible, but too rare to account for more than some of the evil that is prevalent.

Yet a further explanation is that the prevalence of evil is the result of the autonomous but uncharacteristic evil actions of otherwise decent people. They act freely, understand and evaluate the significance of their actions, but they go wrong because their circumstances are exceptional. Great provocation, strong temptation, difficult situations, virulent dislike of their victims, and the like, cause them to act in a way in which they normally would not. This undoubtedly happens, but it can account only for some evil because uncharacteristic actions are necessarily rare. It is a matter of logic, not of psychology, that most people most of the time act in characteristic ways. That is part of what it means to have a character. The characteristic actions of decent people cannot be evil. Their uncharacteristic actions may be evil, but, being uncharacteristic, they cannot be frequent. If, on the other hand, the characteristic actions of some people are autonomous and evil, then they are the moral monsters or amoralists who have already been discussed.

The general difficulty about attributing the prevalence of evil to autonomous actions has long been noticed—and overstated. Perhaps the earliest formulation is the paradox Plato put in Socrates' mouth: no one does evil knowingly. The thought behind it is that insofar as people are rational, they act to bring about what they regard as good. If they nevertheless end up acting in evil ways, it must be that they mistook evil for good. For, the key question is, why would reasonable people act to bring about what they themselves regard as the opposite of the good.

The preceding discussion of the autonomously evil actions of moral monsters, amoralists, and uncharacteristic evil-doers answers that question. Such actions show that it is an overstatement that no one does evil knowingly. Yet Plato may still be thought to have a powerful point: it is not often that people do evil autonomously, at any rate, not often enough to account for more than some of the prevalent evil. The reason for this is that it seems to be natural and basic to human motivation to pursue what one, rightly or wrongly, takes to be good and avoid what one takes to be evil. If people knowingly, intentionally, and frequently do evil, then there must be some special explanation of why they go against what is natural and basic. Such explanations can be given—they have just been—but they cannot tell the whole story of why evil is prevalent.

There are good reasons then to consider the possibility that much evil is the result of non-autonomous actions. The actions are non-autonomous because they lack either the freedom or the judgment component of autonomy. The former failure of autonomy is simple, and it will not go far to account for the prevalence of evil. The latter kind of failure, however, lends itself to a sophisticated and plausible explanation of how people frequently come to perform non-autonomously evil actions.

To begin with, consider simple cases of non-autonomous evil. People cause serious and morally unjustified harm to others because they cannot help it. They may have no choice in the matter because they are merely the unknowing and/or unintentional agents of the evil they cause. They drive the car that kills the child who runs in front of it, even though they are attentive and good drivers. Or they may have a choice, but it is forced on them. They decide that this person will live and that one will die because only one of them can be attached to the only available kidney-machine. In these simple cases, people cause evil non-autonomously as causal rather than moral agents. They are not acting freely, and that is why they are not acting autonomously. In civilized circumstances, barring emergencies, people normally have choices that are not forced on them, so the freedom component of autonomy is routinely met. The murderers, torturers, dictators, terrorists, and other typical evil-doers of the world are usually able to make unforced choices.

The failure of autonomy that results from miscarried judgment, however, is a far more promising explanation of how people come to cause much non-autonomous evil. Bad judgment comes about because the agents fail either in their understanding or in their evaluation of the significance of the choices they have and the actions they perform. As a result, they do evil, but they do not see what they do *as* evil. They see their choices and actions under some other description, and their misjudgments of them reflect a cognitive failure, which may or may not have deeper non-cognitive sources. Such people are cruel, but they see themselves as just; they are dogmatic, but they believe themselves to be principled; they are greedy, but it seems to them that they are taking no more than their fair share; they are prejudiced, but they appear to themselves as objective about their wretched victims. They are, therefore, not monstrous, but obtuse. They fail to see what they ought to see and what they would see if their lack of judgment did not cloud their vision. Such failures led Hannah Arendt to speak about the banality of evil.[3] There is nothing heroic or romantic about the agents of most evil actions; they do not adopt the maxim of Milton's Satan: Evil, be thou my good. They banally mistake evil for good because they are morally deficient.

Implicit in this explanation of how evil often comes to be caused, there is a view of human motivation. According to it, human motivation is complex and motives are morally mixed. Virtues coexist with vices. The inner lives of most people are struggles in which selfishness, cruelty, greed, envy, hatred, and so forth, on one side, and love, decency, pity, kindness, and so on, on the other side, are the soldiers of the ignorant armies clashing in the night. Such people are the sources of much evil. They are vicious in some ways and in some circumstances, virtuous in others—people like most of us. They are the agents of evil and of the good, and they act one way or another, depending on their imperfect understanding and evaluation, mixed motives, contrary feelings, unclear aims, and on the pressures exerted on them by the historical, political, cultural, and other forces to which they are subject.

These agents do not pursue evil as a conscious and deliberate policy. They certainly do evil, but they mistake the moral standing of their actions. In a sense, they know what evil is because they can recognize it in others and may be brought to recognize it even in themselves. Moreover, they choose their evil actions because they perform them uncoerced in circumstances where they could have done otherwise. In another sense, however, they do not know what evil is because they do not recognize their own evil actions as such. Something intrudes between their general knowledge of evil and the recognition that their actions fall under it. Their own cruelty is seen by them as healthy ambition, selfishness as doing what is necessary to succeed in the competition of life, hatred as well-merited contempt, envy as just indignation, or fanaticism as consistency. They know that cruelty, selfishness, hatred, envy, and fanaticism are vices and that the corresponding actions are evil, but they do not know that their own actions exemplify these vices and that they are evil. The reason why they do not know it is that early deprivation, self-deception, brutalizing experiences, egocentrism, fantasy, or some passion that rules them prevents them from seeing the true nature of their actions.

Such people are like those amoralists who subordinate moral to other considerations, but they are also unlike them because they do not do it autonomously. Amoralists do evil autonomously because they know perfectly well what they are doing, but these people do not because they have made a mistake in understanding or evaluating the moral significance of their actions. They cause evil, albeit non-autonomously, because they violate the judgment component of autonomy. Some people act in this way habitually and predictably, others only episodically. The former are wicked, the latter are merely prone to do evil in some circumstances.

To return, then, to Plato's Socrates: do the agents of non-autonomously evil actions do evil knowingly? Yes and no. They know what evil is and they know what they are doing, but they do not connect these two pieces of knowledge. Socrates was right, therefore, in seeing that full knowledge is lacking in the case of non-autonomously evil actions, although he did not see that moral monsters, amoralists, and uncharacteristic evil-doers do evil autonomously, with full knowledge. Socrates was also wrong, however, because he supposed that the extent to which agents possess knowledge of evil, it will motivate them to avoid it. The agents of autonomously evil actions must and of non-autonomously evil actions may possess knowledge of evil without being motivated by it. Socrates missed this possibility because he did not see that in addition to the natural and basic human motivation to pursue the good there are also other equally natural and basic motives that may prompt people to act in ways contrary to the good. The prevalence of evil is the result of these other motives and corresponding actions.

The upshot of the argument thus far is that some of the actions responsible for the prevalence of evil are autonomous, some are not; some are done with full knowledge, some are not. It is extraordinarily difficult to decide in the case of many individual actions how much choice, how deep an understanding, how thorough an evaluation have gone into them, what choices, understanding, and evaluation were actually possible for the agents, and what ought to have been possible for them, given their characters and circumstances. These difficulties, of course, are multiplied manifold when the question is not about the autonomy or its lack in the case of individual actions, but about actions in general. The prevalence of evil therefore is the result of both autonomous and non-autonomous actions, although their relative contributions vary with individuals, societies, and historical periods. The argument was meant to go beyond this truism by exhibiting some of the psychological processes that may lead people to cause both autonomous and non-autonomous evil, and by suggesting that an adequate political morality must be concerned with imposing limits on both autonomously and non-autonomously evil actions. Obvious though this suggestion may appear to be, it is rejected by those who embrace Socrates' mistake as a truth.

Criticizing Socrates is not an exercise in historical impiety, but the identification of a widespread mistake that transcends historical, moral, and political differences. It is a mistake that conservatives are conspicuous for not making, a mistake that allies many of their opponents against them. The mistake is in fact assumed by them to be a truth. This matters because it leads them to misdiagnose what can be done to make evil less prevalent, and that, in turn, is responsible for their inability to respond appropriately to the prevalence of evil. Or, so it will be argued now.

THE ENLIGHTENMENT FAITH

If evil is prevalent, if it is the result of some mixture of both autonomous and non-autonomous actions, and if commitment to morality involves avoiding evil, then one central question that an adequate political morality must answer is about what ought to be done to further this end. The obvious answer is that what ought to be done is to impose and enforce limits that prohibit autonomously and non-autonomously evil actions. The effect of such limits is to interfere with the conduct of evil-doers and restrict the scope they have for causing evil. There are countless ways in which this could be done, but some are as follows: rigorous moral education; social and legal sanctions with teeth in them; swift, predictable, and severe punishment for causing evil; creating a climate of opinion that unequivocally condemns evil actions, vices, and wickedness; and fostering a general tendency to recognize that habitual and predictable evil-doers do not have the same moral status and are not entitled to the same concern and respect as others. Such attempts to make evil less prevalent would involve recognizing that it is important to

know about the moral standing of politicians, teachers, military and police officers, physicians, executives, journalists, psychotherapists, judges,
and others, who are in a position to affect the lives of numerous people,
and that it is important to disqualify evil-doers from holding positions in
which they have ample opportunities to inflict serious morally unjustified harm on others.

This obvious answer, however, does not seem obvious to a large number of people who are as committed to having a good society as conservatives. These people see the conservative answer as a symptom of an
objectionable moralistic mentality that refuses to acknowledge the autonomy and fundamental moral equality of all human beings. Seeing
the conservative approach to avoiding evil in this unfavorable light goes
a long way toward accounting for the prevailing unpopularity of conservatism. The refusal to accept the answer, however, is indefensible because it rests on a modern version of Socrates' mistake: the
Enlightenment Faith.

To understand the Enlightenment Faith, consider again the Socratic
view that no one does evil knowingly, but this time in the light of what
has been said about the autonomous and non-autonomous sources of
evil. The Socratic response to the moral monsters, amoralists, and uncharacteristic evil-doers who have been discussed would be to deny that
their actions were truly autonomous. Defenders of this response would
claim that there must be some failure in the understanding or the evaluation of the agents because otherwise they would not do evil. People act
in ways that seem good to them, and if they do evil, it is because they
make a mistake: what seems good to them really is not. They fail in their
understanding or evaluation of their choices and actions, and that is
why they cause evil. If they have the proper understanding and evaluate
matters rightly, they will do what is good rather than evil. The Socratic
view may be expressed therefore as: no one does evil autonomously. The
prevalence of evil, according to the Socratic view, must be attributed to
non-autonomous actions. In that case, however, it is clear that what
should be done to make evil less prevalent is to make non-autonomous
actions autonomous. They key to avoiding evil, on this view, is to improve the agents' understanding and evaluation because, the assumption is, the prevalence of evil is the result of failures in understanding
and evaluation.

The Enlightenment Faith inherits this assumption from the Socratic view, but it adds to it a component of its own. This addition is an explanation of the most important source of the failures in understanding and evaluation from which the prevalence of evil results. The failures are attributed to the political arrangements of less than good societies. People's understanding and evaluations are corrupted, according to the Enlightenment Faith, by the injustice, exploitation, poverty, discrimination, ignorance, resentment, irrationality, and so forth, that bad political arrangements cause and perpetuate. The Enlightenment Faith, therefore, is that if people do not have choices forced on them, if their judgments are not corrupted by bad political arrangements, then they will act autonomously for the good and they will not act in non-autonomously evil ways. The true sources of evil are bad political arrangements, and the way to make evil less prevalent is by reforming the political arrangements that cause it.

For those who hold the Enlightenment Faith, the conservative response to the prevalence of evil will appear to be misguided, not obvious. If autonomous actions tend to be good, and if evil actions tend to be non-autonomous, then the conservative strategy of restricting both autonomously and non-autonomously evil actions cannot result in making evil less prevalent. The appearance that there are many autonomously evil actions is bound to be mistaken, according to defenders of the Faith, because genuinely autonomous actions tend to be good. Restricting autonomous actions, then, would be to restrict good, not evil, actions. Furthermore, the way to make evil less prevalent is not by restricting the non-autonomous actions that cause it, but by improving the understanding and evaluations of their agents. This would mean transforming non-autonomous evil actions into autonomous good actions. The key to that transformation, according to the Enlightenment Faith, is to reform the political arrangements that interfere with the autonomy of the people who live in the society. The conservative strategy of strengthening the political arrangements that limit evil appears to be utterly wrongheaded, given the Enlightenment Faith, because, as the faithful see it, it will make people less rather than more autonomous, and thus more rather than less likely to cause evil.

The dispute, then, between conservatives and defenders of the Enlightenment Faith turns on the assumptions that autonomy tends to lead to good actions, that evil actions tend to be non-autonomous, and that the prevalence of evil is the result of bad political arrangements.

These assumptions are so patently indefensible that holding them must be matter of faith, not of reason. But before that can be shown, it needs to be appreciated just how widespread the Enlightenment Faith is, so that criticizing it will not seem like the pointless flogging of a dead horse.

Who holds the Enlightenment Faith?[4] To begin with the most influential ones, a large majority of liberals holds it, for these liberals believe that the political arrangements of a good society ought to aim at increasing the autonomy of the people who live in it. Liberals are for freedom, equality, rights, pluralism, and distributive justice because they see them as necessary conditions for the autonomous functioning of human beings. The more autonomy people have, the fewer mistakes they will make in their attempts to understand and evaluate their choices and actions. And the fewer mistakes they make, the more likely it is that their choices and actions will lead to good rather than to evil. Socialists hold the Faith too because they attribute social ills to political arrangements that stand in the way of equality, especially economic equality. According to them, evil is prevalent because people lack the resources they need to live a good life. If the resources were redistributed so as to reduce the prevailing inequality, then evil would thereby also be reduced because people would no longer be forced to satisfy their legitimate needs by illegitimate means. Marxists are also committed to the Faith because they think that if the existing political arrangements ceased to be the instruments of one class exploiting another, then the false consciousness they create in exploiter and exploited alike will be replaced by a perception of social life that is unclouded by people's class interests. There would then be no reason for anyone to cause serious morally unjustified harm to others.

Perhaps the primary source of the Enlightenment Faith is the thought of Rousseau and Kant, as developed by contemporary liberal thinkers, who have been aptly described as deontological liberals. The Enlightenment Faith, however, also has two secondary, less influential, sources in the utilitarianism of John Stuart Mill and his contemporary followers and in the belief in the malleability of human beings held by liberals of John Dewey's persuasion. There are, of course, substantial differences between these two formative influences on the Faith, but what matters for present purposes is the agreement between them. They agree that the requirements of morality and autonomy largely coincide;

that if people act autonomously, they tend to act for the good; that causing evil tends to be a failure of autonomy; and that the way to make evil less prevalent is by transforming political arrangements so as to remove interferences with the autonomous functioning of the people in a society. To express this agreement in the language of autonomy is to adopt the vocabulary of deontological liberals. But utilitarians, followers of Dewey, socialists, and Marxists make the same point in their own vocabularies. The terms do not matter, the Faith they express does. The time has come to say why it is indefensible.

THE INDEFENSIBILITY OF THE ENLIGHTENMENT FAITH

The key idea of the Enlightenment Faith is that the prevalence of evil is a consequence of non-autonomous actions and that avoiding evil depends on making non-autonomous actions autonomous. But why is it supposed that autonomous actions are more likely to be good than evil? Because it is believed by the faithful that if people choose and act without interference from bad political arrangements, if they do not have to contend with poverty, crime, discrimination, and other social ills, if they are not ignorant, indoctrinated, sickened in mind or body, or enraged by injustice, if they have time to think about their choices and actions in peace, then they will do what is good and not what is evil.

It is just this feature of the Enlightenment Faith that makes it a faith. For it is held in a way that makes it immune to falsification by any fact. Morally good choices and actions are interpreted as evidence for autonomy. Morally evil choices and actions are interpreted as evidence for lack of autonomy. If people cause evil, bad political arrangements must have corrupted them. If people act for the good, then good political arrangements must have made it possible for them to act autonomously. The Enlightenment Faith thus leaves no room for the possibilities that much evil may be caused autonomously, that there may be a great deal of evil when the political arrangements are not bad, and that people may refrain from causing evil even if the political arrangements are bad.

Generally speaking, the stratagem of the Faith is to ascribe good to autonomy and evil to political arrangements. That is why autonomous evil is regarded by the faithful as exceptional and non-autonomous evil is blamed on external influences. As John Rawls, perhaps the most prominent contemporary defender of the Enlightenment Faith, puts it:

"men's propensity to injustice is not a permanent aspect of community life; it is greater or less depending in large part on social institutions, and in particular on whether they are just or unjust."[5] All the facts of moral life are thus taken to confirm the Enlightenment Faith: anything good is taken as evidence for autonomy and anything evil is regarded as evidence for bad political arrangements. The Faith is rigged because it excludes interpretations of the facts that are inconsistent with what it holds to be true.

It is a wry thought that the liberal, socialist, and Marxist defenders of the Faith are in a position strikingly analogous to the one that they castigate Christians for holding. As Christians believe that responsibility for evil lies with corrupt human beings and not with God, so defenders of the Faith believe that responsibility for evil lies with corrupt political arrangements and not with human beings. As Christians base their belief on what they take to be the nature of God, so defenders of the Faith base their beliefs on what they take to be human nature. The odd result is that, although defenders of the Faith scorn Christians for not facing the theological problem of evil, they avert their gaze from the secular problem of evil that is as serious for the Enlightenment Faith as its theological counterpart is for the Christian Faith.

That the Enlightenment Faith is held in an unreasonable manner does not show that it is not true. The faithful may arbitrarily exclude interpretations of facts, and yet what they exclude may in fact be false and their own rigged interpretation may be true. Part of the trouble with the Enlightenment Faith is not therefore that it is a faith—embarrassing though that is for its secular defenders—but that it is a false faith. It falsifies reality by substituting illusions for the facts that no reasonable person can deny. These facts are that evil is prevalent in all societies, regardless of their political arrangements; that, although bad political arrangements make evil more prevalent than it would otherwise be, evil is prevalent even if political arrangements foster autonomy; that no society has stressed more than contemporary America the importance of autonomy for everyone, and yet murder, mayhem, addiction, deception, theft, fraud, ruthlessness, and moral indifference are rampant; that it is absurd to suppose that virtues are the autonomous achievements of individuals, whereas vices, like selfishness, greed, malevolence, envy, aggression, prejudice, cruelty, suspicion, and laziness, are foisted on them from the outside; that it is equally baseless to suppose that virtues are somehow natural and basic, but vices are the unnatural products of corrupting political arrangements without which virtue and goodness would reign; and that, notwithstanding moral monsters, amoralists, and uncharacteristic evil-doers, autonomous actions tend to be good. The Faith denies these facts, ignores what is contrary to the illusions it fosters, inflates the importance of what reinforces it, and that is in part why it is indefensible.

There is, however, worse to come. It is not just that the Enlightenment Faith systematically falsifies the facts that are inconsistent with it. The Faith would be indefensible even if it were true—although it is not—that the prevalence of evil is the result of non-autonomous choices and actions and that making evil less prevalent requires making non-autonomous choices and actions autonomous. After all, it is perfectly possible that if the agents whose non-autonomous choices and actions are supposed to be responsible for the prevalence of evil evaluate and understand their choices and actions accurately, and thus stop misjudging their true moral status, then they would continue to do autonomously what they were doing before non-autonomously. Their reaction to the realization that they are cruel, not just, dogmatic, not principled, greedy, not fair, prejudiced, not objective, may just be to embrace these vices and continue to perform the actions that follow from them. The transformation from non-autonomous to autonomous agency may just be the transformation of unknowing and unintentional evil-doers into moral monsters or amoralists who do evil knowingly and intentionally.

People become non-autonomous evil-doers because some preexisting feeling, desire, hope, or fear creates in them a receptivity to vices. The newly acquired knowledge that their character traits are vices, not virtues as they previously believed, need not by itself motivate them to change their characters. They may just shrug and say to themselves: That is the way I am. And even if they do not just shrug, because they are motivated by their new knowledge to change themselves, why should it be assumed that the force of that motive would in most cases be sufficient to defeat the contrary forces of the pre-existing motives that made them receptive to their vices in the first place? That assumption is made even more indefensible by the fact that the vices of the non-autonomous evil-doers in question must be habitual and frequently acted upon to account for the prevalence of evil, so that what would have to be changed are not just individual actions, but ingrained habits.

Suppose, however, that the indefensibility of this assumption is ignored and an effort is made to transform non-autonomous evil-doers into autonomous agents. What would happen in and to a society in which this was done? The society in question suffers from the prevalence of evil, and, let it be supposed, most of the evil is non-autonomously caused. The present suggestion is that the way to improve the wretched *status quo* is to make non-autonomous actions more autonomous. This process would require changing the prevailing bad political arrangements that are responsible for the prevalence of evil. The change would involve such measures as guaranteeing to non-autonomous evil-doers more freedom, greater equality, stronger rights, a richer plurality of options, and more resources through redistribution than they had before. These measures are called for, according to the present supposition, because it is their absence that has made the prevailing political arrangements bad and thus evil prevalent. Suppose that these measures were actually adopted. Is it not obvious that the result would be that evil would become even more prevalent? Bad as the previous political arrangements were, they at least placed some restrictions on evil-doers by depriving them of the opportunity and resources to translate their vices into actions that cause serious unjustified harm to others. The supposed improvement of the political arrangements would remove these restrictions. The effect is bound to be to make evil more, not less, prevalent.

Defenders of the Enlightenment Faith will respond to this objection by pointing out that they have never supposed that autonomy should be given free rein. They will say that they have been centrally concerned with creating political arrangements that foster everyone's autonomy, and such arrangements may well require the restriction of the autonomy of those who exercise it in violation of these arrangements. The autonomy of individuals may thus be justifiably restricted, according to the Enlightenment Faith, if they interfere with the autonomous functioning of others. This, of course, is a perfectly reasonable response. It is in fact none other than the conservative response to the prevalence of evil that has been called obvious earlier and whose obviousness defenders of the Enlightenment Faith have been contesting. The implications of this response, however, are incompatible with the Enlightenment Faith.

If it is acknowledged that evil is prevalent, then it must also be acknowledged that there are very many evil-doers. If defenders of the

Faith are prepared, as they should be, to place restrictions on those who cause evil autonomously or otherwise, then they must embrace the conservative idea that in a good society there will be many restrictions, made necessary by the prevalence of evil. Given its prevalence, a good society will not be one that fosters the autonomy of all the people living in it by political arrangements that promote freedom, equality, rights, pluralism, and distributive justice. For a good society will take cognizance of the plain fact that these undoubted goods will be used by evildoers to endanger the good lives of others. It is, therefore, highly misleading for defenders of the Enlightenment Faith to identify themselves as favoring autonomy. If they are reasonable, they favor autonomy only for those who use it in morally acceptable ways. And if that qualification is understood to hold, then conservatives are just as much in favor of autonomy as are defenders of the Faith.

How much and how severe restrictions ought there to be in a good society depends on how prevalent evil would be in it without the restrictions. What makes a society good is that people in it can live good lives. But that possibility requires decreasing the autonomy of some and increasing the autonomy of others. A good society will make the ratio of decrease versus increase depend on how much evil there is in it. Reflection on the records of past and present societies will readily suggest the conclusion that the decrease of autonomy will have to be considerable. If the obvious need for avoiding evil is conceded, and if it is also accepted that evil is prevalent, then presenting the Enlightenment Faith by concentrating on its good-approximating aspect, while remaining silent about its evil-avoiding one, is a gross misrepresentation.

There remains, however, still one further reason for regarding the Enlightenment Faith as indefensible. Its defenders ascribe the prevalence of evil to bad political arrangements and they think that the way to make evil less prevalent is to make the political arrangements less bad. The problem with this line of thought is that it fails to pose the obvious question of how political arrangements come to be bad.

Political arrangements are made by people. If they are good, it is because they were made well; if they are bad, it is because their makers made them so. If the prevalence of evil is the result of bad political arrangements, then it must ultimately be the result of the deficiencies of their makers. If people would act in morally acceptable ways were it not for bad political arrangements, then how could bad political arrangements come into being? Who would make them bad? If people were made into evil-doers by bad political arrangements, then how could political arrangements ever be improved? If people are not totally at the mercy of political arrangements, and they can actually diagnose them as bad and try to improve them, then it must be possible to act contrary to bad political arrangements. And if that is possible, then the prevalence of evil cannot be the result merely of bad political arrangements, because the people who allow themselves to be influenced by them, even though they could act contrary to them, must also be responsible. Human beings are no doubt malleable enough to be influenced by political arrangements. But they are not sufficiently malleable to be without innate tendencies that make them receptive to both good and bad influences.

The Enlightenment Faith, then, faces the following dilemma. If it is possible to escape the corrupting influences of bad political arrangements, then how could continued adherence to them not have something to do with the pre-existing evil tendencies of the people influenced by them? If these pre-existing evil tendencies were also said to be the products of bad political arrangements, then how did those arrangements become bad? Defenders of the Faith must eventually bite the bullet and blame people rather than the arrangements people make. If, on the other hand, it is supposed to be impossible to escape the corrupting influences of bad political arrangements, then evil could never be made less prevalent because people in a society would be unavoidably ruled by the prevailing arrangements. On that supposition, all attempts to improve matters would be pointless, including those that follow from the Enlightenment Faith. Moreover, the odd implication of this social determinism is that if it held, defenders of the Faith themselves could not possibly have sufficiently freed themselves from the prevailing arrangements to enable them to see that they are bad.

In the light of these criticisms, it may be concluded that the political arrangements of a good society should not be based on the Enlightenment Faith. The arrangements must be based on the recognition that avoiding evil is at least as important to a good society as approximating the good. The political morality of conservatism recognizes the necessity of doing both, whereas its main contemporary rivals—liberalism and socialism—embrace the Enlightenment Faith and are led by it to underestimate the significance of the prevalence of evil. This is one of the main reasons for preferring conservatism to its rivals.

PESSIMISM AND AVOIDING EVIL

The evil-avoiding aspect of conservative political morality is but the working out of the implications of the fourth basic belief of conservatism: pessimism. The first three basic beliefs—skepticism, pluralism, and traditionalism—have been shown, in the preceding chapter, to motivate the good-approximating aspect of conservative political morality. According to pessimism, avoiding evil is necessary and important because evil is prevalent, it is an obstacle to good lives, and its prevalence is the result of the propensity of human beings to cause it. A good society must not only cherish the possibilities that make lives good, it must also impose limits that restrict the scope of evil that results from the vices of people who may or may not be amoral, wicked, or moral monsters.

Pessimism leads conservatives to regard the human propensity to cause evil as a permanent feature of moral life. It is a feature intrinsic to human beings, although, of course, its expression is strongly influenced by the prevailing political arrangements. These arrangements may make evil more or less prevalent, but not even the best arrangements can undo the propensity to cause evil. If the limits set by political arrangements are effective, evil will show itself in private rather than public life, or, in an even more attenuated form, in the prevailing forms of art, in commercial competition, in sports, in the kinds of entertainment that is demanded and supplied, or in demonizing people in other societies. The best hope for avoiding evil, therefore, is to find relatively less harmful ways in which it can be expressed.

Pessimism, however, rejects as shallow the hope that a society will be successful in finding political arrangements that will sublimate evil. Political arrangements are made and implemented by people whose propensity to cause evil is likely to be neither stronger nor weaker than that of others. There is no reason to suppose that there is such a thing as "the best" political arrangements, or that, if there were, their creation and implementation could somehow escape the evil propensities of the people in charge. Whatever arrangements people make is bound to reflect their propensities, and since the propensity to cause evil is one among them, all arrangements will always be imperfect. The aim is to mitigate their imperfections as much as possible in the historical circumstances of particular societies.

The pessimism of conservatives is not a misanthropic counsel of doom. It is a realistic pessimism that recognizes that human propensities are varied, that evil is only one of them, and that good is another. These propensities vie for dominance in the arena of the soul, and sometimes one prevails, sometimes another. People are motivated by the good, not just by evil. If the issue hangs in the balance, political arrangements may well influence its outcome. Political arrangements, therefore, matter, it is just that they do not matter enough and are not reliable enough to hope from them the perfectibility of the human condition. The pessimism of conservatives is the pessimism of Sophocles, Thucydides, Machiavelli, Montaigne, Hobbes, Nietzsche, Stephen, Bradley, Santayana, and T. S. Eliot. The human condition cannot be changed; nevertheless, the efforts to make it better are worthwhile, even though the efforts are as vulnerable to the vicissitudes of contingency as the human condition itself.

CHAPTER 5

The Enforcement of Morality

I must dwell . . . on . . . epithets usually associated with morally impossible action, on a sense of disgrace, of outrage, of horror, of baseness, of brutality, and, most important, a sense that a barrier, assumed to be firm and almost insurmountable, has been knocked over, and a feeling that, if this horrible, or outrageous, or squalid, or brutal action is possible, then anything is possible and nothing is forbidden. . . . In the face of the doing of something that must not be done . . . the fear one may feel is fear of human nature. . . . This fear . . . is an aspect of respect for morality itself rather than for any particular morality.

— STUART HAMPSHIRE, *"Morality and Conflict"*

The preceding two chapters taken together constitute an overview of the political morality of conservatism. It emerges from this overview that commitment to a good society must involve commitment to the possibilities that may make lives good and to the limits on which the avoidance of evil depends. Although conservatism is pluralistic because it acknowledges the existence and the value of many varied possibilities whose realization would make lives good, it stresses that not all possibilities are permissible and those that are depend on conditions whose violation is impermissible. A good society, therefore, must impose limits on people living in it. These limits prohibit the pursuit of possibilities that violate the conditions on which permissible possibilities depend.

The imposition of limits unavoidably restricts the freedom of individuals, and so it is inherently dangerous. The countless historical and contemporary instances in which individuals were and are unjustifiably oppressed in the name of arbitrary religious or political moralities will be abhorrent to everyone whose allegiance lies with the party of humanity. Nevertheless, the limits that protect the conditions that make good lives possible are reasonable, not arbitrary. Any acceptable political morality must therefore give an account of what makes some limits reasonable and others arbitrary. The conservative account is given in terms of a three-level conception of political morality developed in this and the following two chapters.

On the first level, there are limits that protect the universal requirements of good lives, regardless of what form they may take. These limits must be protected by all good societies. Historical and cultural variations among them are small because the limits are set by the barely changing core that remains constant because of the basic physiological, psychological, and social needs that normal human beings living whatever happens to be their routine existence share. These are the limits that distinguish civilized life from barbarism. In civilized life, the universal conditions of good lives are protected; in barbarism, anything goes because nothing is prohibited. The violation of these limits is evil. Observing the limits makes it possible to satisfy basic needs, and that is normally good. These limits and possibilities will be discussed in this chapter.

On the second level, there are traditional limits and possibilities that define the moral identity of the people living in a particular society. In a good society, these limits include but also go beyond the universal ones without which good lives would be impossible. On this level, good lives may be conceived of in many different ways, provided their basic requirements, expressed in terms of primary values, are acknowledged. It is essential, however, to recognize that good lives must be conceived of in concrete ways. A society can be good only if it protects some concrete conceptions of a good life and encourages people to live according to them. These conceptions incorporate also the secondary values of various traditions and conceptions of a good life that may vary individually, traditionally, and historically. Reasonable limits on this second level then protect concrete traditions and conceptions of a good life. The reasonable possibilities are those suggested by the prevailing traditions and conceptions. The protection of these limits and possibilities is normally good, their violation is normally evil, but whether such goods and evils are primary or secondary, and what significance that distinction has, is a complicated matter whose discussion will be deferred until the next chapter.

On the third level, there are limits and possibilities that define the conceptions of a good life that individuals may pursue. These conceptions lead individuals to participate in various traditional activities of their society, adapting themselves to some of them, and in adapting them to their own characters and circumstances. Understanding these activities, coming to know one's character, and seeing one's circumstances realistically are complex and difficult tasks in which individuals need all the help they can get. Moral authorities provide that help. The nature and importance of moral authorities, and an explanation of them as crucial to living good lives, and not as intrusive meddlers, will be the topic of the chapter after the next one. However one forms an individual conception of a good life, such conceptions are formed out of the secondary values of various traditions, and they vary from individual to individual. The protection of a conception of a good life, one that embodies the universal requirements and conforms to the moral identity of a particular society, is normally a secondary good and its violation is normally a secondary evil.

The conservative view is not that these three levels of political morality ought to be imposed in order to make a society good. The conservative view is rather that these levels are found in good societies, and when the possibilities and limits are protected on each level, then a society becomes good. These levels emerge as a result of historical reflection on good and bad societies, and on what makes them good and bad; they are not abstract constructs, but concrete features that have been extracted from an understanding of the political arrangements that actually foster good lives.

Conservatism involves therefore a commitment to this three-level conception of political morality that proceeds from the universal requirements of all good lives, through the requirements of particular societies, to the individual requirements of specific conceptions of a good life. For ease of reference, the three levels will be referred to as universal, social, and individual. Conservatives are committed to this conception and to its possibilities and limits because they are committed to protecting the political arrangements that foster good lives which these possibilities and limits express.

REQUIRED CONVENTIONS

The distinction between primary and secondary values (in Chapter 3) was intended to call attention to the fact that two different kinds of values are required for good lives. Primary values derive from the minimum requirements of all good lives, such as adequate nutrition, health, shelter, rest, and protection against murder, torture, enslavement, and so forth. Good lives are alike because they depend on each of the primary values. But they also differ because they depend as well on secondary values, which vary with societies, traditions, and conceptions of a good life. Some of these secondary values are aesthetic appreciation, religious faith, a good job, carefree love affairs, raising children, and peak physical condition. A good society protects primary and secondary values by means of its conventions. Conventions that protect primary values are "required"; those that protect secondary values are "variable." Required conventions will be discussed now, variable ones in the next two chapters.

Take the primary value of life as an illustration. All good societies must protect the lives of people living in them, so they must have a convention prohibiting murder: deliberate and premeditated homicide. But this necessity leaves open both whether murder can ever be justified and the extent of its prohibition. Does it end at the borders or does it include foreigners? How inclusive is its prohibition in the society itself? Does it apply to the very old, to barely viable babies, to the mentally ill, or to criminals? What is the status of suicide, abortion, capital punishment, war, euthanasia, revenge, feuds, infanticide, and the like? What is recognized as a mitigating or exempting excuse? These are difficult questions that must be answered by all good societies, and they may answer them differently. These differences, however, must not be allowed to obscure the primary value of life and the necessity of the required convention prohibiting murder.

All good societies must recognize that there is a difference between clear cases in which a required convention is unambiguously violated and unclear cases that stand in need of interpretation. Murder for fun, torture for pleasure, enslavement for profit, to mention some examples, are clear cases in which required conventions are unjustifiably violated. People are deprived of a primary value they need to live a good life and the reason for depriving them is morally unacceptable.

There may be disagreements, of course, about whether an act constitutes murder, torture, or enslavement. Such disagreements lead to unclear cases about which two things need to be said. The first is that the existence of unclear cases in no way obscures clear cases. It may be unclear whether an act constitutes murder, torture, or enslavement. But if it does, and if it is motivated by fun, pleasure, or profit, then it is an evil act that any reasonable and morally committed person will recognize as such. Not everyone is reasonable and morally committed, evil acts are routinely done, but unclarity is not among their effects. That there are unreasonable and immoral people who act in evil ways casts no more doubt on the clear requirements of morality than there being stupid and self-destructive people who act in unhealthy ways does on the clear requirements of health.

The second thing that needs to be said is that if unclear cases are the results of disagreements among reasonable and morally committed people, then they strengthen rather than weaken the relevant required convention. For such disagreements presuppose the primary value in question and focus on its interpretation. When reasonable and morally committed people disagree about whether an act constitutes murder, torture, or enslavement, their disagreement is *not* about whether murder, torture, or enslavement, is evil. If their disagreement is *moral,* they are committed to aiming at a good society. This commits them to aiming at the good lives of people who live in their society, which, in turn, commits them to aiming at the protection of conditions that good lives require. Their disagreements, therefore, presuppose their commitment to primary values and to the required conventions that protect them. It is a logical, not a moral or political, point that their disagreements would not be possible without their shared commitment because sharing that commitment is what makes their disagreement moral.

Reasonable *moral* disagreements are not straightforwardly factual. The parties to them agree that a homicide has occurred, that much pain has been inflicted, or that freedom has been drastically curtailed. They disagree about it being right to regard these acts as murder, torture, or enslavement, and, consequently, as evil. These disagreements, however, are not hopelessly intractable. Because the opposing sides are committed to the primary values and required conventions that their disagreements presuppose, the burden of proof can be assigned. If they believe that murder, torture, and enslavement are evil, but that this homicide, this infliction of pain, or this deprivation of freedom is not an instance of these evils, then they owe an explanation of why the act in question is an exception.

Such explanations may be good or bad. Good ones try to excuse an apparently evil act on the ground that it was accidental or done in ignorance, or, if it was deliberate and informed, then on the ground that it was done to avoid much greater evil or to lead to much greater good. Killing a vicious tyrant, painfully extracting life-saving information from a terrorist, or sentencing a serial killer to a life of hard labor may be morally justified. Bad explanations will be unsupported by such reasons. There will also be explanations that are neither clearly good nor clearly bad because it is difficult to weigh the reasons adduced in support of them. Be that as it may, the existence of unclear cases actually reinforces, rather than calls into question, the reasonability of the moral requirement that all good societies must meet: the protection of the primary values of their members by required conventions.

The commitment of conservatives to required conventions, however, is not unconditional. Conservatives are pluralists, and pluralists have no unconditional commitments. Required conventions are of great importance to having a good society, but any required conventions may be justifiably violated if, and only if, the overall aim of protecting the conditions of good lives warrants it. History is full of hard cases in which the commitment to good lives had made it reasonable and morally justified to do what required conventions normally prohibit.

The obvious conclusion that follows from this understanding of required conventions is that a good society must enforce morality on the universal level. A society is good to the extent to which it makes good lives possible. Required conventions protect conditions of good lives no matter how they are conceived. So a good society must enforce its required conventions. This involves encouraging the pursuit of possibilities and prohibiting the violation of limits set by required conventions. The possibilities are defined by primary goods and the limits are defined by primary evils. The enforcement of required conventions is done through the legal system, public opinion, and moral education, which, with varying degrees of severity protect the possibilities and limits of all good lives. A society cannot be good if it fails to enforce the universal level of its morality. All adequate political moralities must make appropriate political arrangements to enforce this level.

The enforcement of morality, however, affects only its universal level, having to do with primary values and required conventions. Morality also has social and individual levels, which concern secondary values and variable conventions. The argument just completed is silent on what should happen on levels other than the universal. So the claim that morality must be enforced on the universal level is a claim about the prohibition of such matters as murder, torture, or enslavement, and it does not address the question of what a society should do, if indeed anything, about suicide, sexual preferences, pornography, prostitution, taxation, university education, high culture, and so forth.

If it is clearly understood that the enforcement of morality is restricted to the universal level, and that its concern is exclusively with required conventions that protect primary values, then it becomes difficult to see how any morally committed person could reasonably oppose its enforcement. If there is reasonable opposition, it must be based on the suspicion that what is being enforced are variable conventions and secondary values. This is just the claim that critics of conservatism often make. They charge conservatives with the perpetuation of irrational prejudices, with forcing repressive moral views on unwilling recipients, and with specious moralizing masquerading as reasoned argument. These critics are mistaken. But showing that requires going deeper into what is involved in the enforcement of the universal level of morality.

REQUIRED AND STRONGLY HELD CONVENTIONS

The question of whether morality ought to be enforced provoked a heated and confused controversy between Lord Justice Patrick Devlin[1] and some of the leading lights of liberalism.[2] It began with a lecture Devlin delivered in 1959 to the British Academy about the conditions under which a society is justified in enforcing some aspect of its morality. The point of departure of Devlin's argument was the recommendation of a British Royal Commission to decriminalize homosexuality and prostitution. Devlin did not say whether he was for or against the recommendation. What he did was to state and argue for the principle that if a society is to endure, then it must use its legal system to enforce a certain narrowly circumscribed part of its morality. Devlin's argument was thus very close to the one advanced in the preceding section.

The liberal response was an avalanche of indignation. Devlin was charged with arguing against the recommendation, approving of the punishment of those who deviate from a Victorian interpretation of Christian sexual morality, and advocating a repressive attitude to conduct that departs from the prevailing norms of a society. The following illustration is one of many: "Lord Devlin concludes that if our society hates homosexuality enough it is justified in outlawing it, and forcing human beings to choose between the miseries of frustration and persecution, because the danger the practice presents to society's existence."[3]

This reaction rests on a bad confusion because liberals themselves are vociferous advocates of the enforcement of morality in numerous cases, such as integration, egalitarianism, foreign aid, and the preferential treatment of women and minorities. Consistency requires, therefore, that they should not object to Devlin's claim that it may be justified to enforce morality. If liberals have a legitimate objection, it must be directed against the particular cases in which they take Devlin to insist on the enforcement of morality. But this objection also misses the point because Devlin has not committed himself to any particular case that would warrant the enforcement of morality. He did not claim, for instance, that homosexuality or prostitution are such cases. His argument centered on the general question of whether morality may ever be legitimately enforced. To that question, however, both Devlin and liberals give an affirmative answer.

Devlin says that "Societies disintegrate from within more frequently than they are broken up by external pressures. There is disintegration when no common morality is observed and history shows that the loosening of moral bonds is often the first stage of disintegration, so that society is justified in taking the same steps to preserve its moral code as it does to preserve its government and other essential institutions." In order to take these steps, it must be known what the morality of a society actually is, and so Devlin asks: "How are the moral judgements of society to be ascertained?" His answer is that the standard by which they are ascertained is "the reasonable man. . . . He is not expected to reason about anything and his judgements may be largely a matter of feeling. [The standard] . . . is the viewpoint of the man in the street. . . . He might also be called the right-minded man. For my purposes I should like to call him the man in the jury box, for the moral judgement of society must be something about which any twelve men or women drawn at random might after discussion be expected to be unanimous." These judgments, according to Devlin, establish what lies "beyond the limits of tolerance." In order to regard something as intolerable "[i]t is not nearly enough that a majority dislike a practice; there must be a real feeling of reprobation. There must be disgust if it is deeply felt and not manufactured. Its presence is a good indication that the bounds of toleration are being reached. Not everything is to be tolerated. No society can do without intolerance, indignation, and disgust; they are the forces behind the moral law."[4]

In their criticisms of Devlin, Ronald Dworkin and, following him, Herbert Hart argue that Devlin may be interpreted as advancing one of two theses. The first is that "morality is valued as the cement of society, the bond . . . or one of the bonds, without which men would not cohere in society. . . . The case for the enforcement of morality on this view is that its maintenance is necessary to prevent the disintegration of society." Dworkin and Hart call this "the disintegration thesis." The second is "that society has a right to enforce its morality because the majority have the right to follow their own moral convictions that their moral environment is a thing of value to be defended from change."[5] According to Dworkin and Hart, this is "the conservative thesis." Their criticisms aim to show that neither thesis is defensible. The conservative view, by contrast, is that both theses are true, provided they are freed from misinterpretations. The disintegration thesis will be explained and defended now, the conservative thesis in the next chapter.[6]

The chief trouble with the disintegration thesis, according to its critics, is that it ignores the obvious fact that there are bound to be moral changes and disagreements in any society without resulting in the society's disintegration. Devlin, however, grants that and also that these changes and disagreements may eventually produce a shift in what is regarded with "intolerance, indignation, and disgust." What he is saying is that at any given time in a good society there must be acts that people who are not depraved would find disgusting. These acts involve a certain sort of violation of what has been called here, although not by Devlin, required conventions. If there is no disgust felt in a society at the relevant kind of violations, then it is already disintegrating because its members have no strong commitment to protecting the minimum requirements of good lives in their context. It ought to be clear, therefore, that Devlin's critics have misunderstood his position. It must be admitted, however, that Devlin is partly responsible for this misunderstanding because he does not say what moral changes and disagreements do and do not contribute to the disintegration of society. This unclarity, however, can be removed by the distinction, which neither Devlin nor his critics drew, between required and strongly held conventions.

Required conventions protect the minimum requirements of good lives. They may or may not be strongly held by members of a society. If they are strongly held, then, at least in that respect, the society is good because its members are seriously committed to protecting the conditions of good lives. If required conventions are not held strongly, then the conditions they protect are at risk, the society is failing to make good lives possible, it is bound to be losing the allegiance of its members, and so it is in danger of disintegration. It is a mark of a good society, therefore, that its required conventions are strongly held.

Another mark of a good society, however, is that *only* its required conventions are held strongly. If members of a society hold some variable conventions strongly, then they allow some secondary value of some particular tradition or conception of a good life to achieve dominance and override primary or secondary values that are incompatible with it. This is indeed a repressive and thus objectionable attitude. If "intolerance, indignation, and disgust" are directed at people who fail to conform to strongly held variable conventions, then they are unreasonable and morally objectionable attitudes. But reason and morality are on the side of "intolerance, indignation, and disgust," if they are responses to certain violations of required conventions, if they are elicited, for example, by murder, torture, or enslavement. If Devlin had made it clear that he favors these responses only when they are directed against certain violations of required conventions, and if his liberal critics had made it clear that what they find morally objectionable is when these responses have the violation of variable conventions as their target, then their heated dispute would have cooled off.

THE MORAL IMPORTANCE OF DISGUST

A much more searching criticism of Devlin's position is that feelings in general, and disgust in particular, are unreliable moral guides. They tend to overpower people, cloud their judgment, and lead them in morally noxious directions. What if twelve randomly chosen citizens of a society happen to find, or not to find, homosexuality, capital punishment, abortion, or the mutilation of criminals disgusting? Are moral judgments to be made on the basis of what the unreflective people in a society agree in feeling about them? Can a society and its members not be swayed by vicious feelings? What about enlightened opinion as a moral force? Is that not often necessary to bring about moral improvement? Devlin does not answer these questions. Even if he is right that agreement in some moral feelings is necessary for the survival of a society, it does not follow that such agreement is good to have. For the society may not deserve to survive, and the agreement may be in regarding evil as good. The question, therefore, is how to tell when disgust is appropriate and when it is not.

The *Oxford English Dictionary* (1961 ed.) lists two current usages for "disgust" as a noun. The first is a specific sense in which it is elicited by some food, drink, or medicine, and it is irrelevant for the present purposes. The second, more general one, is as follows: "Strong repugnance, aversion, or repulsion excited by that which is loathsome or offensive, as a foul smell, disagreeable person or action, disappointed ambition, etc.; profound instinctive dislike or dissatisfaction." Disgust is thus an emotion, and the experience of it depends on finding something revolting. In this respect, there are considerable individual variations. The cases in point, however, are experiences that involve both "profound" and "instinctive" revulsion—experiences that just about everybody in contemporary Western societies would find disgusting. This kind of disgust is a much stronger reaction than mere squeamishness.[7]

A noteworthy feature of the uniformity of the experiences that elicit disgust is that if some people in our context were not disgusted in certain situations, then there would have to be some special explanation in terms of their repression, brutalization, pathological inattention, or the like. The experiences include slowly disemboweling a person, being suffocated under putrefying human corpses, dismembering someone with a chain saw, slaughtering babies and bathing in their blood, or being drowned in excrement. (One must apologize for presenting this list, but the subject requires examples.)

The disgust these and similar situations elicit is a visceral reaction. To say that they are sickening is not a metaphor. If people encounter such situations, they are nauseated, their guts heave, they tremble, their hearts race, they both sweat and shiver, they cannot control their physical responses, or control them only with great effort. It is unthinkable that such experiences could be combined with the enjoyment of a good meal or flirtation, or that people could respond to them merely as annoying interruptions of an interesting conversation or a good book. These experiences are fundamentally unsettling, their memories persist, they are the stuff of nightmares, and people usually find it hard and often therapeutic to talk about them.

There is a sense, therefore, in which disgust is not under voluntary control. It is necessary to be careful, however, not to exaggerate the extent to which disgust is involuntary. If people are surprised by the experience, if it comes to them as a shock, then their reaction tends to be involuntary. But they can also anticipate the experience, prepare themselves for it, steel themselves to the revolting thing that they are about to encounter, and then they can, to some extent, control their reaction. Even in such cases, however, what they usually control is not the feeling of disgust itself, but its severity and expression.

There is, furthermore, a shared sense that learning to control disgust, not on any particular occasion, but generally, is a dubious skill. People who do not feel disgust at the sort of experiences listed above are in some sense diminished. They have been de-sensitized, brutalized, hardened in a way that sets them apart from the rest of their society. It is natural to be vulnerable to certain kinds of shock, to react viscerally to some revolting objects. People's steeling themselves not to buckle under their disgust is one thing, and it may be good to be able to do it in some extraordinary situations, but to learn control to the extent of not having to steel themselves is to have lost a sensitivity that is important to have.

Not all disgust fits the description so far offered. Even among people who judge alike in moral matters there are usually wide variations in what they find disgusting. The food, odor, insect, sexual practice, personal habit, or joke one person finds disgusting may appear to another as an object of indifference or even as something likable or appropriate. Disgust is often a matter of taste. But it is not always so; some experiences of disgust, as the *OED* says, are "profound" and "instinctive." Part of the purpose of the examples given above is to point at some instances where disgust is not a matter of taste. Such experiences will be referred to as "moral disgust."

What makes some experiences of disgust moral is the combination of two elements. One element is the grievous and unjustified harm inflicted on a human being. The other is that it is done in a manner that outrages the sensibility of morally committed witnesses. The infliction of grievous and unjustified harm need not be outrageous, and moral outrage may be provoked in other ways. Moral disgust requires the coincidence of these two elements. It is possible that there may be some few people who are not outraged when they witness such things being done. In that case, however, there must be some explanation of why they do not respond in the same way as most others do in their context. Their profession may have hardened them, they may themselves have been brutalized, they may have particularly strong psychological defenses that shield them, and so forth. The fact remains that moral disgust is the normal reaction for people who witness the kinds of acts that have been illustrated earlier, and if the normal reaction does not occur, its absence requires an explanation.

Much of the time when people experience deep disgust, the cause is the *spectacle* of an outrageous event. They witness the disgusting thing happening to someone else, real or fictional, but it is not happening to them. In civilized circumstances, there is usually some distance between themselves and the object of their moral disgust. This space between subject and object creates room for two other elements essentially connected with moral disgust: imagination and fear.

Through imagination, people put themselves in place of the victims to whom the disgusting thing is happening. The bring themselves to experience vicariously what the victims are observed as experiencing personally. The viewers' disgust is, as it were, both on the victim's behalf and on their own. This gives a clue to why there are variations in individual experiences of moral disgust. Moral disgust is normally a uniform reaction to certain situations, but its intensity is not uniform. On some people, moral disgust, even if it is vicarious, leaves a much more lasting mark than on others. The explanation is that in the mental lives of some people imagination plays a much greater role than in those of others. How much moral disgust affects people depends on how disposed and capable they are of imaginatively putting themselves into other people's positions.

People also vary in their capacity to control their reactions to what they find morally disgusting. They have the experience, but they keep it at arm's length, they control the extent to which their imagination dwells on the experience. How successful they can be at this is determined by how central and vivid the play of their imagination normally is. It has been noted earlier that it is unclear whether the capacity to have this control is a good thing. To have it, makes people less sensitive; not to have it, makes them more vulnerable.

Furthermore, moral disgust has evident pitfalls. People who are provoked by their imagination to feel moral disgust are often suspect. It is natural to ask about them why they go about imagining disgusting things. One answer is that they are tempted by what is disgusting, and their reaction is partly a revulsion at themselves. Much strident moralizing has this source. Such tainted reactions, of course, are morally undesirable. But it is also possible that people's imaginations are understandably provoked because they find themselves in situations in which they cannot help confronting morally disgusting spectacles, and their imaginations subsequently prey on them. Soldiers, members of juries, triage nurses, the police, pathologists, and attendants in psychiatric hospitals are especially liable to be thus assailed. It is a reflection on the current state of movies and television programs that many of them inflict a similar liability on their audiences.

Another element of moral disgust is fear. It is natural to fear what is morally disgusting because it represents a danger. The danger, however, is not necessarily that some immediate harm threatens to befall the subjects of disgust. It is rather that something they find profoundly revolting is going to invade their lives and they cannot keep horror at bay. But why is it that they uniformly find some possibilities so fearful, if these possibilities do not threaten them with immediate harm? This question leads to the fundamental link between moral disgust and required conventions.

MORAL DISGUST AND REQUIRED CONVENTIONS

It is not surprising if Devlin's twelve randomly chosen people in a good society unanimously agree about the clear violations of required conventions being evil. There is no doubt in anybody's mind that murder for fun, torture for pleasure, enslavement for profit are clear cases of evil. Nevertheless, it is a conspicuous fact that required conventions are often violated, even in good societies. Societies can sustain some such violations, but there is a limit to how frequent they can be, since after a while the societies cease to be good. Societies in this state may be held together by inertia, fear, or terror, but they lose their moral justification because they no longer protect the conditions of good lives. That a society may reach this state is one of the worst things that can happen to it. The danger that looms then is disintegration: regression to barbarism in which there are no limits and all possibilities are at risk. What threatens then is the breaching of the bulwark that keeps barbarism out and makes civilized life possible. That bulwark is constituted of the required conventions.

The fear that is one constitutive element of moral disgust is of this danger. The fear is reasonable in proportion to the threat the danger of disintegration presents. The violation of required conventions is threatening in two ways. One is the immediate danger that people themselves or those they care about will become victims. But this is not what is feared when reasonable people feel moral disgust. Moral disgust is often provoked in people by spectacles that present no immediate danger to them. The danger that is reasonably feared in moral disgust is not immediate harm, but the more remote and more devastating collapse of civilized life. What is feared is not that one will suffer, but that life will become barbaric because morality loses its foothold in it. The prospect of the collapse of the whole framework within which people can make a good life for themselves is far more threatening than even serious harm that may befall one. For the latter can be alleviated by compensation, condemnation, sympathy, and the like, whereas the former endangers the very possibility of good lives.

It is crucial to understanding the significance of moral disgust that what makes it a reasonable reaction is not the mere violation of a required convention, but the kind of violation that threatens civilized life. These violations are not banal evil acts motivated by common human vices. They are acts that provoke moral outrage because they transgress required conventions in a gross, flamboyant, flagrant, and contemptuous manner. The required conventions are not just broken, but flaunted. Such acts reveal contempt for morality. Murder, torture, and enslavement are certainly violations of required conventions. But it is one thing to shoot people dead and take their money and another to disembowel children and watch them writhe as they die; it is one thing to deprive captured enemy soldiers of sleep and food in order to extract information from them and another to mutilate randomly selected victims by cutting off their limbs inch by inch with a chain saw to establish one's reputation as an enforcer; it is one thing to restrict the movement of itinerant workers and force them to work for food and it is another to kidnap people, force them into sadistic sexual rituals, while making a pornographic film depicting their humiliation.

All of these acts violate required conventions, and are therefore evil. But the second act in each case normally provokes moral disgust, whereas the first does not. Both cause evil, but they are of a different order. In the first, wicked people use evil means to achieve evil ends. In the second, wicked people use evil means, but the evil of their ends is so extreme as to remove it from the range of understandable human options. These ends are monstrous and their pursuit is incompatible with civilized life. Their agents are not merely wicked, but depraved. These are the acts, real or fictional, to which moral disgust is a reasonable reaction.

Moral disgust, therefore, is revulsion at acts that subvert the moral foundation of a society. The subversion consists in the gross violations of required conventions, violations that involve not merely breaking but flaunting them. The violations threaten the possibility of civilized life. Moral disgust is the secular equivalent of sacrilege. Indeed, an alternative way of describing what provokes moral disgust is the desecration of some person. It is a reaction to seeing the unthinkable happen, to treating a person as no one should be treated, no matter what. Members of a good society are united in being revolted by it. And when the revolting act is seen as done, there looms the dreadful possibility of the removal of all limits. The possibility of this happening is the ultimate object of the fear that is one essential element in moral disgust.

The point about moral disgust, of course, is not that when people are assailed by it, then they are aware of the account just completed. The account is the result of reflection, whereas moral disgust is an instinctive emotional reaction. People feel it because their moral education makes them feel profound revulsion at some acts. They do not come to feel it because they have memorized some rules, but because they have learned what required conventions are and what sort of violation of them is beyond the pale. Knowing those things, they can be relied on to recognize the occasions that outrage morality. If challenged to justify their reaction, they may not be able to do so. But that does not mean that their reaction is not justifiable.

Moral disgust is not the only response to the violation of required

conventions. Other feelings, as well as intellectual and volitional responses, are also standard parts of the moral repertoire. People may
feel, for instance, sadness or dismay at the outrages they witness. These
quiet emotions, however, will surely be felt only later, after the visceral
reaction of moral disgust has somewhat dissipated. People can also
think through what the appropriate response is to a spectacle of moral
outrage they encounter and they can call upon their will to make themselves respond in certain ways regardless of how they feel. But if the
kinds of situations that provoke moral disgust are remembered, then
the very need for reflection and for summoning up an effort will be
seen as morally suspect. Morally committed people ought to feel moral
disgust at some acts and they ought not to have to reflect or make efforts
of will to oppose them.

Feeling moral disgust about the gross violation of required conventions, however, is neither a necessary nor a sufficient condition of moral
commitment. It is not necessary because morally committed people may
become hardened by prolonged exposure to moral outrages. Their experiences may overtax their emotional capacity, and, perhaps as a means
of self-defense, their emotional reactions are deadened. Their moral
commitments have not weakened, but their moral reactions have altered. Nor is moral disgust a sufficient condition of moral commitment
because people may feel moral disgust when they should not. It is not
unusual to confuse a strong commitment to some non-moral convention, say about sexual conduct, with a required convention. People then
mistakenly regard the flaunting of the non-moral convention as endan-
gering the conditions of civilized life, when it is merely the challenging
of a local custom. Moral disgust in such cases is a sign of moral confusion, not of moral commitment.

In a good or not-so-bad society, moral disgust is bound to be a rare experience, because if it were otherwise, required conventions would be
frequently violated in an outrageous manner, and a society in which that
happens is bound to be bad. If that is so, however, then it may be won-
dered why the case for conservatism requires emphasizing this rare experience. The answer is that what matters is not the frequency of moral
disgust, but the shared capacity of people living together in a society to
react with moral disgust to the appropriate situations. The shared possession of this capacity is a good indication that the society is morally
healthy because people living in it would be outraged by acts that flaunt

the required conventions that guide the conduct of most of them. The capacity to react that way and to react that way when circumstances warrant it establishes a bond among those share it. And that bond is at once moral, emotional, and deep, because it informs their moral sensibility and constitutes part of their identity. The stronger that bond is, the better is the moral health of a society; and the weaker it is, the closer a society comes to disintegration.

Conservatives stress the central moral importance of this point. Liberals, by contrast, stress the dangers that moral disgust may be an inappropriate reaction to some situations, that the moral sensibility of a people may be corrupt, and that the moral bond that unites them may be an immoral bond. These are real dangers, as the historical record of numerous societies amply demonstrates. But the fear of this danger leads liberals to question that moral, emotional, and deep bond among a people without which a good society cannot long endure. Surely, the fact that a good and necessary thing may be corrupted is not a sufficient reason to question its goodness. It *is* a sufficient reason to do what is possible to prevent its corruption. That, however, is a reason whose strength conservatives recognize and stress, without making the mistake liberals make of fearing a danger so much as to lose sight of the goodness of the very thing whose corruption they fear.

Nor should it be thought that to emphasize the significance of moral disgust is to deny that will and intellect play an indispensable role in morality. There are countless moral situations in which reflection and effort are essential, whereas feelings are an unreliable guide. It is just that the situations involving the desecration of individuals, situations in which required conventions are outrageously violated are not like these. These are the situations in which feelings in general and moral disgust in particular do and ought to play a dominant role.

CONSERVATISM AND THE UNIVERSAL LEVEL OF POLITICAL MORALITY

The central argument of this chapter has been that conservatism, as any reasonable political morality, must be committed to the enforcement of required conventions, which protect the universal requirements of all good lives. The conservative argument, therefore, is not that a society is justified in enforcing whatever its strongly held conventions happen to be. Nor is it that a society is justified in forcing on its members some traditions or conceptions of a good life. What a society is justified in doing is enforcing the universal level of morality: required conventions protecting primary values. This justification is independent of what political, moral, or religious beliefs, sexual preferences, racial, ethnic, or cultural identities, economic circumstances, or individual aspirations people have. It depends only on being committed to a good society, which is made good by enabling its members to live good lives, which, in turn, depends on the protection of the possibilities and limits that all good lives require.

This is not a reactionary view, for it is compatible with the recognition that the future should bring a much needed corrective of the past. It is not a plea for maintaining the status quo, for it allows that the status quo may be bad. It is not a plot to repress any reasonable conception of a good life, for it is not committed to any particular view about how people should live. It is an attempt to identify reasonable limits that a good society must protect. Because these limits protect civilized life from barbarism, their violation by actions that reveal a contemptuous disregard of the limits rightly provokes moral disgust. Such actions threaten not just individuals who are their victims, but also the conditions on which everyone in the society depends. Moral disgust is a justified reaction to the outrageous violation of required convention.

The argument is not that if an act disgusts some people, then it should be condemned. Nor is it that if an act disgusts the majority or everyone in a society, then the society is justified in repressing it. The argument is not even that if disgust is moral and it is provoked by the outrageous violation of a convention, then the offending act should be placed beyond the pale. The argument demands in addition that the convention be a required one. Meeting that requirement does not depend on whether or how strongly moral disgust is felt, or on what percentage of a population feels it, but whether the required convention does indeed protect a condition required for civilized life and a violation of it reveals a contemptuous disregard for such life.

CHAPTER 6

Moral Tradition and Moral Identity

> Social life would be psychologically intolerable if each of its moments required from us full attention, deliberate decision, and high emotional involvement. . . . Triviality is one of the fundamental requirements of social life. . . . If we understand this . . . we will see that there are limits not only to disorder and discontinuity, but also to the frequency of "significant events." We will then become very careful how we view "meaningless rituals," "empty forms," or "mere routines" in social life—simply because we will recognize that if social life in its entirety were charged with profound meaning, we would all go out of our minds.
>
> —PETER L. BERGER, *Facing Up to Modernity*

The aim of the argument in the last, present, and next chapters is to develop a three-level conception of political morality. On each level, there are distinctive possibilities and limits the protection of which, according to conservatives, make a society good. On the universal level, the possibilities are presented by primary values and the limits by required conventions. They jointly protect the minimum conditions of all good lives. The disintegration thesis that has been defended in the last chapter is that a society is justified in enforcing the universal level of its moral tradition because without it good lives are impossible and the society would disintegrate if it failed to secure the minimum conditions its people require.

The topic of the present chapter is the second—social—level of political morality. The relevant possibilities are presented by some secondary values and the limits by some variable conventions. Together they protect the moral identity of the people living in that society. The conservative thesis is that a society is justified in defending the social level of its political morality because failing to do so would jeopardize the moral identity of its people. Moral identity is another indispensable constituent of good lives, even though moral identities vary with societies, moral traditions, and individuals. Another way of explaining the topic of this chapter is that it aims to work out the implications of one of the basic beliefs of conservatism: traditionalism.

MORAL TRADITION

Some of the conventions of a society are moral, others are not. A convention is moral if its primary purpose is to secure the conditions required by good lives. Required conventions are obviously moral since they protect universal and minimum conditions of good lives. It is equally obvious that some variable conventions are moral and some are not. Whether or not women are mainly responsible for household chores has an effect on the careers they may seek and how they conceive of good lives. Since societies differ in this respect, their relevant conventions are variable; but since the conventions affect the goodness of many lives, they are also moral. On the other hand, societies also have variable conventions regarding favored games, for instance, which have normally no bearing on the goodness of lives, so that they are non-moral.

It complicates matters that variable conventions may have an effect on the goodness of lives in one society, but not in another. Teenage sex, alcohol consumption, and nepotism are moral offenses in some societies and accepted parts of life in others. Just about anything may come to be thought to affect the goodness of lives in the context of some society. It is futile therefore to try to draw a sharp distinction between moral and non-moral variable conventions. The most that can be said in the service of clarity is that if a variable convention is treated as moral, then its justification must exhibit its effect on the goodness of lives.

In order to make concrete the hitherto abstract idea of variable conventions, here is a list of them drawn quite unsystematically from the moral tradition of contemporary America. Parents are responsible for their children; breaking a promise requires an excuse; politicians should not tell public lies; winners ought not to gloat over losers; people should not brag about their achievements; a life of idleness is wrong; following one's conscience is right; animals should not be treated cruelly;

disagreements should not erupt into violence; it is wrong to spread malicious gossip about one's opponent; permission must be asked before borrowing anything; confidences ought to be kept; white lies are permissible; people should not rejoice publicly about the misfortune of their enemies; handicapped people should be helped; the expression of unpopular opinions should be protected; chastity and parsimony are obsolate virtues; elitism is suspect; sincerely held religious beliefs ought to be respected; one's financial affairs are private; physical labor is not shameful.

This list is impressionistic and illustrative, not exhaustive or representative. The variable conventions it contains, and the countless others that could be added to them, form an intricate, interlocking, sometimes mutually reinforcing, sometimes inconsistent system. Much of it is uncodified and unconscious, and conformity to it is habitual and customary. Many people who by and large observe these conventions may go through life without having or needing an opportunity to articulate or to declare allegiance to them. Variable conventions are of course often violated. But when that happens, the violators either accept blame or they can be shown its appropriateness. If people habitually violate the variable conventions of their moral tradition, they are immoral, abnormal, or, in rare and exceptional cases, moral reformers whose violations are conscientious acts of protest, which may or may not be justified. If there are many people who, for whatever reason, habitually violate the prevailing variable conventions, then the moral tradition is radically changing or disintegrating.

The moral tradition of a society is the evaluative background of the conduct of its members. It is what moral lapses are deviations from. It provides criteria for determining what kind of conduct requires excuse and what sort of excuse is acceptable. This is not the whole of morality, for room must be left for individuals to construct their own conceptions of a good life and live accordingly (see the next chapter), for supererogatory conduct, and for relationships with people outside of the context of one's society. It is not meant to be a guide in moral crises, extreme situations, or radical changes. It is the morality of everyday life. Since for most people much of life is everyday, their moral tradition is bound to have a significant influence on how they live their lives.

It will deepen this account of moral traditions to distinguish, following Oakeshott, between two kinds of tradition.[1] The first is guided by a specific goal. It provides the framework of practices, rules, ideals, skills, historical precedents, and outstanding achievements with the aid of which people may pursue their common goal, whatever it happens to be. It may be profit, world domination, the composition, performance, and appreciation of music, historical research, athletic achievement, helping the poor, and so on. There will be many such traditions in a society.

The other is an endeavor to defend the conditions necessary for the existence and continuation of the first kind of tradition. This kind of tradition does not aim at some specific goal; it aims to make possible the pursuit and achievement of specific goals. Legal, political, managerial, and law enforcement traditions are some examples of this kind of tradition, and moral traditions are others. Moral traditions, then, are enabling rather than productive; defensive rather than venturesome; regulative rather than goal-directed. A moral tradition is working well if no one in a society needs to be aware of its existence. A society in such a felicitous state shows itself to be morally untroubled. People in it can get on with their lives, pursuing what specific goals they may happen to have.

It is a great and rare achievement if a society reaches such moral spontaneity during some moment of its history. The vast majority of past and present societies falls more or less short of this desirable state. Its approximation depends, in the first instance, on moral education, which consists in handing down the required and the variable conventions from one generation to the next. Moral education begins with imitation and the rote learning of these conventions expressed as simplified rules. But these will not take novices very far. Morally well-educated people do not merely know how to do what others have done in their situation, they also know how to recognize which situations are moral and what specific types of responses are appropriate in them. Imitation and unthinking rule-following must be replaced by intelligent performance. Such a performance, however, involves more than knowing how to act in conformity to conventions. It also involves knowing what conduct is appropriate in new situations. It requires creative participation in the moral tradition.

This kind of participation is based on experience and requires an appreciation of the spirit of the tradition. It is based on knowing which of several possible conventions ought to guide agents in a particular situation; when steadfast adherence to a convention is right and when consis-

tency turns into soulless rigidity; when some prevailing variable convention is at odds with the spirit of the tradition; when individual interests
should take precedence over the common good, and when they should
not; when the good that may be achieved is great enough to risk the evil
that failure may produce; when kindness or respect is actually warranted
in particular cases; and so forth.

One reason for trying to acquire the requisite moral knowledge is
that moral traditions inspire it. Moral education is initiation into possibilities whose realization may make a life good. It is the cultivation of a
sensibility in terms of which participants in a moral tradition perceive
good and evil. Belonging to a moral tradition therefore is not merely habitual conformity to conventions, but also having particular motives for
doing so and sharing those motives with others who also belong to it.
These motives derive from a moral vision about the possibilities of a
good life.

Vision is perhaps too grandiose a term to describe this aspect of moral
traditions. People belonging to a moral tradition are rarely visionaries.
Moral traditions in fact often restrain their adherents' flights of fancy.
Yet people receive much more from a moral tradition than just a conventional outlook. Such an outlook need not guide action, it need not
inspire, it need not provide a framework of interpretation and evaluation in terms of good and evil, and it need not engage the emotions of
those who share it. But moral traditions do all these things and more.

The evaluative dimension of a moral tradition is deep. It goes beyond
knowing how to use general moral terms such as good and evil, or right
and wrong. The depth comes from familiarity with the discriminations,
nuances, judgments of importance and priority, from attention to
sources of conflict and tension, all of which are part of the texture of
everyday life guided by the tradition. What participants know is not
merely that this person is good and that evil, but also what makes them
so, why one is better or worse, more or less culpable or admirable,
weaker or stronger, more capable of improvement or more hopelessly
corrupt than another person in similar circumstances. They know what
is outrageous, shocking, offensive; what is a sophomoric attempt to provoke, a cry for help, or an assertion of independence, which may be pre-
mature, timely, or overdue; they know the distinctions among actions
that should be encouraged, tolerated, forbidden, and respected; they
know what is shameful, dishonorable, forgivable, or a sign of weakness

or wickedness; they know how to tell what is morally significant or negligible, and what lies in between.

Full-fledged participants in a moral tradition know these and thousands of similar things in a particular manner. They do not know them as an umpire knows the rules. They do not normally reflect and then carefully select the appropriate rule that best fits the case on hand. Moral knowledge for such people has become a second nature. Making the distinctions, noticing the nuances, being alive to the conflicts, priorities, pitfalls, and temptations no longer requires much thought. Just as an accomplished violinist knows how to play adagio and a rock climber knows how to manage an overhang, so participants in a moral tradition know about moral matters. There are times and situations, of course, when they have to stop and think. But that happens only in difficult cases. The daily flow of moral life can be handled spontaneously by people whose moral tradition is in good order.

Nor is the required knowledge like that of anthropologists observing another society. The crucial difference is that anthropologists stand outside of what they observe. They may privately approve or disapprove of its moral tradition; they may feel sympathy, revulsion, or indifference; and they may compare it favorably or unfavorably to other traditions with which they are familiar. Participants in a moral tradition are necessarily inside it. They can observe it perhaps as accurately as any anthropologist. But they cannot be indifferent. It is not that they are bound to judge their own tradition superior to others. It is rather that whatever moral judgments they make is made in terms their tradition provides. Their belonging to it means that they see the moral dimension of life in that way.

This could not be otherwise. For a moral tradition gives people their view of what the possibilities are whose realization may make life worth living, what it is to be a morally good person, what personal characteristics are virtuous and admirable, how people should treat each other, what the acceptable forms of personal relationships are, how to cope with misfortune, adversity, and the prospect of failure, and what the duties and privileges are of the various positions in life afforded by their society. These possiblities constitute the substratum of their moral life and inform their sensibility in terms of which they evaluate the moral significance of whatever happens. Indifference would mean the loss of the evaluative dimension of their lives.

Moral traditions leave their imprint on the individuals who participate in them. They shape the way they think and feel about their own
lives and the way they interpret the disclosures of their experiences. But
by being so shaped, they come to belong to a community whose members share an outlook and sensibility. Moral traditions then unite their
participants by providing them with a common way of interpreting and
responding to the world.[2] At other times, when societies were smaller
and more homogeneous, contemporary members of a moral tradition
were likely to know each other personally or by reputation. If they did
not, their clothing, demeanor, and language would have identified their
allegiances. This system of identification has been changing because societies have grown larger, less homogeneous, and more impersonal. Yet
moral traditions need visible marks of belongingness and these, at the
present time, are behavioral clues, rituals, and ceremonies.

The behavioral clues are the gestures, frowns, smiles, nods, scowls,
laughter and tears, sniffings and cluckings, winkings, head scratchings,
yawns, clearings of throat, stares, gazes, looks and taking care not to
look, gaze, or stare, the speed and emphasis with which something is
said, the occasion and direction in which it is said, blushes, blanches,
and the multitude of others ways in which people emphasize, embellish,
soften, indicate the seriousness or levity of what they say and do. But the
clues are telling only if they communicate what the agent has intended
or meant, and this, of course, requires that the actor and the spectator,
the agent and the recipient, the speaker and the hearer should share an
interpretation of the significance of what has passed between them.
This process, once again, is rarely conscious or reflective. The clues are
frequently given and understood without either party being aware of
their passage. To a very considerable extent, people feel comfortable
and familiar with each other because they can depend on being thus
understood.

These sentiments are enhanced by the rituals and ceremonies that
permeate everyday life. The rituals are the greetings, handshakes, open-
ings of doors, taking off of coats, jackets, ties, the sharing of a meal, having coffee or a drink together, kissing and embracing, telling of secrets,
sharing confidences, exchanging gossip, expressing respect, condo-
lence, enmity, or sympathy.

The ceremonies mark significant occasions, such as birth, marriage,
death, graduation, birthdays, anniversaries, arrivals and departures, pro-

motion and retirement, holidays and festivities. They too are unifying forces which deepen, strengthen, and sustain those who participate in them. Fellow members of a moral tradition share the knowledge of what is appropriate to the significant events of their lives and they share also the knowledge of the manner in which these events are to be marked. This remains true even of those rebels, eccentrics, non-conformists, and iconoclasts who refuse to do what is appropriate. For the moral tradition that they reject determines the occasions on which they express their opposition. Only genuine indifference, uninvolvement, and ignorance of what is appropriate place people outside of a moral tradition.

When individuals participate in a moral tradition in the manner just described, they derive a considerable portion of their moral identity from it. This identity is something that they both share with each other and makes them the individuals they are. The basis of their shared moral identity is not that they know, love, or even like each other. There need be no fundamental principle to which they all subscribe, no overarching ideal whose inspirational force motivates them. Their solidarity may be real and strong without having a unitary base. Their conduct is largely spontaneous, unreflective, and customary, and they have an unarticulated feeling of ease in each others' company. Their shared identity guarantees that there is much that need not be said, and that when something needs to be done, they know how to do it. The signs of a shared moral identity are the behavioral clues, rituals, and ceremonies, and the consequence is that people recognized as fellow members are given the benefit of the doubt. They are regarded as agents and recipients who are owed and who, in turn, owe respect and can be expected to act with decency.[3]

Moral identity then essentially involves knowledge of the conventions of the agents' moral tradition. Such knowledge has become their second nature, so it no longer involves the conscious application of rules. The knowledge, moreover, is that of committed participants who cannot be indifferent to what they know in this way. But what kind of knowledge is it, how is it acquired, and what claim does it have to yielding truth?

MORAL IDENTITY AND THE KNOWLEDGE INVOLVED IN IT

The knowledge is intuitive. Reliance on moral intuition was traditionally thought to involve unquestioning obedience to an authoritative inner voice—often identified with the agents' conscience—which requires no justification. This view is dogmatic and obscurantist and has done much to discredit appeals to moral intuition. But it is possible to proceed differently, as W. D. Ross has shown.[4]

Before Ross, moral intuitions were generally regarded as involving self-evidence and unconditionality, and as being the product of a moral sense. Self-evidence was supposed to guarantee that intuitions could not be mistaken. Unconditionality led to categorical moral judgments that expressed the intuitions. And the psychological apparatus that made intuition possible was assumed to be an inborn human faculty whose proper functioning required only maturity and normality. This view was rightly criticized on the grounds that intuitions change over time, that the intuitions of decent and reasonable people are often incompatible, that a person's or a society's intuitive truth is frequently rejected by other people as dubious, and that no trace of an inborn moral faculty can be found.

Ross jettisoned the idea that intuitions were produced by a moral sense, and he attributed prima facie status rather than unconditionality to them. He gave a celebrated list of six types of prima facie duties which were vouchsafed for by moral intuitions, and he claimed that all normal adults recognize them as duties, provided they were not in conflict with each other. In cases of such conflicts, Ross suggested, reasonable agents must put themselves, actually or imaginatively, in the concrete situation and judge on the basis of reasons available to them which of the conflicting prima facie duties should override the other. Such judgments are difficult and they could be mistaken. The home of moral intuitions, however, is in situations where there are no conflicts. Conflicts therefore do not show that intuitions are unreliable; they show that in some situations it is inappropriate to rely on them. Ross thus recognized that moral intuitions are fallible and conditional. Nor did he think that it is necessary to postulate a mysterious moral sense whose deliverances moral intuitions are. Moral sense should be conceived of metaphorically, on the analogy with a sense of humor or honor.

It should also be recognized that "there are vast areas of belief necessary for survival within which intuition is not discreditable, and in which the mind operates by a mechanism of causes and effects normally unknown to the thinking subject. . . . If it were possible to count beliefs, one could say that most of one's beliefs about the environment are of this character."[5] Examples are the recognition of color, pattern, size, persons, sounds, tastes, smells, and texture. But intuitions are also involved in logic, when a conclusion is just seen to follow from its premises; in mathematics, when, if a proof is understood, then it is directly evident that it is a proof. We use intuition in judging people, estimating distance, getting the point of a joke, and so on. Reliance on intuition is an indisputable part of many areas of life, and morality is one of them.

Consider now some examples. A man is walking on the street and an old lady in front of him stumbles and falls. He rushes to her assistance. Doing so requires no thought, he does not ponder the facts. The connection between his perception of the facts and his action is immediate. In the second case a woman witnesses a lie being told. One of her colleagues wants to have a beautiful summer day off to go to the beach, so he asks another to fill in for him, because there is an illness in his family. The woman is not personally affected, yet her instantaneous reaction is indignation on account of the wrong that is being done. In the next situation, a man receives a bill. As a matter of course, without having to remind himself that the facts make him owe it, he pays it. Lastly, a teacher learns that a young man who had been her student committed suicide because he had neurotic doubts about his intellectual ability. She recalls the occasions on which she criticized his work, but she is confident that she had been just and not harsh. She blames herself for nothing, yet she feels spontaneous and unavoidable regret.

In all these cases, agents react intuitively to a moral situation. There occurs a point at which the facts jell into a pattern and the agents come to see them, then and there, in a certain moral light. The seeing of these facts in the way described is an immediate, sudden realization that involves no conscious reflection. There is nothing odd or idiosyncratic about the people in question seeing the facts as they do. Other people in their places would have seen them in the same way. If they did not, there would have to be some special explanation for it. They may be foreigners or psychopaths, or they may suspect that the facts are not as they appear to be. But if people are raised in the moral tradition in whose context these cases occur, and if the facts are as they appear to be, and if both the people and the circumstances are normal, then the moral intuitions of these people will be routine and shared by just about everybody.

Intuition is a complex psychological process that has cognitive, emotive, and volitional elements. The cognitive element is what the agents believe about the situation: what the facts are and what moral significance they have. Helping the old lady, disapproving of the colleague's lie, paying the bill, and regretting the student's suicide all involve beliefs that the agents take to be true and could turn out to be false. But when a situation is intuited in a certain way, the agents' feelings are usually also engaged. They are alarmed on behalf of the stumbling old lady, made indignant by the lie, and feel sorry about the student. It is natural to have these feelings, for people normally cannot remain indifferent to the moral dimension of their lives. These beliefs and feelings prompt actions. Circumstances, prudence, or contrary motives may prevent performing a particular action, but having an intuition moves the agent toward action, even if it is no more than voicing, perhaps only privately, approval or disapproval.

There are countless situations which would routinely be seen in a certain moral light by the vast majority of people in a moral tradition. That they see in such a way is part of their moral identity. If some people in the moral tradition of contemporary America did not see the four cases in the ways described, it would be appropriate to suspect them of immorality or abnormality. On the other hand, there are numerous complex situations whose intuitive apprehension is likely to be mistaken. Perhaps there are a few people who are capable of seeing immediately and without reflection some patterns formed by the complicated facts, but for most people careful thought must take the place of intuition. It would be foolhardy nowadays to rely on one's intuitions about gender-related matters, welfare legislation, or childrearing.

The intuitive knowledge of the moral significance of simple situations may then be said to have the following characteristics. It is immediate. There is no conscious inference, reflection, or thought involved in recognizing their moral significance. People spontaneously perceive them that way. As soon as the facts present themselves, they fall into a pattern. And the pattern is normally the same for all normal adults who belong to a moral tradition. This, of course, is not to deny that the intuitions of individuals and the agreement in the intuitions of different people rest on learning, trial and error, and much thought, all of which have taken place in the past. The fact that intuitions are now immediate is no doubt explained the fact that one has learned from one's moral tradition to see the world in a certain way. This moral education, however, has been so thoroughly absorbed that people no more have to recall their lessons now than they have to remember how to walk or talk. There certainly is a need to think in morality, but only in complex situations in which moral intuitions are inappropriate.

Moral intuitions occur routinely. They are not sudden revelations or striking discoveries, but rather pedestrian, ordinary perceptions of something being so. They are, therefore, not to be sought in cases of moral conflicts, but in the innumerable spontaneous transactions of the morality of everyday life in which people do their jobs, keep their appointments, help others if they can without too much trouble, pay their bills, and spontaneously feel such reactive emotions as shame, guilt, resentment, outrage, or disgust.

Moral intuitions appear to people as imperatives that call for action. The action may be arrested for many reasons, but unless something intervenes, the agents feel called upon to do something about the intuited situation. In this respect, moral intuitions differ from sensory intuitions. People can sense some aspect of the world intuitively—that the poplar is closer than the birch—and be quite indifferent to it. But it is not a sufficient explanation of the action-guiding force of moral intuitions that, unlike sensory intuitions, they are evaluative. For aesthetic intuitions are also evaluative, yet they need not move people to action. Aesthetic intuitions are contemplative, moral intuitions are practical. Beautiful objects are uplifting and ugly ones are repellent. But good people and actions are not merely admired and publicly praised; they also act as examples that others wish, perhaps vainly, to emulate. Wicked people and evil actions similarly call forth an active response: people feel obliged to do something, if only to express disapproval.

Moral intuitions are fallible. They establish no more than a prima facie case for the moral significance of a situation. This feature should be contrasted with the infallibility that used to be attributed to intuitions. It was dogmatically supposed that nothing could overrule the deliverances of bona fide intuitions. It is more reasonable, however, to allow for the possibility that there may be good reasons for doubting the reliability even of bona fide intuitions. Ross restricted this possibility to cases in which moral intuitions conflict with each other, and he thought that in such cases reflection must replace reliance on intuitions. Ross was right about this, but it should be recognized that intuitions may be overruled for another reason as well. Moral intuitions are interpretations that impose a pattern on the facts and attribute greater or lesser significance to them. There are therefore two components of moral intuitions, although they are separable only in thought. One is the identification of the facts and the other is the recognition of their significance. Reasonable people may identify the same facts as constituents of a situation, but they may err in the significance they attribute to them.

The recognition of significance is not a conscious process of establishing priorities. The significance of the facts simply appears to normal agents in normal circumstances. In the case of the lying colleague, for instance, no sooner did he lie than those familiar with the situation came to see that his self-serving deception had much greater moral significance than his desire to go to the beach. Witnesses need not express all this in an explicit moral judgment. If they were called upon to do so, however, they would have said: "He should not have done that," where the "that" has buried in it the understanding of the situation.

The interpretation on which this judgment rests is open to argument. Reasons can be adduced for or against it. The good nature of the colleague, the triviality of the desire of the liar, the need for trust among colleagues, the lack of respect shown by the liar each provide a reason supporting the interpretation that what he did was wrong. If people were to contest the interpretation, they would have to show why these reasons are weak and why some other reasons are strong enough to overrule them. There may always be such reasons, and that is why moral intuitions must be seen as fallible.

That they are fallible does not of course mean that they are unreliable. It means that they may be mistaken. But whether it is reasonable to suppose that they are mistaken depends on adducing reasons to show why the interpretation that seems obviously correct to normal and reasonable people who share a moral identity is actually incorrect. May be the old lady who stumbled is a vicious drug dealer; may be the student's suicide should occasion self-doubt in the over-confident teacher; may be paying the bill should be seen as strengthening a deplorable economic system; may be the lying colleague wants to go to the beach because he has only a few days to live. If this additional information were true, the situations would appear in a different moral light, and then the initial intuition would have to be replaced by reflection. The point, however, is that in the absence of such considerations it is perfectly reasonable to regard moral intuitions as reliable, provided the facts are not in dispute, the intuitions are of everyday moral situations, and the agents who have them are normal, reasonable, and share a moral identity through belonging to the same moral tradition.

THE JUSTIFICATION OF MORAL INTUITIONS

Consider people in a moral tradition who rely on their moral intuitions. They are confronted with a situation and they recognize it as moral. They interpret the facts immediately and spontaneously, and they are moved to respond to them. Their beliefs, feelings, and motives are focused on the situation, even if they may remain unarticulated and untranslated into action. Their interpretations are fallible, although they seem natural and obvious to them. Nevertheless, reasons may lead them to recognize that the situation is more complex than they have supposed, that their intuitions are unreliable in that context, and then they may attempt to correct them. Suppose, however, that no such reason is presented. The people then have no reason to doubt their shared intuitions of a particular situation. If they were asked to justify them, their understandable reaction would be incomprehension. For why should they need justification for the obvious? They bought the goods, and that is why they pay the bill; their friend asked and that is why they help. What more needs to be said? What more could be said?

Situations of course are not always simple; there may be hidden facts, unrecognized complexities, deeper conflicts. Reliance on intuition is then misplaced. When complications occur, reasonable people recognize the need for reflection. Intuition is appropriate only in routine situations. It is a logical point, however, that the routine is what occurs most of the time. In the morality of everyday life, therefore, intuition is an appropriate and reliable guide. If people think that a situation is simple, even though it is complex, then the resulting intuition is likely to be mistaken. If the request for justification is based on the suspicion that this has happened, then it has a serious point and deserves an answer. But if there is no reason to doubt the obvious, then there is no need to justify it either.

Furthermore, moral intuitions do not occur in a solipsistic universe. People act on them, compare them, and one person's intuitions figure in other people's moral responses. There is thus a ready public test of intuitions. If one's intuitions are contrary to those of informed others, then, once again, there is ground for doubting them. But if what seems obvious to an agent is reinforced by the concurring intuitions of others, then there is no reason for the agent to doubt it.

The concurrence of moral intuitions presupposes education in a shared moral tradition, and a resulting common moral identity. Moral intuitions seem obvious and compelling only against such a background. If people have been taught from a very early age on to see certain situations in a certain way, then it is not surprising that they will so see them.

It is just this admittedly central feature of moral intuitions that makes reliance on them appear irritatingly shallow to critics of the conservative thesis. They may concede that the minimum requirements of good lives are protected by required conventions. They demand a justification, however, for the supposed value of moral identity that derives from unquestioning acceptance of the variable conventions of some moral tradition. They want to know how moral education in that tradition is to be distinguished from indoctrination with a moral outlook whose variable conventions may seem quite arbitrary to outsiders. They point at the intuitions suggested by charismatic, fundamentalist, puritan, rigidly hierarchical, or guilt-ridden moral traditions. And they refuse to grant even a presumption in favor of the moral standing of the consensus prevailing in such traditions, unless the moral standing of the tradition is first established.

This demand is reasonable, but it is so easily and obviously met that it is hard to understand why it is thought to be telling against reliance on intuitions. The justification of moral traditions is that they enable people who participate in them to make good lives for themselves. If the moral traditions fail to do that, then they are indeed unjustified, the moral identity they foster is valueless or worse, their variable conventions are defective, and the intuitions of their participants are unreliable moral guides.

The distinction between external and internal goods will help to give detail and add force to this justification.[6] External and internal goods are alike in being benefits obtainable through participation in a moral tradition. But they differ because these goods stand in different relations to the good lives which the tradition aims to make possible. External goods are related to good lives as means are to ends. The most important type of external good is the protection of primary values by required conventions. A good moral tradition will provide this protection because it is a requirement for all good lives. The failure to do so leads to disintegration, which has been the subject of the preceding chapter.

Internal goods are related to good lives as parts are to the whole of which they are constituents. A moral tradition is logically connected with the good lives and the internal goods that are obtainable through participation in it. The tradition is what it is because it provides those particular forms of good lives and internal goods and the particular forms of good lives and internal goods are obtainable only through participation in that particular tradition. But obtaining internal goods is not like winning a prize, understanding a joke, or solving a difficult problem. Internal goods are to be found by continued engagement in activities which are constitutive of living according to a conception of a good life. If all goes well, these activities are enjoyable. Enjoyment however is not the end at which they aim, but a by-product of engagement in them. The enjoyment pervades the activity, and its quality and the nature of the activity are inseparably connected. Examples of internal goods are the enjoyment people take in the activities central to their way of life, musicians in making music, athletes in the disciplined use of their body, couples in loving and being loved by each other, or citizens in approving and being approved by their society.

The internal goods of a moral tradition are secondary values. They are by-products of the activities that constitute part of living according to their conceptions of a good life. One important kind of variable convention in a moral tradition is concerned with guiding and protecting these activities, and thereby securing internal goods, and hence secondary values, for participating agents. This kind of variable convention, setting standards of appropriateness for the activities, has numerous instances. It will give further content to the idea of internal goods to describe some of them.

The first of these internal goods is self-direction. This is the activity of individuals through which they construct for themselves a conception of a good life. The material for it is provided by the variable conventions of the moral tradition and the construction consists in individuals selecting and adapting those among the conventional possibilities which seem to them to fit their character and circumstances. Self-direction involves some view of what they want to make of themselves, and what character traits they need to have and cultivate in order to succeed. They must ask and answer such questions as whether they want to live a retiring private or a gregarious public life; whether they have the talents and skills required by their chosen way of life; whether that way will be scholarly, artistic, commercial, or athletic; whether they prize a quiet life, achievement, contemplation, service, or risk-taking; whether they will be casting their net wide, or concentrating on a specialized endeavor; whether they aim at wielding power, enjoying the luxuries wealth can provide, receiving the recognition status and prestige bestow, basking in the love of a few intimates, or devoting themselves to a cause. Through self-direction, individuals decide which secondary values they should aim to include in their conception of a good life, beyond those primary values that must be recognized by all reasonable conceptions.

Intimacy is a second kind of internal good. Conceptions of a good life must leave room for personal relationships based on love, friendship, or joint dedication to some shared project. It is hard to imagine that a life could be good without prolonged contact with at least a few other people who engage the agents' deep and positive feelings. But it will vary from life to life whether these contacts will be provided by marriage, parenthood, solidarity with comrades, shared admiration of some ideal, love affairs, discipleship to someone great, or by the affection and loyalty of one's students, family members, colleagues, or fellow inquirers. The variable conventions of the agents' moral tradition will make the various forms of intimacy available, and the task of individuals is to find and cultivate those appropriate to their conception of a good life.

A third kind of internal good is civility. This is a reciprocal relationship that exists among members of a good society who are not intimates and who may not even be personally acquainted with each other. Their contacts occur in the routine conduct of affairs. They meet each other in queues, audiences, airplanes, waiting rooms, and stores; they are connected as clerks and customers, nurses and patients, buyers and sellers, fellow drivers on the road, providers and recipients of various services, homeowners and repairmen, officials and clients, and so on. If all goes well, the internal good that characterizes these impersonal encounters shows itself in the presence of casual friendliness, spontaneous good will, and courtesy, and the absence of hostility, distrust, surliness, and a litigious disposition bent on exacting one's pound of flesh.

Some important types of internal goods in a moral tradition are then the local forms of self-direction, intimacy, and civility. In a good moral tradition, the variable conventions protect these internal goods and thus individuals can participate in the activities which produce them. In such a tradition, these internal goods may be available in more forms than individuals can reasonably try to incorporate into their conception of a good life. Conventional conduct therefore does not appear to people in such contexts as rigid codes, rules that bind, or ideals exacting obeisance. Conventional conduct will seem to provide secondary values, and the possibility to live according to them, thereby enabling people to make a good life for themselves. A moral tradition of which this description is true will be pluralistic, in virtue of the multiplicity of variable conventions, and it will be free, because its members can choose among the forms their lives could take. The moral tradition will not be the enemy of individuality, but a necessary condition of its development.

Part of the justification of a moral tradition is, then, that it defends the required conventions which protect the primary values and make possible the enjoyment of external goods all reasonable conceptions of a good life require. If a moral tradition is unjustified in this respect, it will disintegrate. The disintegration thesis, properly understood, claims that a society has good reason to exclude conceptions of a good life which violate its required conventions. Another part of the justification of a moral tradition is that it defends the variable conventions which protect the secondary values and make the enjoyment of internal goods possible. Secondary values and internal goods, however, vary with moral traditions and conceptions of a good life, so that this part of the justification of a moral tradition consists in the defense of those specific values and goods that the tradition creates, that define the tradition, and that distinguish it from other traditions. The local forms of self-direction, intimacy, and civility are some examples of these secondary values and internal goods. It needs to be stressed, however, that they are merely examples, although central ones, and conceptions of a good life are not anywhere near fully specified by these examples.

A moral tradition is good if through moral education it makes available to its participants a wide plurality of possible forms that good lives can take, and if it thereby creates a shared moral identity for the individuals who adhere to it. According to the conservative conception, moral education and moral identity do not dictate what form of good life individuals should choose; rather, they provide a wide variety of secondary values and internal goods—forms of self-direction, intimacy, and civility included—out of which individuals can select some to incorporate into their conceptions of a good life.[7]

The conservative thesis is a defense of the variable conventions of a moral tradition on which the moral identity of its participants rests. Since reasonable people will recognize that a shared moral identity is necessary for living a good life, they will want to embrace the conservative thesis.

CRITICISM, CHANGE, AND TOLERATION

The argument just completed for the conservative thesis must not be interpreted as ruling out criticism, change, and toleration. Even good moral traditions can be legitimately criticized, moral identities do and often should change, and conceptions of a good life that conform to required conventions but are at odds with variable conventions should be tolerated. To begin with criticism and change: moral traditions can be situated on a continuum ranging from the good to the bad. A tradition is bad if it fails to provide the conditions its participants require to make a good life for themselves. This failure may result from many causes, but the one relevant for present purposes occurs if the required and/or variable conventions of a moral tradition are defective or inadequately protected. The task of criticism is to point out this flaw and to recommend remedial changes.

A moral tradition, however, has usually endured through several generations. It must therefore command the allegiance of a substantial number of people in a society. And even if it is defective, continued adherence to it is usually preferable to the chaos and disorientation that follow the overthrow of a whole way of life. There certainly are moral traditions that should be condemned in their entirety, but they are few, even if those few are monuments to evil. Most bad moral traditions, however, are not beyond redemption. It is possible to point at changes that would make them morally better: ante-bellum South without slavery; Second World War Japan without the samurai ethic; India without the caste system; South Africa without apartheid; Sicily without the Mafia; and so forth. To be sure, these changes would be radical, they would reverberate throughout the tradition, and the society that emerged may bear little relation to the *status quo ante*. The point, however, is that the conservative thesis encourages rather than obstructs the criticism and change of bad moral traditions.

The same point holds for good moral traditions. They do defend the conditions required by their participants for living a good life. It is most unlikely, however, that even they are in perfect order. They may be faulty because some of their strongly held conventions are mistaken for required ones. They are then falsely thought to protect some minimum requirement of all good lives, when they merely register prevailing prejudices, such as thinking of homosexuality as an abomination. Or they may fail to have a required convention that is really needed to protect some basic requirement of good lives; they may lack, for instance, prohibition against serious domestic violence.

Further defects may affect variable conventions. Some of them may be regarded as absolute, rather than prima facie, and then they constrain rather than enhance the possibilities of life, as the inflation of family honor into a value that overrides all others may do. Or the available variable conventions may be too few, so that lives are impoverished because they must conform to some small number of rigid patterns, like the lives of properly brought-up girls in Catholic countries before the First World War. Variable conventions may be inconsistent with each other, they may be unresponsive to technological, demographic, or other changes in the non-moral circumstances of life; they may provide insufficient guidance for resolving conflicts between conventions or people; they may be too inflexible to incorporate changes suggested by contact with other traditions; or they may fail to inspire the young because of the unwillingness of the old to adjust the conventions to changes in expectations and sensibility. Not even good moral traditions are therefore beyond reasonable criticism. The better they are, the more open and responsive they are to such criticism. The reason for such receptivity is that the justification of the tradition is its contribution to the good lives of its participants, and legitimate criticism and warranted change make that contribution more substantial than it would be otherwise.

The criticism of a moral tradition and resulting changes to it will of course affect the moral identity of the people. If the tradition is by and large good, then changes in it will be piecemeal, and the corresponding changes of moral identity will be gradual adjustments rather than radical alterations. There are two reasons for this. One is that the changes will affect only what are taken to be the morally bad aspects of the prevailing moral identity, while those thought to be in good order will be left intact. The other is that people come to see the need for changing their moral identity because they find some aspect of it incompatible with other aspects. They will then opt for the aspects they regard as deeper or more important and change the one they have grown to see as anomalous. The effect will be not just a change in their moral identity, but also a strengthening of those aspects of it which prompted the change and whose moral importance they now better appreciate.

It is a crucial point about the central importance of moral identity that, apart from the extreme case of irredeemably evil moral traditions, the impetus for change is felt because, and only because, some convention, practice, custom, or institution is seen to be inconsistent with the rest of the moral tradition. For a moral tradition, it will be remembered, is the substratum of the evaluative dimension of people's lives. It provides the standards to which they appeal in their evaluations, it establishes what counts as a morally relevant reason, and it defines the acceptable possibilities of life. As an illustration, consider the current changes in American society about sexual matters. Attitudes are changing about family, monogamy, contraception, homosexuality, AIDS, pornography, the relation between the sexes, abortion, and so forth. It is impossible to live in the society and not to be aware of the strong passions and of the conflicts between defenders of older attitudes and advocates of newer ones.

One highly significant feature of the disputes about the morality of these changes is that all parties argue their cases by appealing to the moral views of the people whom they wish to enlist on their side. The conflicts about the relation between the sexes is debated in terms of the more basic values of equality, respect, and justice; the controversy about abortion takes for granted a shared commitment to the value of life; one issue about homosexuality is how far the undoubted values of freedom and privacy should extend; and so forth. In all these cases, the proposed changes in the moral tradition involve the reaffirmation of its more fundamental aspects.

Another noteworthy feature of these disputes is that the very questioning of some aspects of the moral tradition implies the acceptance of other aspects which no one wants to change. Whatever may be the morally acceptable attitude toward sexual matters, there is no doubt that honesty, integrity, courage, conscientiousness, and kindness are good, and that cruelty, hypocrisy, dishonesty, and irresponsibility are bad. The arguments of both the defenders and the critics of some aspect of the prevailing moral tradition have as their subtext the tacit message that the unquestioned aspects of their shared moral identity are better served by opposing or advocating the changes. Gradual changes, therefore, reinforce rather than threaten a moral tradition. And although there may be moral traditions so inundated with evil as to deserve destruction not reform, the gradual change of most moral traditions is preferable because their destruction would leave people without the moral resources to try to live a good life.

Even if the conservative thesis allows for criticism and change, the question remains: what moral attitude does it suggest toward conceptions of a good life that are at odds with the prevailing moral identity? This question is about the status of toleration in conservatism. It will be answered in two steps. The first is to specify the limits of toleration. The second is to distinguish between toleration and respect.

To begin with the limits of toleration: what lies within the limits is what conforms to the conditions whose protection all conceptions of a good life require; and what lies outside the limits is the violation of these conditions. The conditions are specified partly by the required conventions, which protect the minimum requirements of good lives regardless of how they are conceived, and partly by the requirement that there be some system of variable conventions, which protects the prevailing moral identity. The minimum requirements are by and large the same for all good moral traditions, but the moral identities are likely to vary because self-direction, intimacy, civility, and other secondary values may take a wide plurality of forms. What does not vary is that a moral tradition must protect both the minimum requirements of good lives for its members and their moral identity. For the justification of a moral tradition is that it provides the conditions its members require for living a good life, and the minimum requirements and moral identity are among these conditions.

Conceptions of a good life that conform to the required conventions that protect the minimum requirements and to the variable conventions that protect moral identity deserve not just toleration, but also respect. That toleration and respect must be distinguished is obvious if it is borne in mind that different attitudes are appropriate to the Ku Klux Klan and the Red Cross, the American Nazi Party and the American Academy of Sciences, pornographic movie stars and Shakespearean actors, faith healers and physicians, or lawyers specializing in the defense of wholesale drug dealers and those sitting on the Supreme Court. It is less obvious, however, how the distinction is to be drawn.

Toleration is a doubly negative attitude. It involves allowing something to go on without interference, even though it is morally suspect. It combines a hands-off attitude with a moderate degree of moral disapproval. If the disapproval is severe, it excludes toleration and it calls for condemnation and interference. Toleration is thus not of evil, of serious morally unjustified harm, but of morally questionable activities that have not yet caused evil. Respect, by contrast, is a positive attitude toward activities that range from the permissible to the admirable. Toleration implies moral doubt; respect implies some degree of moral approval.

Conceptions of a good life that violate the required conventions do not deserve even toleration. The problem is how to treat conceptions of a good life that conform to the required conventions but not to the system of variable conventions. The problem is not caused by conceptions of a good life that reject all variable conventions, for lives could not be good without self-direction, intimacy, and civility, which depend on the variable conventions. The problem is presented by conceptions of a good life that do conform to variable conventions, and thus confer a moral identity on those who live according to them, but the variable conventions violate the moral identity that prevails in the moral tradition. From the perspective of the prevailing moral identity, the contrary identity is suspect because it is committed to dubious forms of self-direction, intimacy, and civility.

Here are examples from contemporary American society: religious cults whose members accept the revelations of a charismatic leader as self-direction; radically egalitarian communes whose members strive to develop equal intimacy with each other; political groups that require their members to exclude from civility certain races, religions, or ethnic groups. All are maintaining morally questionable forms of moral identity. The problem is what to do about them if they conform to required conventions, but violate the system of variable conventions.

The conservative solution is to tolerate, but not to respect, them. Toleration without respect means to regard conceptions of a good life that are at odds with the prevailing moral identity as suspect, but nevertheless put up with them. It means that they should be allowed to exist, but that they should not be aided in doing so, and that people should be discouraged by moral education and public opinion from adopting them. It means that they should not be given an equal share of resources, that children should be taught that they represent some of the many morally dubious conceptions of a good life, and that they should not be on the same footing as morally acceptable conceptions. The reason conservatives have for tolerating them is that human fallibility and pluralism make it prudent that questionable conceptions of a good life should be allowed to exist, provided they do not threaten other conceptions of a good life. The reason for not respecting them is that there are good reasons for regarding them as morally suspect.

CONSERVATISM AND THE SOCIAL LEVEL OF POLITICAL MORALITY

It is an odd and significant fact that the argument presented in this chapter would be unnecessary in the vast majority of past and present societies outside of the contemporary Western world. Of course a society is justified in protecting its way of life and the moral identity of its people. What else are societies for if not for sustaining a moral tradition that enables people to make good lives for themselves? Different societies have different moral traditions and conceptions of a good life, but each society must protect those it has, for otherwise life in it would become chaotic, insecure, and, as Berger says in the epigraph to this chapter, psychologically intolerable. Moral traditions and conceptions of a good life, of course, could be good or bad, better or worse. Which they are depends to a large extent on how well they protect, on the universal level, the minimum requirements of good lives, and, on the social level, the prevailing forms of self-direction, intimacy, and civility, and through them the moral identity of their people. But few people outside of the current Western orthodoxy doubt or have doubted that a society is justified in protecting the possibilities required by good lives and in setting limits that prohibit their violation.

The advanced—and largely liberal—thinkers of contemporary Western societies, however, think otherwise. They take it to be the mark of a good society that it welcomes the possibilities of other moral traditions and that it relaxes at least those limits that protect the moral identity of its own people. They think that a society ought not to regard its own values as privileged, that the better a society is, the more open it is to ways of life other than its own. They do not advocate merely a civilized attitude of toleration and a reasonable willingness to learn from the experiences of other societies. They think that a good society ought to guarantee equal respect, encouragement, resources, and moral status to ways of life that accord with and those that are contrary to the moral identity of its own people.

The result of this well-intentioned but utterly misguided indiscriminateness is a climate of moral uncertainty. It prompts those who suffer from it to eagerly embrace alien possibilities taken out of the context which nourishes them. It leads to such absurdities as the search for inner peace through 15 minutes of daily transcendental meditation; the Zen of stockbrokering; the confusion of drug-induced hallucination with mystical experiences; the surrender of autonomy that has become burdensome to the insane certainties of authoritarian cults; the deadening of the mind through the repetitive rhythms of chants, tam-tam drums, and mantras; the acceptance of the solemn fatuities of emigré gurus as the deliverances of wisdom; the retreat from moral and political responsibilities into the fine-tuning of one's soul according to the prescriptions of ill-understood and poorly translated oriental manuals; martial artists in strip malls; ashrams in penthouses; and yogis in gyms.

The real damage, however, does not come from the moral vacuum that is filled by this half-ridiculous and half-dangerous jetsam washed to our shores. The danger is the creation of the vacuum that needs to be filled. This vacuum increases as moral identity decreases, and it voids the moral sensibility of those who mistake their vice of moral indiscriminateness for a virtue. Such deluded people are typified by the morally half-educated person of the present age and society who "may be defined as the man who has acquired a degree of critical self-consciousness sufficient to detach him from the standards of his time and place, but not sufficient to acquire new standards that come with a more thorough cultivation. . . . The characteristic of the half-educated man is that he is incurably restless; that he is filled with every manner of desire. . . . He craves various things, but is not willing to pay the price—not willing to make the necessary renunciations."[8]

These renunciations have to do with the acceptance of the possibilities of some one moral tradition or another; with the realization that their acceptance entails placing beyond limits the possibilities of other moral traditions; with the rejection of that restless indiscriminateness that characterizes the morally half-educated people of contemporary Western societies; with the recognition that there comes a point where greater breadth is inimical to the depth that good lives require; and with valuing one's moral identity above the alienation from one's moral tradition that casts one adrift in a sea of moral uncertainty.

Since these lines are likely to be read by at least some people unsympathetic to them, it must be stressed that the protection of moral identity, as conservatives conceive of it, is not contrary to pluralism, to the criticism and change of one's moral tradition, and to toleration. A good moral tradition will be pluralistic because it will be hospitable to a wide variety of forms of self-direction, intimacy, and civility, but it will not allow its pluralism to go to seed. It will insist on the need for limits that prevent reasonable pluralism from turning into unreasonable relativism. Inside the limits are conceptions of a good life that embody the prevailing and plural forms of self-direction, intimacy, and civility; outside the limits are conceptions that violate them. These limits are open to criticism and change in the light of the primary and secondary values of the moral tradition. Moreover, conceptions of a good life that are placed outside the limits are tolerated, provided they do not violate the primary values and required conventions; although their toleration is not to be confused with respect.

If unsympathetic readers find it hard to swallow the lack of respect for some possibilities that follows from conservatism, they should ask themselves what it is that they regard as the appropriate attitude to racists, anti-Semites, creationists, paedophiles, pornographers, and so forth, who live according to their beliefs without violating any required convention. As they give the obvious answer, so they will recognize the merit of the distinction conservatives draw between toleration and respect.

CHAPTER 7

Moral Authority

> There are some minds that give us the sense that they have
> passed through an elaborate education which was designed to
> initiate them into the traditions and achievements of their civi-
> lization; the immediate impression we have of them is an impres-
> sion of cultivation, of the enjoyment of an inheritance.
>
> — MICHAEL OAKESHOTT, *"Rationalism in Politics"*

The political morality of conservatism aims to protect the conditions in which people can live according to one or another of a plurality of morally acceptable conceptions of a good life. This of course
requires conservatives to provide an account of moral acceptability. The
two preceding chapters, as well as the present one, are intended to meet
this requirement. Moral acceptability sets limits and excludes conceptions of a good life that transgress them. There are, however, different
limits, different responses to their violations, and different justifications
for conforming to them on each of the three levels of the political
morality of conservatism.

The most basic limits are universal, and they are set by the required
conventions that any good moral tradition must have. The justification
of these limits is that they protect primary values, which embody the
minimum requirements of all reasonable conceptions of a good life.
The violation of these limits is prohibited and, under normal circumstances, it is not tolerated. Even if these limits are generally observed
however, there is still need for further ones, since the minimum is not
sufficient for good lives. Some of the additional limits are social, and
they are set by the system of variable conventions of a moral tradition.

Their justification is that they protect the secondary values required by people for maintaining their moral identity. Moral identity is the evaluative social background without which individual conceptions of a good life could not be formed. The violation of these limits is normally tolerated, but their violators do not deserve respect, concern, and resources equal to those who observe them because the violators are opting out of civilized life, as it is understood in their society. The argument in this chapter is that in addition to limits on the universal and social levels there are limits of a third kind also required. These limits operate on the individual level, and they are set by the need for moral authority. The argument concerns the nature and justification of moral authority.

AUTHORITY IN GENERAL

Discussions of authority tend to go wrong from the beginning. They start with considering authority, and then, usually without notice or excuse, switch to the consideration of political authority. This tendency is shown equally by those who regret its loss and wish to shore it up,[1] by those who deny its legitimacy,[2] and by those who want to defend some suitably circumscribed and attenuated version of it.[3] They all assume that authority is a relation in which the authority makes those subject to it conduct themselves as the authority directs. The authority is thus thought to have a power, which it uses to get people to do things that they would not do otherwise. Opinions vary across the political spectrum as to the legitimacy of the power that authorities have and use, but they all respond to the supposed tension succinctly expressed as follows: "The defining mark of the state is authority, the right to rule. The primary obligation of man is autonomy, the refusal to be ruled. . . . Insofar as a man fulfills his obligation to make himself the author of his decisions, he will resist the state's claim to have authority over him."[4] The standard discussion thus begins with a suspicion of authority, and it goes on to consider how far the suspicion is justified.

The trouble with this approach to understanding authority is that it leaves no room for the thought that authorities are individuals, not states or other political units, and that what makes someone an authority is experience and good judgment, rather than power. That this approach got it wrong is made obvious by the fact that the everyday lives of most people are permeated with various relations in which they seek out, willingly follow, and regard themselves as lost without authorities. These attitudes need not be unreasonable, craven, bamboozled, indoctrinated, or intellectually or morally slothful. That this is so becomes obvious if some of the prevalent forms of authority are recognized as more reasonable starting points than the exclusive concentration on political authority. Such forms are the relations between parents and children; teachers and students; physicians and patients; coaches and athletes; lawyers and clients; directors and actors; masters and disciples; established practitioners in a field and beginners; the clergy and the faithful; experienced old friends and inexperienced young ones; management consultants and floundering firms; superiors and subordinates in the army, police, religious orders, and other hierarchical organizations; plumbers and homeowners; judges and juries; mentors and advisees; umpires and competitors; editors and authors; pilots and passengers; and so forth. Given these forms of authority, the idea that reason and morality dictate resistance to them must be seen as perverse. To be sure, authorities may be phoney rather than genuine, and then it would be folly to do as they say. But if an authority truly is one and if people rely on it to help them to do something that they have difficulty with doing on their own, then folly is to fail to do as they say.

The right question to ask therefore is how to tell real from spurious authorities, rather than the politically inspired one of why reasonable people would subject themselves to authorities. The wrong question, however, has dominated discussions of authority: "There has been a remarkable coalescence of opinion around the proposition that authority and authority relations involve some species of 'surrender of judgment' on the part of those who accept, submit or subscribe to the authority of persons or a set of rules or offices."[5]

The attempt to understand authority through the notion of the surrender of judgment is highly misleading. It stresses submission, subordination, and the abandonment of responsibility. It implies that the recognition of authority is demeaning and detrimental to self-respect, and that people with integrity and courage would reject it. And then one should ask how this fits people who recognize the authority of their parents, teachers, older friends, physicians, mentors, or plumbers? The recognition of authorities may be unreasonable, but only if they are unnecessary or unsuccessful. If they are genuine authorities, however, then they respond to the needs of those who turn to them. To recognize them in that case does not merit suspicion. The question is whether those who recognize an authority are in need of it and whether the authority they recognize is genuine. This is why the salient fact about authority relations is whether it is reasonable to recognize the supposed authority as such, and not the fact that those who recognize it have surrendered their judgment. People often turn to authorities precisely because they cannot rely on their own judgment: they do not know how to judge some complex situation, or they feel the need to reconcile the conflicting judgments of other people.

In trying to arrive at a better understanding of the nature of authority, it is necessary to start by distinguishing between a descriptive and a normative approach. The descriptive one is a historical, sociological, or anthropological inquiry about the authorities that are recognized in some particular context and the reasons that are given in that context for regarding the authorities as such. The normative approach aims to discover whether these reasons are good. The normative approach presupposes the descriptive one, and the two often go together, but they are nevertheless different because they aim to answer different questions. The approach to understanding authority in this chapter is normative. The descriptive element will enter only by way of illustration, so that abstract notions can be made concrete. The normative question is whether a particular authority is legitimate. The question is not whether it is recognized as an authority, nor whether it is thought to be legitimate by those who recognize it. But the question is even more specific. The particular form of authority that will be discussed is moral. The discussion of authority in general is meant merely to help to clarify the nature and justification of moral authority in particular.

Continuing then with the discussion of authority in general, but with the qualification that the discussion is normative, not merely descriptive, it is useful to distinguish between *de facto* and *de jure* authorities.[6] *De facto* authority is one who is actually recognized as an authority in a particular context. *De facto* authorities, however, may or may not have official status. Authorities that have official status are *de jure*. They derive their status from some formal procedure, training, rule, institution, or custom which gives them the right to exercise authority. *De facto* authorities may or may not be *de jure*, and vice versa. In the weeks before his resignation, Nixon had *de jure,* but no *de facto,* authority. If gossip is to be believed, Hillary Clinton has *de facto* political authority, but not, of course, *de jure* political authority.

Both *de facto* and *de jure* authorities may be legitimate or not. *De facto* authorities are legitimate if people have good reasons to recognize them as such. Legitimate *de facto* authorities not only exercise authority, but also possess the qualifications necessary for it. Similarly, the legitimacy of *de jure* authorities derives not merely from the fact that the method by which the status is conferred has been followed in their case, but also from the additional fact that the method is successful in identifying those who ought to be in a position of authority.

Many legitimate authorities have no official standing because their status is not conferred on them by any formal method. Friends, mentors, teachers, religious, financial, aesthetic, literary, or mechanical advisers may be legitimate *de facto* authorities, without being *de jure* ones. One reason why thinking about authority in political terms leads to misunderstanding is that in politics legitimate authority is *de jure.* If political authority is thought to be the model for all authority, then, if an authority is *de facto* without being *de jure,* the suspicion naturally arises that it is illegitimate. If the suspicion could be allayed only by identifying and justifying the formal method by which the status has been conferred on it, then *de facto* authorities could not be legitimate. The reasonable alternative, however, is not to take political authority as the model and to recognize that the legitimacy of *de facto* and *de jure* authorities is established in different ways.

A further distinction will help to understand better what is involved in an authority being legitimate. The distinction is between being *an* authority and being *in* authority.[7] Being *in* authority is being in a position that carries authority with it. Those who are in that position are necessarily *in* authority. The position may be *de jure,* such as that of an elected official, or it may be *de facto,* like that of a mentor. Being *an* authority is to possess qualifications which make the judgments of the authority better than the judgments of other people. But an authority may or may not be in authority, because the comparative excellence of the authority's judgment may lack either *de facto* or *de jure* acknowledgment. A person thus may be an authority and not be recognized as such. The ideal case is when the person who is in authority has that position in virtue of being an authority. In that case, the authority is legitimate because the status and the qualifications required for it coincide.

The ideal case, of course, often fails to obtain. A person may be an authority, but not be in authority; and the person in authority may not be an authority. If the suspicion of authority is based on thinking that the person in authority is not really an authority, then it deserves to be taken seriously. But if there is good reason to think that the two coincide, then suspicion is misplaced and the judgments of the person in authority should be accepted. It must be added, by way of caution, that, even in the ideal case, authority holds only in a particular context and in some particular respect. It is an illegitimate use of authority to exercise it beyond its proper sphere. Once again, however, if the authority is exercised in the appropriate context and respect, then it is legitimate and it ought to be recognized as such.

The nature and legitimacy of different forms of authority vary with the context and the respect in which they are candidates for recognition. Their legitimacy varies because their contexts determine who should recognize them. The legitimate authority of an older friend has a different scope than that of a music critic, or a President. Authorities are authorities for a specifiable range of people who are their potential subjects. Their nature also varies because the respects in which they are supposed to hold are determined by the different qualifications that make people an authority.

In trying to understand the necessary qualifications, it is crucial to bear in mind that the topic is considered normatively, not descriptively. The question is not what qualifications make people recognize an authority as legitimate, but what qualifications make an authority legitimate. The descriptive question is answered if it is explained why people recognize someone as an authority. The normative question is answered if it is explained why people ought to recognize someone as an authority. The attempt to answer the descriptive question must begin with the distinction between three ideal types of authority: traditional, rational-legal, and charismatic.[8] Much has been written about this topic,[9] but it is irrelevant to the present question, which is the normative one.

When people recognize an authority, they do not so much as surrender their judgment, but rather realize that they do not know how to judge or that their judgment is defective, and that the authority's judgment is better than the one they could arrive at on their own. As it has been perspicuously put: "He who accepts authority accepts as a sufficient reason for acting or believing something the fact that he has been so instructed by someone whose claim to do so he acknowledges. . . . It is to act or believe not on the balance of reasons, but rather on the basis of a second-order reason that precisely requires that one disregard the balance of reasons as one sees it. Likewise, to exercise authority is precisely not to have to offer reasons, but to be obeyed or believed because one has a recognized claim to be." [10]

There are countless cases in which it is reasonable to accept authority in this sense and in which it would be unreasonable not to do so. The cases are those in which people need to form some belief and/or perform some action, but they are confused or uncertain about what the belief or action should be, they realize this about themselves, and they have good reason to follow the direction of someone else. In this manner, a student may accept a teacher's authority when studying a difficult work, a patient may accept a physician's authority when taking medication, a novice may accept an experienced practitioner's authority about when routine operations have become so defective as to require not reform but drastic change, and a young person may accept an older friend's authority when considering a lucrative job offer that would be corrupting. In all these cases, the authority has reasons for its judgment. These reasons can be stated, explained, and argued for. They are capable of what has been aptly called "reasoned elaboration." [11] But the people who accept the authority's judgment are not in a position to appreciate the reasons or their elaborations. They are confused and uncertain because they lack the qualifications that the authority has. The reasons support the authority's judgment, but their significance, weight, and contestability are not available to the people.

The legitimacy of authority depends on its qualifications. People are reasonable in recognizing an authority if they have good reasons to believe that it possesses the necessary qualifications. These reasons, of course, cannot be derived by people from a direct evaluation of the authority's qualifications, since for that they would already have to have the qualifications which they *ex hypothesi* lack. But the reasons can be derived indirectly by considering such matters as the authority's official status, if it has one, its reputation, the success or failure of its past judgments, and so forth.

This way of thinking about the qualifications that make an authority legitimate is derived from the private realm in which one individual recognizes the authority of another. Not all authority relations, however, are like these. There are also public, especially political, authorities whose qualifications need not involve any particular personal excellence. Their qualifications derive simply from the procedure that is followed in placing them in a position of authority. The reason for having public authorities of this kind is to cope with what has been called the "coordination problem." That problem is to impose order and predictability on the otherwise chaotic actions of people living together in populous societies. Someone has to decide what forms contracts should take, when elections are to be held, what days are holidays, where public buildings should be built, and so on. If public authorities of this sort perform their tasks competently and if their status is conferred on them by the appropriate procedure, then they too are legitimate and it is reasonable to recognize them as such.

In conclusion, it may then be said that authorities in general may or may not be legitimate. Their legitimacy depends on their qualifications. If people lack the qualifications an authority has and if they need to make judgments about beliefs and actions to which the qualifications are relevant, then they are reasonable in accepting the authority's judgment in place of their own. If these conditions are met, there is nothing intellectually or morally questionable in recognizing someone else's authority over oneself. If suspicion of authority is motivated simply by a desire to make sure that a putative authority has the qualifications that make it legitimate, it is a healthy attitude. But if the suspicion is based on the very nature of authority relations, then it is groundless.

THE NATURE OF MORAL AUTHORITY

If authority is the genus, then moral authority is a species. There has not been much written on the latter.[12] The characteristics of moral authority vary with historical and social contexts, but the discussion will concentrate on moral authority in the context of a pluralistic society. The salient feature of such a society is that it neither has nor desires a single generally recognized moral authority. At other times and in other kinds of societies, the Pope, the King, the Party Leader, the Oracle, the Elder, the President, and so forth may have been publicly recognized moral authorities, but times have changed. There still are moral authorities of course, but they are many, not one, and they tend not to be public, but private. Moral authority relations hold between individuals, and even if the authorities happen to have some official status, that is not what gives them authority.

Legitimate moral authorities are *in* authority because they are *an* authority. What makes them so is that they possess the appropriate qualifications. Since pluralistic moral authority relations tend to be private, moral authorities tend to be *de facto,* not *de jure.* The latter requires some formal method to confer the status of authority, but in private relationships there is no such method. One individual may recognize the moral authority of another, but the recognition is a personal matter based on the belief that the authority possesses the relevant qualifications. This belief, of course, may or may not be justified. If it is justified, then the moral authority is legitimate and it is reasonable to recognize it as such.

To understand what moral authorities do, consider an account of one occasion on which Confucius exercises moral authority: "we read of the Master teaching a return to the purity and sincerity of the ancient ceremonies. He deplores superstition and the mere outward observance of forms. Then Tzu-kung, one of the disciples, asks about the monthly ceremony at which the new moon is announced. . . . Would it not be better, he queries, if the practice of sacrificing sheep were done away with? Confucius reproves him gently. He calls him by his familiar name. 'Ssu,' he says, 'You care for the sheep. I care for the ceremony'."[13]

This story reveals several significant features of moral authority. First, Confucius responds to a question that is put to him. He speaks because he was asked. He does not issue a command, impose his will, or tell Tzu-kung what he should do. He rather shows how he, Confucius, thinks about the matter. There is, to be sure, the clear suggestion that Confucius' way of thinking is better than Tzu-kung's, but let that go for the moment. Second, in thinking as he does Confucius mediates between the moral tradition that both he and Tzu-kung recognize as their own and the moral problem that Tzu-kung raises. The problem is a problem for them only because their allegiance lies with the tradition. Confucius then thinks about the problem in the light of the shared tradition in the background. Third, in Confucius' opinion, the tradition is defective because the significance of ancient ceremonies has been lost and they have become empty forms. Tzu-kung's problem arises precisely because of this defect in the tradition. The ceremonies used to mark important occasions in the lives of people who belong to the tradition, but they no longer do that. An important part of their moral identity, therefore, has been lost. They are impoverished in the same way as Christians are who think of Christmas without religious sentiments or as Americans are who think of Fourth of July without patriotic feelings. It may be, of course, that the religiosity and patriotism would be misplaced, but there is no doubt that even if that were so, it would be a serious loss for those in whose lives they used to be significant values. Fourth, the question Tzu-kung is asking is difficult. There is no simple solution to the problem of how to cope with the defects that people recognize in their own moral tradition. Should they reaffirm the old values that are being violated or should they seek to replace them with new values that reflect changing circumstances? Answering that question requires understanding both the moral tradition and the new circumstances, judging the importance of the old values, and weighing whether the possible new values would be adequate substitutes for the old ones. It is not to be expected that most people, kept busy by the demands of their lives, would have the understanding, judgment, and sense of proportion, as well as the inclination, time, and seriousness, to ask and answer these questions. That is why they need a moral authority.

Consider now why and how moral authorities mediate between their moral tradition and some particular problematic case. The mediation of moral authorities is needed chiefly because the knowledge that most people in a moral tradition can be expected to have has become insufficient. As a result, they cannot rely on their moral intuitions. They encounter an increasing number of situations in which the simple connection between a hitherto morally acceptable variable convention and a particular case that clearly falls under it has been broken. The case is there and it is pressing for evaluation and response, but it is unclear how it ought to be seen.

Is the sacrifice of sheep just an act of cruelty? Is it a waste of livestock? Is it a hypocritical show of piety? Is it a stalwart adherence to old values in a changing world? There is no intuitively persuasive answer because the old variable convention governing the sacrifice is no longer generally observed. So people do not know whether they should evaluate the sacrifice of sheep according to some other convention, or whether they should continue to stick to the old one that is falling into desuetude, or whether they should just do as they please because the case no longer falls under the jurisdiction of any convention. What is happening is that their moral identity has been changing. In a particular area of their lives their intuitions have become unreliable, and they feel uncertain in their moral outlook. Their situation is not unlike that of contemporary Americans in respect to marriage. It is called into question by secularization, countless people living together without marriage, the frequency of divorce, single-parent families, and homosexual unions. It is in just such cases that individuals need moral authorities to help them evaluate the situations they face in the no longer clear light of their moral tradition.

In order to answer the question of how moral authorities provide the needed help, it is important to remember that they offer a judgment, not a command. They do not say: do this, rather than that; they say: if you look at the situation in this way, then it will become clear to you what you should do. Their judgment is not a decision, which they hand down, but an interpretation of a complex situation formed of a particular case, conventions of uncertain relevance, and the moral tradition itself. Do not think of the sheep, says Confucius, think of the ceremony. What really matters, he suggests, is that human lives should be meaningful, not the life expectancy of sheep or the money that it takes. Or, as it might be said in response to current uncertainties about marriage, what matters is that people should form lasting intimate relationships with one another, that they should face the world together, that they should be united by love, appreciation, and delight in each other. To focus on whether they can or cannot have children, whether their relationship is sexual, whether their sexual relationship takes one form or another is to misjudge what is important. The judgments of moral authorities are based on an appreciation of their moral tradition that is deeper than what other people have, and on their ability to see through the complexities that bedevil others.

THE QUALIFICATIONS OF A MORAL AUTHORITY

The judgments of moral authorities are better because they possess qualifications that people who solicit their judgments lack. The first of these qualifications is a thorough familiarity with the required and variable conventions of the moral tradition and considerable experience and skill in evaluating particular cases by subsuming them under the appropriate conventions. For the sake of brevity, these qualities may be described as knowledge of the moral tradition. It should be understood, however, that the knowledge is both factual, involving knowledge of the required and variable conventions, and practical, having to do with the application of these conventions. It is, moreover, moral knowledge because its subject matter is living a good life, as it is understood in a particular moral tradition. The tradition, according to conservatives, ought to be pluralistic, so the moral knowledge will be of one or few of a large number of morally acceptable conceptions of a good life. The more pluralistic a tradition is, the less likely it is that there will be moral authorities whose knowledge ranges over all the morally acceptable conceptions of a good life in the tradition. Pluralistic moral authority is likely to be confined to specific conceptions, such as those involved in artistic or academic life, business, politics, athletics, criminal justice, scientific research, social work, or news reporting.

This knowledge is not particularly hard to acquire. Experience and continued participation in a way of life are normally sufficient for it. People who possess it know how to distinguish between simple and complex, routine and controversial, banal and surprising cases. They know what it is to treat someone in that context fairly or unfairly, harshly or indulgently, generously or meanly. They know what counts as negligence, scrupulousness, diligence, efficiency, or going beyond the call of duty. They know when they can trust their intuitions and when they have to stop and think. They are in general experienced practitioners who are skilled in applying the vocabulary of their moral tradition to evaluate relevant conduct. Anyone with sufficient motivation, moderate ability, and long enough practice will meet this elementary, but by no means sufficient, requirement of moral authority.

That this kind of knowledge is not sufficient for moral authority becomes obvious once it is seen that its possession is compatible with the rejection of or indifference to the moral tradition. Anthropologists studying the society, hypocrites living in it, and wicked people violating it may all be familiar with the conventions and be skilled in mediating between the tradition and complex cases. They may know what the moral tradition prescribes, but they do not accept its prescriptions. They may act according to them, but only when expediency dictates.

It is necessary therefore to add a second qualification required for being a moral authority: commitment to the moral tradition. People who are committed do not just know what the conventions are and how to apply them in complex situations, they also believe that morality requires living and acting according to the conventions, and they endeavor so to live and act. Such people do not merely know what conceptions of life are regarded as good in a moral tradition, they also think that they really are good. This, however, is still insufficient for moral authority because much depends on the manner in which the knowledge and commitment are acquired and acted on. This knowledge and commitment may just reflect a rigorous moral education in the course of which people's minds and hearts are so thoroughly influenced as to make it impossible for them to regard any other moral tradition or basic dissension from their own as a live option for themselves. These people know of course that others at other places follow different conventions and have different commitments, but they know it only intellectually. There are cannibals, samurai, shamans, men with harems, and women with bordellos, but what has that got to do with them? They are immersed in their lives, they have no doubts about their moral tradition, what they can spare of their intellectual and emotional energies for moral purposes is fully engaged in it, they see the world from its perspective, and, insofar as they are morally motivated, their motivation has no contrary sources.

It is much easier to sustain this attitude in an absolutistic than in a pluralistic moral tradition. But even in an absolutistic one, the prevailing moral tradition, with its one or few approved conceptions of a good life, is bound to be challenged by the failure of many people to follow the conventions. As it has been stressed, evil is an unignorable feature of all moral traditions, and its existence and prevalence raise questions that cry out for an answer. If the countenanced conceptions of life are good, then why do so many people live in violation of them? If they so live, how could it be that they often flourish? And why are good lives so difficult and chancy? Why is it that living reasonably according to the conventions often fails to result in a good life?

To these questions, which will be asked in any moral tradition, others will be added, if the tradition is pluralistic. For if pluralism prevails, competing conceptions of a good life will be spatially and temporally contiguous, and thus evident in everyone's life. People do not then have to go far afield to see others live in ways that cannot but appear as challenges to their own way. It is therefore not only the prevalence of evil, but also the existence of moral possibilities other than what they have adopted that will pose questions to most people. Moral authorities ought to be able to give convincing answers to such questions. If, however, their knowledge and commitment are formed without awareness of such questions, they will lack the means to do so.

It is necessary therefore to add a third qualification to the making of a moral authority: reflectiveness. This is a large topic that cannot be treated fully here.[14] In general, however, reflectiveness may be said to be directed more deeply into the moral tradition and more broadly to compare the moral tradition with other moral traditions. The greater depth and breadth that result enhance the appreciation of the moral tradition, if it is a morally acceptable one, or they lead to its criticism and possible improvement or abandonment, if it has moral defects.

One object of reflectiveness is to understand the moral vision that is meant to be expressed by the conventions of a moral tradition. The vision is of human possibilities and limits and of how best to pursue the first and recognize the second. It is to penetrate to the deepest level of a moral tradition and understand what motivates it. For Christians, it is the imitation of Christ; for Jews, it is the covenant with God; for liberals, it is autonomous life; for utilitarians, it is the happiness of humanity; for Plato, it is the transformation of the self as guided by knowledge of the Good; and so on for each of the major religions and moral philosophies. If the conventions of a moral tradition are seen as the forms in which the underlying vision is given concrete expression, then there will be a principled way of justifying, criticizing, or changing the conventions. For it will then be understood that it is not conformity to the conventions that is of the greatest importance, but the translation of the vision into concrete forms. Conventions are the means by which this is done, and they can be more or less adequate to their purpose.

The conventions may change with times and circumstances, and they may become more or less faithful, practical, or realistic. Having understood the vision, however, one will have a ready way of evaluating actual or proposed changes. Part of the authoritativeness, attraction, and persuasiveness of moral authorities comes from their possession of greater depth than most people have. Depth creates the ability to cut through the moral complexities caused by changing conventions. It involves judging the adequacy of conventions in the light of the underlying moral vision that they were meant to express. The judgment may not be favorable, and so moral authorities may be critics of the moral *status quo*.

Reflectiveness is directed also toward understanding that the vision of one's own moral tradition is merely one among many. The possibilities and limits protected by required conventions will be largely the same in all morally acceptable traditions, but those defined by variable conventions will differ. To have the breadth of this kind of understanding is to see that here "there are truths but no truth."[15] It is the essential feature of conservatism that it recognizes that the morally acceptable visions of a good life are many. The fact remains, however, that of the many only one is one's own. One of the most difficult tasks of a conservative moral authority in a pluralistic society is to combine the recognition of the plurality of morally acceptable traditions with allegiance to a particular one. If one knows that there are many truths, why live according to one of them?

The answer is that people's knowledge of the truths of other moral traditions is not like knowledge of their own. Moral traditions other than their own do not provide the perspective for evaluating the lives and conduct of themselves and others, they do not protect their conceptions of a good life, they do not inspire and motivate them, and they do not engage their feelings and imagination, at least not to the same extent as their own. And if two conceptions of a good life derived from two moral traditions were found to be equally attractive, it would still be necessary to opt for one of them, for one person can live and act reasonably only by trying to follow one of two incompatible moral visions. One task of conservative moral authority therefore is to remind people whose allegiance to a moral tradition is challenged by the possibilities of another that the evaluative dimension of their lives is defined by their own tradition, that its moral vision is theirs too, and that their conception of a good life is intimately connected with the moral tradition whose framework makes living according to that conception possible.

Of course, people may have reason to exchange their commitment to one morally acceptable tradition for another. The role of moral authority is not to dictate what commitments people should have, but to make vivid to them the moral vision which lies behind the commitments that they have made. The vision may fade; limited energy, lack of emotional agility, and the demands of everyday life often hinder concentration;

wickedness, weakness, and love of comfort frequently act as countervailing motivational forces; and the inevitable defects of the prevailing conventions further cloud the original vision. People often turn to moral authorities for help when they find themselves beset by such conflicts, doubts, and weakening commitments. The way to help them is to remind them of what they already know, but tend to forget under the pressure of their lives and circumstances: the moral vision that provides the rationale for living as they do.

Implicit in this account of reflectiveness is the further qualification that moral authorities must be morally articulate. They can make simple the situations others find complex because they have reflected more deeply and broadly on their moral tradition than those who turn to them for help. But they could not help if their reflectiveness merely enabled them to see clearly what appears to be obscure for others. They must also be able to communicate what they have seen, and to communicate it in a way that would make those who have not seen it see it too. Moral authorities must therefore be teachers, and as teachers they must know how to bring those who want to learn from the point of being lost in complexities to the point where their own efforts will suffice.

The plain statement of the plain truth will rarely accomplish this because what is plain to someone who has reflected sufficiently will not be plain to those who have not. This is why moral authorities in widely different contexts tend to communicate through stories, allegories, parables, myths, and striking images. The imaginative and emotive aura with which they surround the truth is not sugarcoating that will make swallowing it easier, but a method of making its significance apparent. One of the greatest of these literary devices is Plato's allegory of the cave.[16] It is most apposite in the present context because it is not only a classic illustration of how moral authorities can communicate successfully, but also a depiction of the predicament of both moral authorities and those in need of them. Plato writes: "the eyes can become confused in two different ways . . . it can happen in the transition from light to darkness and also in the transition from darkness to light."[17] Moral authorities must overcome the clouding of their vision as they proceed from light to darkness when they return to the cave; and they must do so in order to help those in the cave to see better as they try to proceed from darkness toward light.

There are, however, two significant differences between Plato's and the conservative ways of thinking about moral authority. The first is that Plato thinks that ultimately there can be only one authoritative moral vision, whereas conservatives think that there are many. The second is that Plato thinks of moral authority in a far more intrusive way than conservatives do. For Plato, the vast majority live in darkness, and they must be made to see, otherwise they will not be able to see by themselves. For conservatives, the darkness is not unrelieved; most people can see, if only obscurely; they may come to realize this about themselves and then ask for help. It is only then that moral authorities, according to conservatives, should do what they can to show them how their own moral vision can illuminate the obscurities they face.

There is one further qualification that moral authorities must possess in addition to the four already discussed. Its necessity emerges if we bear in mind that people's recognition of someone else's moral authority is always a matter of trust. Such recognition involves the belief that the judgment of the moral authority is better than their own. What is it about moral authorities that would make it reasonable for people to trust their judgment more than they trust their own? The answer cannot just be that the moral authorities possess the necessary knowledge, commitment, reflectiveness, and articulateness, for how could people know that they actually have these qualifications, and not just claim them. Putative moral authorities, after all, can be pretended, phoney, false, or deluded. There must, therefore, be something about the moral authorities themselves that would make it reasonable to trust them. It must not be hidden; it must be readily observable to anyone who cares to look. These requirements are met by the conduct of moral authorities being exemplary in the area of life where their authority holds.

The trust in moral authorities is warranted, therefore, by the way they live. They are placed in authority by others because they have shown how to live well according to a particular conception of a good life. Their authority derives from the successful experiments in living that their lives represent. They show to those interested that their conception of a good life is indeed good, that it is possible to live that way and succeed, and so they stand as examples to those who want to live that way. The qualification that the conduct of moral authorities must be exemplary bridges the gap between being a moral authority and being recognized as such. Articulateness alone is insufficient because it is unclear whether verbal facility is evidence of knowledge, commitment, and reflectiveness, or merely of rhetorical talent. But if the life and conduct of putative moral authorities are of a piece with the moral vision they articulate, then they demonstrate in the most convincing way possible that they mean what they say, that it is reasonable to trust them, and that they are moral authorities indeed.

Moral authorities do not set themselves up as such, rather they are discovered. They are found to be conspicuous successes at living according to their conception of a good life, and that is why authority is attributed to them. The possession of moral authority, however, is only an unintended by-product of their conduct, not its goal. What primarily matters to them is to live what they regard as a good life. That is and must continue to be the true center of their conduct. If others turn to them for help, then decency and good will prompt them to try to give it. Their ability to help, however, is contingent on their lives remaining exemplary. It would undermine that very ability to use their authority in a way that would interfere with living as they have been. The exercise of moral authority, therefore, must always be a subordinate activity for those who genuinely possess it.

The point, of course, is not that moral authorities must be self-centered, but rather that they must be centered on living according to their conception of a good life. If it is a reasonable one, it will include, as it was argued in the preceding chapter, not only self-direction, but also intimacy and civility, and, through them, concern for the well-being of others. But the nature of that concern will not be to impart a vision to them or to teach them how to resolve the complexities they face; it will not be didactic or pedagogical. It will be to interact with them in the ways appropriate to the conception of a good life. That there are other people similarly engaged, and that they see their conspicuous success, and therefore recognize them as moral authorities, may often come to those so recognized as a surprising and unsought honor. It may also come as a burden because it may interfere with living the life they want and enjoy. This is probably part of the reason why moral authorities seem often distant and somewhat removed to those who turn to them. In any case, it will perhaps be obvious why genuine moral authorities will not aim to impose their will on others and why they are likely to find their status an embarrassment of riches.

A further implication of the present account is that moral authorities are not exceptional figures who are hard to find, but familiar people

often encountered in everyday life. If the knowledge, commitment, reflectiveness, articulateness, and exemplary conduct were thought of in
absolutistic terms approaching perfection, then moral authorities would
indeed be rare. But this is not how they should be regarded. Being a
moral authority is a relation that holds between individuals. Moral authorities, therefore, are such for particular persons. Their authority derives from the possession of the qualifications to an extent sufficient to
enable them to judge better than others who turn to them for help and
who distrust their own judgment about the complexities they face.
Moral authority relations thus depend on the respective qualifications
of the people who participate in them. Moral authorities may themselves need moral authorities and people who recognize a moral authority may themselves be recognized as moral authorities by others. The
essential feature of these relations is that a moral authority is recognized
as having better judgment about complex situations than the people
who turn to them. And having better judgment depends on and it is
demonstrated by the authority's possession of the qualifications to a
high enough degree so that they could help those who cannot help
themselves. The possession of the qualifications, however, is always a
matter of degree, and that is why a person who is a moral authority in
one context may be in need of moral authority in another context. The
determining factor is whether people possess the qualifications to a sufficient degree to resolve the complexities they face when the variable
conventions of their moral tradition do not provide clear guidance.

One last implication of the account of moral authority remains to be
made explicit. The possibility of being a recognized moral authority presupposes allegiance to a shared conception of a good life and to a moral
tradition upon which living according to that conceptions depends. A
moral authority excels at living in the way those who recognize it want to
live. Their shared allegiance provides participants in moral authority relations with an objective standard of evaluation: that set by the conception of a good life. Moral authorities excel because they approximate it
more closely than others. That achievement is what makes them authorities, and not that they are charismatic, possess the trappings of status,
command a large audience, or speak powerfully.

The recognition of the objective standard and the shared allegiance
to it provide two vitally important components of good lives. First, they
make it possible to distinguish between genuine and pretended moral

authorities. They enable people thereby to know whom they could reasonably trust with judging for them when the complexities are too great for them to judge for themselves. Second, they motivate people to continue to adhere to their moral tradition and conception of a good life in the face of difficulties which are not of their own making. They are thus antidotes to alienation, ennui, cynicism, and resignation, which the difficulties of living a good life often provoke.

THE JUSTIFICATION OF MORAL AUTHORITY

The preceding account was meant to provide two considerations that jointly require that moral authorities be recognized by all morally acceptable conceptions of a good life. The first concerns the necessity to recognize the possibility of moral authority. This is a logical requirement, and it follows from understanding the nature of good lives and of moral authority.[18] Those who commit themselves to living according to some conception of a good life thereby commit themselves to recognizing that conception as an objective standard with reference to which both their own conduct and the conduct of others who share their commitment could be compared and evaluated. The standard is objective in the sense that how closely lives and conduct approximate it is a factual question whose answer is independent of what anyone thinks, feels, hopes, or fears. The standard is not objective in the sense that any reasonable person would have to accept it. There are many reasonable conceptions of a good life, and people can accept or reject any of them without violating reason or objectivity. What cannot be done without the loss of reason and objectivity is to make a commitment to a particular conception and then refuse to recognize it as a standard of moral evaluation that applies to all those who are similarly committed.

It follows that other people's lives and conduct may approximate the standard more closely than the agents' own. Others may have done better than they have done themselves at the most important endeavor of their lives, which is to make them good. If it is accepted further that at least some of those who have done better have done so deservedly, through their own talents and efforts, and not undeservedly, through injustice or luck, then reasonable people will see them as possible moral authorities from whom they may be able to learn how they themselves could do better.

The second consideration is that people's recognition of moral authority is not just an abstract possibility, but a pressing practical need. For, as a matter of moral psychology, no longer of logic, in trying to live according to a conception of a good life, people are often confronted with complexities they find themselves unable to resolve. These complexities arise because the variable conventions of the moral tradition provide inadequate guidance about how people should respond in some particular situation. They recognize that their intuitive responses have become unreliable, but they do not know how to find a reliable response because they are wanting in knowledge, commitment, or reflectiveness. In this situation, people feel the need to rely on the judgment of others. If they are reasonable, they will rely on those whose lives and conduct are better than their own and who therefore can be supposed to have to a greater extent the qualifications which they themselves lack. If they receive the help they need because the people to whom they turn have the qualifications to provide it, then it is justified to recognize them as moral authorities, with all that such recognition entails.

This justification is in no way committed to the infallibility of moral authorities. Moral authorities are legitimate if they possess the appropriate qualifications. It is reasonable to recognize them as moral authorities if their qualifications enable them to make more reliable judgments about complex situations than the people for whom they count as authorities. This does not mean that such judgments could not be mistaken; it means only that they are less likely to be mistaken than the judgments of those who lack their qualifications. There are three importantly different ways in which moral authorities may be mistaken.

The first is that they may be insufficiently informed about or attentive to the complex situations they are called upon to judge. These failings may or may not be culpable. They may lack the relevant information because they have been lied to, or because they have not bothered to look. Similarly, their lack of attention may be due to fatigue caused by the great demands placed on them, or to laziness and indifference. Assume, however, that they do not fail in these ways, that they are informed and attentive.

The second way in which they may fail is that their qualifications are unequal to the task at hand. Their knowledge, commitment, reflectiveness, conduct, articulateness, and the judgments based on them, are, to be sure, better than those of the people who rely on them, but they are not sufficiently better to make their judgments reliable. They judge in good faith, and as well as they can, but that is still not good enough. If they had the qualifications to a greater extent, they could make better judgments, but lacking them, culpably or otherwise, they cannot. But even if their qualifications are adequate and they do not fail on that account, they may still fail for another reason.

The third kind of failure stems from the defects of the moral tradition within which they are recognized as legitimate authorities. Their judgments are good in mediating between the moral vision of their tradition and complex cases, but the tradition is morally defective. They judge well how complexities could be resolved in conformity with the tradition, but they end up making a mistaken moral judgment because in some respects their tradition is morally unacceptable. Confucius may be right that his tradition requires caring about the ceremony and not about the sheep, but he and his tradition may still be wrong to sacrifice sheep.

Suppose, however, that there is no reason to think that some moral authorities are defective in any of these ways, that their lives and conduct are exemplary, and that the judgments they have made seem to be reliable. There are then good reasons to recognize them as moral authorities and to rely on their judgments when the complexities of some situation make people distrust their own.

It needs to be added as a reminder that, although legitimate moral authorities always judge from the point of view of their moral tradition, it is by no means the case that their judgments must always reflect the conventions of their tradition. Moral authorities are bound to be traditional because they bring the fundamental moral vision of their tradition to the judgment of complex situations. But they need not be conventional because they may think that some conventions prevailing in their tradition are defective expressions of the fundamental vision. Their judgments then serve the direct purpose of resolving the complexities they face, as well as the more indirect purpose of criticizing and trying to remedy the defective conventions of their moral tradition.

CONSERVATISM AND THE INDIVIDUAL LEVEL OF POLITICAL MORALITY

If the possibilities and limits established by the required and variable conventions of a moral tradition are protected, if, that is, the

universal and the social levels of morality are in good order, then individuals can make good lives for themselves. They can then form and
conduct themselves according to conceptions of a good life that they derive from their moral tradition and adapt to their own characters and
circumstances. This task is often difficult, and moral authorities may
help individuals to make it less so. It may be thought, however, that living according to one's conception of a good life requires autonomy that
is incompatible with the appeal to moral authority.

Recall the account of autonomy in Chapter 4: an action is autonomous if the agent chooses to perform it; the choice is unforced; the
significance of the chosen action is understood by the agent; the agent
evaluates the available choices and actions; and the agent chooses and
performs the favorably evaluated action in preference to other available
choices and actions. The first two conditions jointly form the freedom
component of autonomy; the last three jointly compose its judgment
component.

People come to recognize the moral authority of others partly because the complexities of the situations they face make them distrust
their own evaluations and understanding and partly because the qualifications of a moral authority make them trust its evaluations and understanding instead. They then rely on the judgment of a moral authority
rather than on their own. In doing so, they violate the judgment component of autonomy. They are acting freely because they perform the action they have chosen and their choice was not forced, but they are not
acting autonomously because they have neither evaluated nor understood the significance of their action. It appears therefore that there is a
conflict between autonomy and moral authority.

The conservative response to this conflict is to acknowledge that it
may occur in some cases, but to deny that it is a threat to good lives. The
reason why the conflict need not be a threat is that there are many conceptions of a good life in which autonomy plays only an insignificant
role; that if autonomy and moral authority appear incompatible in some
conceptions of a good life, then there may be good reasons to subordinate autonomy to moral authority; and that they may not be incompatible because their conflicting claims can be balanced in numerous
conceptions of a good life. Let us now consider these reasons in turn.

To begin with, autonomy is neither a necessary nor a sufficient condition of those numerous conceptions of a good life that essentially in-

volve the subordination of the judgment of individuals to some religious, communal, political, military, commercial, or other similar authorities. For countless people, living a good life involves having a niche in a hierarchical system that is dedicated to the pursuit of some ideal that the participants accept as their own. Participation in such a system requires them to follow willingly the guidance of those whose superior position is owed to a deeper and broader understanding than they possess themselves of how they can best pursue the ideal that they share.

Conceptions of a good life such as these are viewed with great suspicion by those whose sensibility is informed by the stress the Enlightenment Faith places on the centrality of autonomy to living a good life. It must nevertheless be recognized that privileging autonomy in this manner is a local phenomenon largely restricted to modern, upper middle class, prosperous, moderately well-educated Westerners. The vast majority of humanity outside of that narrow context and countless people within it—orthodox religious believers, soldiers, the police, athletes, executives in tightly organized corporations, and so forth—live under discipline that they accept and on balance welcome. It must also be recognized that the elevation of autonomy into a requirement of all good lives is incompatible with the pluralism to which defenders of the Enlightenment Faith profess themselves to be committed.

The mistake underlying the over-valuation of autonomy is to slide from the true belief that autonomy is essential to some conceptions of a good life to the false belief that without attributing a central place to autonomy no conception of a life can be good. It has been well said that "There is an intellectual error that threatens to arise whenever autonomy has been defended as fundamental: This is that the notion is elevated to a higher status than it deserves. . . . Theories that base everything on any single aspect of human personality, on any one of a number of values, always tend toward the intellectually imperialistic." [19] Those who avoid this intellectual error will not suspect conceptions of a good life merely on the ground that moral authority plays a central role in them and that autonomy does not. In such lives, autonomy and moral authority may conflict, but their conflict is readily resolved in favor of moral authority because autonomy has little significance in them.

There are many conceptions of a good life in which autonomy is important and in which autonomy and moral authority may conflict. Conservatives will be in favor of resolving this conflict in favor of moral authority under one or both of two conditions. The first is if people living according to such conceptions of a good life have good reasons both to distrust their own judgment and to trust the judgments of moral authorities whose knowledge, commitment, reflectiveness, exemplary conduct, and articulateness make their judgments better than their own. To prefer autonomy over moral authority under this condition is not a key to good lives, but a guarantee of bad ones.

The second condition under which conservatives favor moral authority over autonomy is when the individuals exercising their autonomy are moral monsters who cause evil autonomously, or amoral who autonomously subordinate moral to other considerations, or episodic evildoers acting under great provocation, temptation, or stress that mislead their autonomous judgments. No one committed to morality could consistently favor autonomy over moral authority if doing so would make evil more rather than less prevalent. According to conservatives, there are therefore conditions in which the conflict between autonomy and moral authority ought to be resolved in favor of the latter, even if the former is accorded great importance.

There will still remain many conceptions of a good life in which these conditions do not obtain, those who live according to them do value autonomy highly, and autonomy conflicts with moral authority. These are lives in which people have some autonomy, but not enough. Their judgments draw on their understanding and evaluations, but they are not sufficiently reliable to make their judgments good. If their judgments conflict with those of moral authorities, what ought they to do? The conservative view is that such conflicts do not show that autonomy and moral authority are incompatible because the conflict can be defused by reaching a balance between them. Reaching this balance, however, is a complicated matter because ways of weighing conflicting claims vary with moral traditions, conceptions of a good life, and individuals. It is futile, therefore, to seek a general answer that will cover all such cases and provides a blueprint for the resolution of this kind of conflict. The reasonable approach is to try to understand the complexities that are involved in the conflict and to bear in mind that their resolutions depends on striking a balance that will differ from case to case.

In such cases, however, conflict between autonomy and moral authority is not absolute, but proportional. One does not exclude the other, but rather the more there is of one, the less there can be of the other.

They are not incompatible approaches to trying to live a good life. The appeal to moral authority is a remedy for insufficient autonomy. What moral authorities may do in such cases is not to preempt but to improve the agents' judgments. They teach, not command. Their aim as parents, teachers, older friends, therapists, and so forth, is to bring those who turn to them to the point at which they can turn away because their judgments have become good enough. The more autonomous such people become, the less need they have to rely on moral authority. People who value autonomy highly may thus be reasonable in relying on the judgments of others when they are likely to be better than their own because doing so will increase their own autonomy. The preference for moral authority over autonomy therefore is often a way of improving insufficient autonomy, rather than a threat to it.

The conservative view, therefore, is that moral authority plays an important role on the individual level of political morality. It helps individuals to cope with complex situations in which their judgments are unreliable; it limits the autonomously evil actions of moral monsters, amoralists, and episodic evil-doers; and it is an essential component of countless conceptions of a good life which involve participation in traditional hierarchies and which any consistent pluralist will recognize as a widely favored moral possibility. The conservative view, however, is regarded with suspicion and hostility by defenders of the Enlightenment Faith. They suppose that good lives must be autonomous because they suppose that if people live autonomously, then they will tend to seek the good, and if they seek evil, it is because their autonomy has in some way been limited. These suppositions have been shown to be groundless, and they can be adhered to only by denying the plain facts of moral life on which the conservative view is based.

CHAPTER 8

The Ideal of Justice

> If there are powers beyond man, their justice is so alien, so slow,
> so indifferent, as to make impossible even the hope of . . . under-
> standing. But man continues to demand justice and an order
> with which he can live . . . against the whole tenor of his experi-
> ence, in the teeth of universal indifference and the inconsistency
> of fortune.
>
> —WILLIAM ARROWSMITH, *"Introduction to* Hecuba*"*

The political arrangements of a good society will protect the conditions of good lives on each of the three levels of political morality. The question to be considered in this chapter is how a good society should proceed in providing that protection. And the answer is that it should do so in accordance with justice. It is necessary, therefore, to give an account of how conservatives think about justice. The argument will begin with an overview of the three levels and then concentrate on what justice is and how it is connected with these levels.

THE THREE LEVELS OF
CONSERVATIVE POLITICAL MORALITY

The three levels of conservative political morality are the universal, the social, and the individual. On each level, there are possibilities, whose realization makes lives better, and limits, whose acceptance avoids evil. On the universal level, the possibilities and limits are set by the basic physiological, psychological, and social aspects of human nature that are by and large historically unchanging, socially constant, and individually invariant. From these aspects, there follow primary values—primary goods and evils—whose protection or prohibition constitutes the minimum requirements of all good lives. They are protected or prohibited by required conventions whose enforcement is a moral necessity because good lives require having the primary goods and avoiding the primary evils.

On the social level, the possibilities and limits are set by the traditions that define the moral identity of the people who live together in a society. From these traditions, there follow secondary values—secondary goods and evils—whose protection or prohibition constitutes a requirement of all good lives beyond the minimum and in the context of a particular society. These secondary values are protected by variable conventions whose enforcement is a moral necessity generally, but not individually. It is necessary for good lives that there be some system of variable conventions in any good society, conventions that define acceptable forms, among others, of self-direction, intimacy, and civility, but there is considerable latitude in a good society and variety among such societies in respect to the specific variable conventions that constitute the overall system.

On the individual level, the possibilities and limits are set by conceptions of a good life that individuals form by participating in some of the various prevailing traditions of their societies and by finding a fit between the traditions and their own characters and circumstances. From these conceptions of a good life, there follow secondary values—secondary goods and evils—whose protection or prohibition constitutes a condition of that particular conception of a good life. These secondary values are also protected by variable conventions, conformity to which is a requirement that varies from one conception of a good life to another, but for all conceptions there must be some specific secondary values protected by specific variable conventions. Judging the significance, respective importance, suitability, and requirements of these specific variable conventions and secondary values is a complex matter for help with which individuals may often and reasonably turn to moral authorities whose lives and conduct demonstrate their qualifications.

The three-level conception of conservative political morality is intended to capture the structure of what ought to be the political morality of a good society. There is of course more to morality than its political dimension, but that dimension is indispensable because it is concerned with some conditions that are necessary for all good lives. Conservatives acknowledge, indeed they insist, that good lives depend also on conditions that no political arrangements can secure. The political morality of conservatism, therefore, aims to identify and defend some necessary conditions of good lives, while recognizing that those conditions, individually or jointly, are not sufficient.

If a society is good, it is because this three-level structure is in place. The reason for thinking of such a society as good is that through the three levels it makes good lives possible for people living in it. But the relation between a good society and good lives is not that of means to an end. If it were, then the end, good lives, could be obtained by means other than a good society. This, however, is not possible. Lives cannot be good unless their universal, social, and individual requirements are met. And meeting them partly depends on having the political arrangements that protect the possibilities and limits on each of the three levels. A good society, therefore, is not a means to but a constituent of good lives. To live a good life is to engage in activities aiming at the realization of the possibilities and at the acceptance of the limits set by the universal, social, and individual requirements of good lives. If this is understood about good lives and good societies, a number of consequences will be seen to follow.

First, it gives deeper meaning to the catch phrase, repeated by countless political thinkers since Aristotle, that human beings are social. They are social not merely in the descriptive sense, in which they are, say, featherless bipeds, but also in the evaluative sense, in which good lives are inseparable from good societies. That human beings are social is not just a factual truth, but also a practical guide to how they should live. Second, it makes it obvious that conservatives are not committed to a consequentialist approach to justification, although such an approach is compatible with conservatism. If living a good life partly is to live in accordance with the possibilities and limits of a good society, then a good life is not to be understood as a consequence that a good society aims to bring about. The goodness of a society just is the social dimension of good lives. Third, conservatives are not committed to a deontological approach to justification either, although, as before, such an approach is not incompatible with conservatism. Deontologists hold that moral justification is a matter of ascertaining the requirements of reason, quite independently of consequences. Conservatives think that reason requires conformity to the conditions of good lives. It is true that they also think that such conformity will contribute to good lives, but surely deontologists would not find that objectionable. Fourth, the inseparability of good societies and good lives does not mean that there is one, and only one, true morality and that the goodness of societies and lives depends on the extent to which they conform to it. This is true only on the universal level, having to do with the minimum requirements, and partly true on the social level, insofar as the protection of the moral identity of a society is concerned. But it is not true on the social level apart from that, and it is not true on the individual level at all, because on these levels good lives depend on traditions and conceptions of a good live that vary with societies and individuals. To say, as conservatives do, that a good society must have in place this three-level structure of political morality is to make a claim about the indispensability of some possibilities and limits, but the claim remains pluralistic because it leaves open what many of these possibilities and limits are and how they are met on the social and the individual levels.

THE CONCEPT OF JUSTICE

In the history of political thought Plato, Aristotle, Hobbes, Locke, Hume, Hegel, and John Stuart Mill, among others, gave notable accounts of justice, and contemporary thought is awash in controversies about justice since John Rawls opened the floodgates.[1] This vast literature on justice, however, will be ignored here, with one significant exception, because the way in which justice is connected with conservatism is largely independent of the outcome of these controversies. Let it be acknowledged that the concept of justice allows numerous evaluatively charged and incompatible interpretations. The concept nevertheless must possess some core of uncontested meaning, for without it there would be no reason to suppose that the numerous interpretations are of the same thing. This point may be expressed in terms of the distinction between the concept and various conceptions of justice: "it seems natural to think of the concept of justice as distinct from various conceptions of justice and as being justified by the role which these different . . . conceptions have in common."[2] The main concern of the argument then is with the concept of justice. The connection between justice and conservatism depends on the agreed-on core of justice that is encapsulated by the concept and not on the controversial aspects that lend themselves to the conflicting interpretations of different conceptions.

What then is this agreed-on core? The first step toward identifying it is Aristotle's general formula that justice requires treating equals equally and unequals unequally.[3] As it stands, this formula is much too vague because there is nothing that connects it specifically with justice. It is a condition of consistency in any context that the same cases should be treated alike and different cases differently. This is as true of sorting apples, classifying fauna, diagnosing illness, judging wine, appraising antiques, and so forth, as it is of justice. The general formula, therefore, is too general to tell us specifically about justice. What is needed is an account that goes beyond simple consistency and adds something that would permit the identification of particular cases as coming under the jurisdiction of justice. Considerable care must be exercised, however, about what is added. It would be wrong, for instance, to add to consistency the requirement of equal economic status, for this would make economic equality just by definition, and that of course would be question-begging. It would arbitrarily identify the concept of justice with a particular conception of justice, and the result would be that conceptions of justice that allowed for economic inequality could be challenged not merely on moral or political grounds but also for being logically self-contradictory. Whatever is added to consistency, therefore, has to be specific enough to identify the cases that come under justice and yet remain sufficiently general to allow for conflicting conceptions of justice.

The second step toward identifying the core of justice is to reflect on the insistence of Socrates in *The Republic* that there is a deep connection between justice and living a good life. Socrates thought that a life is good only if it is lived in accordance with reason and morality. He also thought that such a life cannot fail to be satisfying, and satisfaction with one's life must be derived from its being reasonable and moral. And he thought both because he supposed that reason, morality, and satisfaction have the same source: conformity to the Form of the Good, which is Socrates' name for the moral order in reality. The appearance that a reasonable and moral life may lack satisfaction, or that satisfaction may be derived from an unreasonable or immoral life deceives only people who are ignorant of the good. Those who know the good will be satisfied with their lives in proportion to their conformity to reason and morality. Justice, according to Socrates is pivotal to good lives because it maintains a harmonious balance among the elements of one's character and of one's society, thereby enabling both to conform to the moral order in reality.

The commitment to pluralism, skepticism, and pessimism prevents conservatives from accepting Socrates' claims. Conservatives believe that even if there is a moral order in reality, reliable knowledge of it cannot be had. It is certainly important to balance the elements of one's character and society with a view to making good lives possible, but there are many ways in which this can be done. Provided that the conditions of good lives on each of the three levels of political morality are met, reason and morality allow living according to any one of these many ways Socrates was right to think that good lives combine reason, morality, and satisfaction, but he was wrong to suppose that reasonable and moral lives must be satisfying or that satisfying lives must be reasonable and moral. History and personal experience provide ample evidence to show that reasonable or moral lives may lack satisfaction and that unreasonable or immoral lives may be very satisfying. The fundamental reason that underlies this conservative attitude is doubt about the possibility of knowledge about a supposed moral order in reality. This doubt is strengthened by the facts whose importance Socrates underestimated: the contingency of life and the prevalence of evil. Conservatives agree with Socrates in deploring these facts, but they do not agree with him that they are merely the products of human ignorance that clear and honest thinking could overcome.

The third step conservatives take toward identifying the core of justice, then, is to recognize that contingency and evil are obstacles to good lives, deny that they can be overcome in the way Socrates had thought, and propose instead another way of coping with them. The name for this way is justice. The clue to its core is suggested by Socrates' mistaken belief that reasonable and moral lives will be satisfying. Conservatives think that this belief is true only if it is reformulated to hold that reasonable and moral lives *ought to* be satisfying. The belief then implies that if the connection between reasonable and moral lives, on the one hand, and satisfying lives, on the other, is severed, then justice is violated. And if the divergence between these necessary components of good lives is too great, then justice is not merely violated but outraged. This belief, unlike that of Socrates, is not falsified by the failure of reality to conform to it because it is not about how things are, but about how they ought to be.

It must be asked, however, why reason and morality should lead to a good life and unreason and immorality to a bad life? The answer finally provides the basic moral belief that, according to conservatives, and not just them, is at the core of justice: people ought to have what they deserve. The conservative view, then, is that justice is the human attempt to arrange that people consistently have what they deserve. Justice may be thought of in individual terms, having to do with the way individuals ought to treat other individuals. Conservatism, however, is a political morality, its concern is with justice from a political point of view, and so it aims at political arrangements in a society that guarantee that people have what they deserve and do not have what they do not deserve. This of course raises the question of how to think about what people do or do not deserve.

What people deserve are some benefits or harms, and they deserve them because of some fact about themselves. This fact is the *basis* of desert and that someone should have some benefit or harm on that basis creates a *claim* of desert. Desert is thus relative to agents because its basis is a fact about them, and the claim is for some benefits or harms that they ought to have on that basis.[4] The fact that forms the basis of desert may be a character trait, such as a virtue or vice, an excellence or a fault, a skill or deficiency; or it may be a relation, for instance, being a taxpayer, a competitor, or an employee; or it may be an explicit or implicit agreement, like having made a promise, married, or enrolled as a student; or it may be a way in which someone has acted, for example, kindly or cruelly, thoughtfully or unthinkingly, fairly or unfairly. The basis of desert, then, is some characteristic, relation, agreement, or conduct of some agent. Each of these bases allows for considerable variety within it. Desert, therefore, does not have any one particular basis; it is a pluralistic notion.

The claim of desert is that some agent ought to enjoy some benefit or suffer some harm on the relevant basis. The claim need not be one that the agent makes; indeed, it is not often that agents lay claim to some deserved harm. Nor need there be any particular person or institution that makes the claim on behalf of the agent. The claim should be understood in the very general sense that the agent has a certain benefit or harm coming and that it would be good, right, proper, or fitting if the agent received it. The claim sometimes could and should be enforced, but it need not be. It need not even be enforceable because there are perfectly legitimate claims of desert that are not directed toward any person or institution, such as that wicked people do not deserve to live happily until they die of old age or that good people do not deserve the misfortune that befalls them.

The ascription of desert is partly backward and partly forward-looking. It looks backward toward its basis, and it looks forward from there to lay claim to the appropriate benefit or harm. The ascription of desert thus always requires a particular type of reason and the claim it creates always requires a particular type of justification. Both requirements are met by the basis of desert. It may thus be said that hard work deserves success, employees deserve wages from their employers, acts of kindness deserve gratitude from their recipients, just as hypocrites deserve to be exposed, incompetent physicians deserve to lose accreditation, and criminals deserve punishment. The justification of these claims is to point at the relevant characteristic, relation, agreement, or conduct of people that provides the basis for claiming that they deserve the appropriate benefits or harms.

The basis for justified claims of desert, however, has a further requirement because not just any characteristic, relation, agreement, or conduct provides the required reason. For the basis to serve as a reason there must be an explanation of what it is about it that makes it fitting that the agent should receive some benefit or harm. Why does hard work deserve success or kindness gratitude? The appropriate explanation then strengthens the reason that can be derived from the basis of desert by pointing at the feature that makes the characteristic, relation, agreement, or conduct in question a fitting basis for the appropriate benefits or harms. The required explanation therefore must point at some specific excellence or fault, achievement or failure, personal nexus or its lack, compliance or non-compliance, commission or omission that provides the basis for claiming that the agent in question deserves the corresponding benefits or harms.

This account suggests several ways in which the ascription of desert may be mistaken. The first is a factual mistake about the basis of desert. The person who was thought to be a burglar really was not, so punishment is inappropriate. The second is a mistake in thinking that the basis of desert warrants the benefits or harms that it is thought to do. This may involve a mistaken evaluation of the basis, such as thinking of chastity as a virtue. Or it may involve the mistaken application of a correct evaluation, for instance, thinking correctly that conscientiousness is a virtue, but mistaking compulsiveness for it. The third is a mistake in proportion. The agent in question does indeed deserve benefits or harms on the appropriate basis, but the benefits or harms received exceed what is appropriate. The burglar deserves imprisonment, but not for life; the novelist deserves good reviews, but not a Nobel Prize. The fourth is the logical mistake of ascribing desert without regard for its basis. The mistake is not that there is thought to be a basis when there is none; rather, the ascription of desert occurs in disregard of whether or not it has an appropriate basis. In this way, benefits or harms may be distributed not on the basis of some properly evaluated characteristic, relation, agreement, or conduct, but for some other reason.

The significance of this fourth kind of mistake about the ascription of desert is considerable, and it will shortly be discussed further. The mistake, it needs to emphasized, is logical. Just as a person cannot be held to a promise if none has been made, or be guilty of a crime if none has been committed, so desert cannot be ascribed unless it has a basis. The reason for this is that without a basis the benefits and harms received cannot—logically cannot—be deserved. Benefits and harms may be received because of need, want, love, prudence, generosity, paternalism, religious belief, political expediency, and so forth. But they can be deserved only on the basis that the recipients' characteristic, relation, agreement, or conduct makes it fitting that they should enjoy or suffer specific benefits or harms.

Suppose, however, that the ascription of desert is reasonable because it is free of the mistakes in fact, evaluation, proportion, and logic. The claim it creates, then, is that deserving agents ought to receive some benefit or harm. How strong is this claim? It cannot be unconditional because it may be impossible to provide the benefit or the harm that is reasonably claimed. One obstacle to it may be the unavailability of the deserved benefits or harms, due to non-culpable scarcity of resources. Another obstacle may be that the available resources cannot be distributed proportionally to what is deserved. How could people who have been negligently blinded or who have been maimed by prolonged torture be fittingly compensated? What benefit could be provided for those who nobly died in the line of duty or chose a life devoid of most satisfactions in order to make others less miserable? Underlying these obstacles is the fact that contingency renders the human control over the distribution of deserved benefits and harms insufficient. People are often unavoidably prevented from having what they deserve and ought to have.

If reasonably based claims of desert are not unconditional because conditions beyond human control may make it impossible to meet them, may they be said then to be overriding? They could perhaps be expressed as claiming that insofar as it is possible to arrange that people have what they deserve, it ought to be done. But this interpretation of these claims is still too strong. Desert is one basis that makes it fitting for people to enjoy some benefits or suffer some harms, but there are also other bases, and they may make it fitting that people should have more or less than what they deserve. Love, friendship, family ties, and so forth may place an obligation on people to be generous rather than punctilious in benefiting others. Relationships of this sort often provide good reasons to benefit others more than they deserve. A similar case can be made for making people suffer less than they deserve. Mercy, forgiveness, hope of reform, remorse of the wrong-doer, the uncharacteristic nature of the wrong that has been done, and the like may provide reasonable bases for not inflicting harm proportional to what is deserved. The claim that people ought to have what they deserve may be overridden, therefore, by a stronger case that rests on some alternative basis for benefiting or harming others.

The most reasonable interpretation of the strength of the claim that people should have what they deserve is, therefore, that it is prima facie. It should be assumed to hold, unless some stronger consideration overrides it. It would be neat if a general account could be given of what consideration would be stronger than desert, but no such account is to be had. Just as there is a plurality of bases of desert, so there is a plurality of ways in which the claims of desert can be reasonably defeated. Desert is a basic moral consideration, but there are also other basic moral considerations, and their claims may conflict with and override the claims of desert. The best that can be done *a priori* is to indicate the logic of a claim that could reasonably defeat the claim of desert.

The context of the claims of desert and whatever conflicts with them is people's aspiration to live a good life, understood as one in which reason, morality, and satisfaction coincide as closely as possible. The prima facie case for desert derives its strength from the importance of desert to this aspiration. What a claim that reasonably overrides that of desert would have to show is that in a particular case some consideration other than desert, such as love or mercy, is more important to making reason, morality, and satisfaction coincide. But what such considerations may be cannot be specified *a priori* because there is a plurality of conceptions of a good life, and what is reasonable, moral, and satisfying in one may not always be so in another. The fact is that in this context a reasonable case must be particular, and a general case can only be prima facie.

The result of this account of the concept of justice is that justice has at its core the combination of consistency and desert. Consistency requires that like cases be treated alike and different cases differently. Desert provides the basis on which the likenesses and differences should be evaluated. On that basis, benefits and harms ought to be made proportional to the appropriate characteristics, relations, agreements, or conduct of their recipients. The political aim of justice is to create and maintain political arrangements that would contribute to good lives by making the agents' satisfactions proportional to the reasonability and morality of their lives.

THE CONTENT OF JUSTICE

The account of justice has so far been entirely formal. A full account would have to specify the particular characteristics, relations, agreements, and conduct that form the appropriate bases of desert. This would require going beyond the concept in order to formulate a particular conception of justice. And conceptions of justice, of course, vary with societies and historical periods. The defense of a particular conception of justice is beyond the scope of the present argument. But it is possible to specify some content that any adequate conception of justice must have. This, in turn, makes it possible to make the present account of justice less formal.

The most obvious aspect of justice is the maintenance of arrangements whose purpose is to guarantee that people get the benefits and harms that they deserve. These arrangements may or may not be political, but no society can do without political arrangements that have this purpose. For instance, there has to be a criminal justice system to allocate deserved harms and a welfare system to allocate deserved benefits. Both systems may and often do fail egregiously, and the extent to which they do, they are unjust. This aspect of justice may be called distributive.

Another aspect of justice is the need to correct the injustice that occurs in the distribution of benefits and harms. This injustice may be culpable, if it is the result of deliberate or negligent acts, or it may be no one's fault, if it results from circumstances beyond human control. The political arrangements that make the necessary corrections possible have to do with the redistribution of benefits and harms. There is a strong temptation to think of benefits and harms in terms of wealth and poverty. It is easy to see how wealth could be redistributed through taxation and welfare checks. But the temptation should be resisted because security, health, education, freedom, and so forth, are also benefits, their opposites are also harms, and they cannot be so easily redistributed as wealth. The appropriate political arrangements, therefore, must be concerned with some form of compensation in case of undeserved harms and some form of deprivation in case of undeserved benefits. This is the corrective aspect of justice.

A further aspect of justice is necessary because there are likely to be deep disagreements in any society about what benefits and harms are deserved or undeserved and about what forms of compensation or deprivation are justified or unjustified. All societies need to have political arrangements for adjudicating between such disagreements. These adjudications will be just if they are impartial, based exclusively on the respective strengths of the conflicting claims. The legal system is the most obvious of the political arrangements that have this purpose, but it is by no means the only one. Legislation, ombudsmen, arbitration panels, judicial committees in various institutions, appeals boards, and so forth, are other examples. This aspect of justice is adjudicatory.

The account of the concept of justice, then, can be made less formal, without becoming a partisan case for a particular conception of justice, by recognizing that any adequate conception of justice must specify the political arrangements that the distributive, corrective, and adjudicatory aspects of justice require. These political arrangements, however, may take quite different forms in different societies, or in different periods in the history of the same society. And political arrangements are likely to vary not just in their forms, but also in their contents because different characteristics, relations, agreements, and conduct may be recognized as appropriate bases for different benefits and harms in different societies.

It is possible to go still further in specifying the content of justice without abandoning neutrality regarding particular conceptions of justice. The key is the distinction between the universal, social, and individual levels of political morality. There is need for justice on each level, but there are significant differences in the operation of justice on each level. The rule of thumb is that the movement from the universal, through the social, to the individual levels is the movement from more to less political, institutionalized, codified, rule-governed, impersonal forms of justice. The requirements of justice become less general as they change from the universal to the individual levels.

On the universal level, it is possible to formulate rules of justice that apply to everyone equally in a particular society. The benefits and harms that may be deserved or undeserved are recognized as such by everyone because the enjoyment of the benefits and the avoidance of the harms are the minimum requirements of all good lives. The object of justice on this level, then, is to formulate and enforce rules that make it clear to everyone in that society how the relevant benefits and harms ought to be distributed, how the discrepancy between deserved and undeserved distribution ought to be corrected, and how disagreements about distribution and correction ought to be settled.

Different societies will have different rules, but this does not make justice on the universal level merely the result of whatever local rules happened to have been developed. For the necessary aim of justice in all societies is to help make good the lives of people living in it, and that aim is served only by rules that make people's satisfactions proportional to the reasonability and morality of their lives. The benefits and harms on the universal level bear on satisfactions that all good lives require, and it is these satisfactions that provide an objective standard by which the relevant rules of any society can be justified or criticized. A good society, therefore, will have an explanation of how its rules of distribution, correction, and adjudication concerning basic benefits and harms contributes to making the satisfactions of individuals proportional to the reasonability and morality of their lives. How good a society is partly depends on how convincing that explanation is.

There are rules of justice on the social level as well, but they are of two general kinds. It will be remembered that the social level comprises the system of traditions that prevails in a particular society. There are two kinds of rules of justice on this level, depending on whether they are meant to apply to the system of traditions taken collectively, and thus concern the moral identity of the society, or whether they concern particular traditions, and thus apply only to individuals who participate in particular traditions.

The rules of justice that concern the whole system of traditions aim to protect and perpetuate the moral identity of a society. Their justification is that the maintenance of moral identity is as important a condition of good lives as is the satisfaction of the minimum requirements. For moral identity is but the evaluative dimension of life as it is lived in a particular society. It provides, as it were, the language of conduct. Or, less metaphorically, it provides the forms of self-direction, intimacy, and civility, the acceptable ways of earning a living, raising children, making friends, competing with others, excelling in one's endeavors, facing illness, old age, grief, and death, and so forth. The benefits associated with moral identity are then the possibilities that individuals have available in particular societies out of which they can construct good lives for themselves. With possibilities come limits on how the possibilities can be realized and what possibilities are excluded altogether. The harms connected with moral identity have to do with the transgression of the limits. The first kind of rules of justice on the social level then establishes the benefits that are deserved by those who live according to the possibilities of the prevailing moral identity and the harms that are deserved by those who live in violation of the limits.

The second kind of rules of justice on the social level concerns the rules that are internal to the particular traditions that jointly form the moral identity of a society. These rules govern ways in which benefits and harms ought to be distributed within a tradition. The rules are numerous and variable because of the variety of benefits and harms that may be enjoyed or suffered in different traditions. But even here it is possible to discern patterns that are likely to exist in quite different traditions. Traditions may be artistic, commercial, scholarly, athletic, literary, religious, academic, political, and so on. But they all have some purpose or another, and what unites the participants in the tradition is that they have made its purpose their own. Their activities are, on the appropriate occasions, directed toward that purpose. Traditions, therefore, are likely to have rules for evaluating the activities of their participants.

The rules will make it possible to distinguish between success and failure, to recognize conspicuous achievements, to compare and rank the excellence with which the activities are performed; they will determine what counts as a proper performance of the activity, what is an innovation, what is a departure so radical as to constitute a break with the tradition, what is imitative, original, idiosyncratic, or self-indulgent; they will help to identify talent and its lack, assign honors, status, and rewards. In short, they will distribute such benefits and harms as are proper to the tradition, correct mistakes in their distribution, and define some procedures for settling disputes about the appropriateness of benefits and harms.

The rules of justice on the social level, of course, vary with the moral identities of different societies and with the traditions that form parts of moral identities. But this variation is compatible with there being an objective standard that can be appealed to in determining whether or not the rules serve justice. That standard is the continued and unforced allegiance of many people in a society to its moral identity and to some of its traditions. Their allegiance shows that they have historically conceived of good lives in terms of the prevailing moral identity and its traditions, and that they must have had some success in actually living good lives when they lived according to them, because otherwise they would have transferred their allegiance to more promising possibilities.

There is justice also on the individual level, but it is not political. It is not a matter of formulating and applying general rules, and so conservatives, being concerned with questions of political morality, need only to recognize and leave room for this form of justice. On this level, individuals try to make good lives for themselves. In a good society, the political conditions of their endeavors are guaranteed. The minimum requirements are met, the moral identity of the society is secure, and there is a generous variety of traditions in which individuals can participate without being forced to do so. Their task is to construct a conception of a good life for themselves by adapting to their characters and circumstances some of the possibilities that participation in traditions provides. They construct good lives by the reciprocal adjustments of traditional possibilities and their desires and aversions. Such conceptions of a good life will have to conform to the rules of justice that exist on the universal and social levels, for if they did not, they would fail as conceptions of a *good* life. Justice, however, is relevant to individual conceptions of a good life in two additional ways.

The first of these ways is constituted of the intimate relationships individuals have with others. In these relationships, they represent nothing and no one but themselves, and they interact with others as husbands, wives, parents, children, brothers, sisters, colleagues, comrades, neighbors, friends, lovers, and so forth. The universal and social rules of justice set limits within which acceptable forms of such relationships ought to fall, but there is, of course, much more to intimacy than what can be captured by rules. Nevertheless, it is an essential part of intimate relationships that people should treat each other as they deserve to be treated. Justice, therefore, is part of intimacy, even if it is recognized, as it ought to be, that love, generosity, forgiveness, loyalty, and so forth, may take precedence over justice. But what it is that people connected by such ties deserve from each other depends on their characters and circumstances, on their history together, and on their respective conceptions of a good life. These vary with relationships, and that is why there can be no rules of justice here, even though there can be justice.

The second way in which justice plays a role on the individual level has to do with the success and failure of individuals to live according to their conceptions of a good life. Let us assume that their conceptions are of a good life indeed, that they do as well as they can to live reasonable, moral, and satisfying lives, and that their society is good, so that they are not handicapped by injustice on the universal and social levels. Such people deserve to succeed in living good lives, but they may fail regardless of what they deserve, because the contingency of life derails them through illness, accident, grief, chance, social change, and the like, which they could not have foreseen and for which no one can be blamed. It is just that some people's lives are good and it is unjust that some fail to be so.

Justice in intimate relationships and in making a good life for oneself is an important part of morality, but a political morality has, and ought to have, little to say about it, because its concern is only with the political conditions of good lives. In fact, it is a strong reason against a political morality if it favors interference with how people conduct themselves on the individual level. Part of the reason why conservatives favor limited government is to avoid such interference.

MORAL INEQUALITY

The just completed account of the concept and the partial content of justice was intended to make explicit what is implicit in the common understanding of justice. The account was meant to be analytical, not original or controversial. It was to identify the core that must be shared by all conceptions of justice, and it was to terminate at the point beyond which controversies begin about what particular forms justice ought to take. The account, therefore, was to be neutral toward the numerous conflicting conceptions of justice. It must now be recognized that there is a limit to its neutrality, and that there is a conception of justice that is incompatible with the account that has been given. If it is recognized further that this conception of justice is accepted by a large number of contemporary political thinkers, then it becomes unavoidable to consider it. The conception of justice in question is the egalitarian one, and its most prominent defender is John Rawls.[5] The incompatibility between the present account of the concept and the egalitarian conception implies either that the account of the concept is faulty or that the conception fails as a conception of justice. The argument will show that the latter is the case. Fortunately, this can be done by concentrating only on a portion of Rawls's egalitarian conception of justice. Readers interested in a full account and an overall criticism of it need to look elsewhere.[6]

We may begin with noticing that it is a consequence of the account of the concept that justice by its very nature is inegalitarian. Justice involves people getting what they deserve, and different people are bound to deserve different benefits and harms. The reasons for this are, first, that the characteristics, relations, agreements, and conduct that form the bases of desert differ from person to person; and, second, that the benefits and harms that people deserve on these bases are greater or lesser because there are differences among people in their moral merits, on the basis of which desert can be ascribed to them. It is just a fact of life that characteristics, such as honesty, kindness, courage, or self-control, are possessed to different extents by different people; that the responsibilities created by relations, such as friendship, family ties, being neighbors or colleagues, are more or less faithfully discharged; that agreements, such as contracts, promises, or informal understandings, are honored in various degrees; and that conduct is morally better or worse. These facts make it plain that people differ both in the bases of their desert and in their moral merits.

Justice, then, is essentially inegalitarian because people have different moral merits, and so they deserve different kinds and amounts of benefits and harms. This, of course, is not to deny that justice requires that people with the same moral merit deserve the same treatment and those with different moral merits deserve different treatment. But it is to deny that people have the same moral merit in the typical cases that are to be evaluated from the point of view of justice. It is amazing that anyone might think that justice requires the equal treatment of different people. What justice requires is the equal treatment of people with the same moral merits, but moral merits are rarely the same because people differ in their characteristics, relations, agreements, and conduct, as well as in honoring the obligations they create, and so they differ in the bases of their moral merits.

It may be conceded that this is so, and simultaneously claimed that justice requires the recognition that there is a basic respect in which everyone deserves equal treatment. This line of thought acknowledges that people differ in their moral merits and goes on to insist that there are some basic benefits that everyone deserves and some basic harms that no one deserves. But what reason is there to think this? Why should one think that benefactors and scourges of humanity, terrorists and their hostages, criminals and their victims, and cruel and kind people are equally deserving of some basic benefits and equally undeserving of some basic harms? Why should one think that when such basic benefits as security, health care, decent jobs, or pleasant housing are scarce, then all people, regardless of their moral merits or demerits, should get the same share of them? And why should malefactors, terrorists, criminals, and wicked people be as undeserving of the harms that they have merited by their way of life as those who have lived and acted decently?

One answer to these questions, if it can be called that, is that the basis for all people being equally deserving of some benefits and equally undeserving of some harms is not any actual characteristic, relation, agreement, or conduct of theirs, but rather a capacity. Different people have realized this capacity to different degrees, and consequently they have different moral merits, but the possession of the capacity itself does not depend on its realization. The enjoyment of some basic benefits and the avoidance of some basic harms is warranted by people's equal possession of the capacity in question. Those who favor this answer have to identify, of course, the capacity they have in mind. And they do identify it in various ways, all of which ultimately boil down to the claim that the capacity is for living a good life. It is because all human beings have that capacity that they are supposed to be equally deserving of having some basic benefits and of avoiding some basic harms.

This answer is untenable because people have great many capacities, among which the capacity to live a good life is one, but the capacity to live a wicked life is another. There are also capacities to live foolish, wasted, unreasonable, useless, self-indulgent lives, as well as capacities for the opposites. Which of their capacities people will develop with the help of basic benefits depends on many things. There is no good reason to single out the capacity to live a good life as the basis for equal basic desert because the advantages thereby gained may be used to develop capacities other than the one for living a good life. Those who are committed to justice because they regard it as indispensable to good lives will not base desert on any capacity because capacities may be misused, unused, neglected, or overwhelmed by other capacities. Good lives depend on how people live, not on how they might live. Justice must be based on what people deserve on the basis of their actual characteristics, relations, agreements, and conduct. That makes justice inseparable from moral merit and demerit, and, since people's moral merits and demerits are greater or lesser, justice is essentially an inegalitarian concept.

This understanding of the concept of justice, however, is rejected by Rawls and his egalitarian followers. Rawls writes: "There is a tendency for common sense to suppose that . . . the good things in life . . . should be distributed according to moral desert. . . . While it is recognized that this ideal can never be fully carried out, it is the appropriate conception of justice, at least as a prima facie principle, and a society should try to realize it as circumstances permit. Now justice as fairness [Rawls's theory] rejects this conception. . . . The principles of justice [as Rawls sees them] do not mention moral desert, and there is no tendency for distributive shares to correspond to it."[7] On Rawls's conception, therefore, the concept of justice does not include desert; the just distribution of benefits and harms is not determined by what people deserve; and, although common sense, and, one might add, the history of political thought about justice from the Greeks on, regard the connection between justice and desert as essential, Rawls thinks otherwise.

The reason Rawls gives for this radical departure from common sense and considered opinion is that the distribution of benefits based on desert is morally arbitrary because desert depends on natural endowments and "no one deserves his place in the distribution of natural assets any more than he deserves his initial starting place in society. . . . [T]he initial endowments of natural assets and the contingencies of their growth and nurture in early life are arbitrary from a moral point of view. The precept which seems intuitively to come closest to rewarding moral desert is that of distribution according to effort. . . . Once again, however, it seems clear that the effort a person is willing to make is influenced by his natural abilities and skills and the alternatives open to him. The better endowed are likely, other things equal, to strive conscientiously, and there seems to be no way to discount for their greater good fortune. The idea of rewarding desert is impraticable."[8] If justice does not call for rewarding desert, what does it call for? According to Rawls, it calls for "treat[ing] all persons equally. . . . The idea is to redress the bias of contingencies in the direction of equality" and that requires that the "basic structure [of society] . . . be arranged so that these contingencies work for the good of the least fortunate."[9]

The fundamental defects of this view of justice are so great and glaring as to make it hard to understand how it could be taken seriously. The view, in effect, erects a theory on the logical mistake noted earlier. It severs the connection between justice and desert; it supposes that the just distribution of benefits and harms is independent of what their recipients deserve. This cannot but lead to absurd consequences. Suppose that a man and a woman are both among the least fortunate members of a society. The man is a hitherto unapprehended mugger; he has never held a job; he is vicious when he can get away with it; he has moderate natural endowments, but he has made no effort to develop them. The woman is the mother of several children; she and the children have been abandoned by her husband and their father; she earns meager wages by working part-time at a menial job; she is doing her best to raise the children well; she has the same natural endowments as the mugger but, unlike him, has used them to make great, although unsuccessful, efforts to improve her situation. According to Rawls, the mugger and the mother are entitled to the same benefits. Their positions of inequality are the result of contingencies that are arbitrary from the moral point of view. The mugger's viciousness and lack of effort and the mother's decency and unsuccessful efforts create no morally relevant differences between them insofar as the distribution of benefits is concerned. Rawls's theory of justice requires that the basic structure of society be such as to entitle them to the same distributive shares.

Changing the scenario a little illustrates another absurd consequence of Rawls's position. The mugger continues as before, but the mother is no longer unsuccessful. Through her efforts, she considerably improves her position. She now has a moderately comfortable and secure, but by no means affluent, middle-class existence. She has a good job, she bought a house, the children are doing well at school, and they can even afford an occasional family vacation. According to Rawls, the mugger's lack of effort and the mother's successful effort are among the contingencies of life and they are to be redressed in the direction of equality. On Rawls's view, therefore, the basic structure of society should be arranged so that some of the mother's resources should be taken from her and used to support the mugger. And this should be done in the name of what Rawls calls justice!

Something has gone dreadfully wrong here. A first approximation of its cause is that the charge that Rawls so memorably leveled against utilitarianism also convicts his own position: "it does not take seriously the distinction between persons."[10] For it is a consequence of Rawls's view that people are merely the creations of contingencies. They have no control over their lives because "the effort a person is willing to make is influenced by his natural abilities and skills and the alternatives open to him. The better endowed are likely . . . to strive conscientiously, and there seems to be no way to discount for their greater fortune."[11] If people act in accordance with reason and morality, they just happened to have been arbitrarily favored by fortune; if they act unreasonably and immorally, they are the arbitrary victims of misfortune. The mother was just lucky, and the mugger was just unlucky. And what Rawls calls justice requires is "to redress the bias of contingencies in the direction of equality,"[12] that is, it requires political arrangements that will redistribute benefits from the mother to the mugger.

Conservatives will certainly agree with Rawls that contingency affects human conduct and that it may do so in ways that escape the control of those affected. But Rawls's view rests on a claim much stronger than this. His claim is that when people "strive conscientiously," it is just a matter of "their greater fortune," and, by implication, if they do not strive conscientiously, it is because they were arbitrarily short-changed "in the distribution of natural assets." If Rawls were right, no one would be responsible for anything. The mugger would deserve no blame and the mother would deserve no praise. This is an untenable position, and what Rawls says at other places makes it clear that he does not hold it. In that case, however, he must recognize that, although the contingencies of genetic endowment and post-natal environment influence human conduct, they often leave enough room for individual control; that people may or may not exercise the control they have; and that the control they do exercise may be for good or for evil. It is a belief basic to morality, a belief without which morality would not be possible, that people deserve praise or blame, benefits or harms, for the actions they have performed and over which they have control. The importance of the concept of justice that Rawls rejects is that it embodies this basic belief.

Rawls rejects this concept of justice because what mainly interests him is not justice but economic equality. He finds it objectionable that there are differences in the economic conditions of people, and he thinks that in a good society there ought not to be such differences. Now he might have said this forthrightly, and given for it such reasons as he could find. But this is not what he does. He claims that economic equality is a matter of justice, and, to defend his claim, he rejects the concept of justice that common sense and political thought historically recognizes, he invents a conception of justice of his own, and from its point of view he criticizes common sense and political thought for not conforming to his invention. The chief reason he has against the concept of justice he rejects and for the conception of justice he invents is that the first opposes and the second favors economic equality. The strategy of redefining a concept to suit one's purposes is an old rhetorical device, but age has not improved its cognitive credentials.

The reason to think that this is indeed the strategy behind Rawls's conception of justice is strengthened by recognizing that it explains several glaring omissions from Rawls's theory. It concentrates exclusively on one part of one aspect of justice: the distribution of benefits. There is nothing in it about the distribution of harms. It does not seriously consider the corrective and adjudicatory aspects of justice. There is a great deal in it about how the distribution of benefits makes lives better, but it says nothing about how to avoid evil. If a theory were about justice, these omissions would be fatal to it. But if a theory were mainly about economic equality, then its inattention to these matters would be neither a failure nor an objectionable omission. Rawls's theory focuses on the distribution of benefits because it is a theory about the desirability of greater economic equality and about the political arrangements that would lead to it. It is not a theory of justice at all, and if it were, it would be indefensible because a theory of justice cannot ignore what people deserve, it must specify the conditions in which inflicting harms is justified, it must address the question of how to avoid evil, and it must give an account of the corrective and adjudicatory aspects of justice, not just part of the distributive one—none of which is done by what Rawls calls his theory of justice.

Suppose that the unlikely happens and it is conceded that Rawls's theory is not of justice but of economic equality. Would conservatives find it acceptable under that description? They would not because, as the theory stands, the economic equality it champions is unjust. Conservatives and economic egalitarians may agree that in their society there is substantial inequality between people at the top and the bottom of the economic scale. Egalitarians point at this fact, find it morally objectionable, and, as Rawls says, want to redress it in the direction of equality. Conservatives recognize the fact, but, before they make a moral judgment about it, they ask how it came about. Why are the people at the top there, and why are the people at the bottom at the bottom? What conservatives want to know is whether or not people deserve whatever positions they have on the economic scale. If they are at the top because they have made legitimate efforts and succeeded, then they deserve their position, and it is not morally objectionable that they have it. If they got there illegitimately, they do not deserve to be there, and it is morally objectionable that they are there. Similarly for those at the bottom. If they are in that position because misfortune doomed them to it, then they do not deserve it. But if they are at the bottom because they have been profligate, took risks and lost, lived unreasonably, or did not do what they could to improve their lot, then they deserve to be where they are. Conservatives, therefore, differ from egalitarians because they think that whether or not economic inequality is deserved makes a great moral difference to what ought to be done.

The difference it makes is great, but it is not all the difference. Economic inequality may be just, and yet conservatives may still think that it is morally objectionable. Justice is an important consideration, but there are also other important considerations. One may be that people at the bottom are very badly off and, even though their position is deserved, decency, solidarity, charity, prudence, pity, or come combination of them, calls for political arrangements that will improve their lot. Conservatives may favor such arrangements, but they will not pretend, as Rawls and his egalitarian followers do, that the arrangements are called for by justice, and that the failure to adopt them is unjust. Conservatives certainly want political arrangements to be just. But they also want them to be free, orderly, and lawful, to foster peace and prosperity, to protect the environment, and so forth. What conservatives ultimately want is a good society. It is good because its political arrangements enable people in it to make good lives for themselves. The claims of justice, equality, freedom, or whatever, may be overridden by other claims if, and only if, the overall aim of having a good society warrants it.

THE LIMITS OF JUSTICE

This chapter has been about the *ideal* of justice, rather than about justice as it exists in any past or present society. The aim of the chapter has been to describe this ideal, show what the reasons are for pursuing it, and how it fits into the political morality of conservatism. The ideal of justice, however, is unattainable, and the acknowledgment that this is so is one of the distinctive features of conservatism. The system of justice that particular societies create and maintain unavoidably falls short of the ideal that reasonable and moral lives ought to be satisfying and that unreasonable and immoral lives ought not to be. This ideal is pursued through the distributive, corrective, and adjudicatory aspects of justice, but the contingency of life presents insuperable obstacles to achieving it.

Contingency affects the distributive aspect of justice by way of scarcity. The simplest form of scarcity is the insufficiency of material resources. There is never enough money, food, medicine, prison or hospital space, police protection, leisure time, interesting work, and the like, to provide everything that people deserve. It is not only material resources, however, that may be scarce, but also the expertise needed to create and deliver them. Physicians, teachers, administrators, research scientists may be as scarce as food, shelter, or medicine. The result of the chronic scarcity of resources is unavoidable injustice because their distribution requires favoring some among equally deserving people. It is useless to try to avoid such injustice by distributing scarce resources equally among all the deserving people because the equal distribution of scarce resources often results in the even greater injustice of no one getting what is deserved. If there are not enough oxygen tanks, it does not help to ration the suffocating to the same brief periods of breathing. Furthermore, there are numerous scarce resources whose equal distribution is impossible. Experienced surgeons, good teachers, or efficient administrators must restrict their activities to particular contexts, but if there are not enough of them, then deserving people outside of those contexts will not get the treatment, education, or efficient service that they deserve.

It would be a mistake to underestimate the seriousness of scarcity as a limit on just distribution by thinking that a more efficient system of distribution could overcome it. Improved efficiency may ameliorate some aspects of economic scarcity, but not all scarcity is economic. Scarcity often stems from the human condition, and in that case no improvement in efficiency could ameliorate it. Societies routinely have to choose between the good things that people in them deserve because there is not enough time, energy, or opportunity to provide all of them. Should limited funding go to deserving artistic or scientific talent? Are the worst off more or less deserving of scarce resources than those who generate future resources? Do the old deserve to hold on to the jobs they do well or do the young deserve them so that they can have a start in life? Freedom and order, justice and patriotism, the free market and high culture, private life and political power are often so related that the more there is of one, the scarcer will the other be. Regardless of its causes, the effect of scarcity is that it prevents people from having what they deserve because there is not enough. Justice requires distribution according to desert, scarcity often makes that impossible, so scarcity imposes unavoidable limits on justice.

The corrective aspect of justice is concerned with remedying injustice. People may not have what they deserve because systems of distribution failed to establish proportionality between benefits and harms and what their recipients deserve. The purpose of correction is to redress this imbalance. Disproportionality often cannot be remedied, however, because the contingency of life makes it impossible to reestablish the lost balance in the cases of numerous forms of undeserved harm that people have suffered. The simple idea guiding correction is that benefits and harms caused ought to equal benefits and harms received. If there is an imbalance, correction consists in adding or removing the appropriate kind or amount of benefit or harm, so that the balance will be reestablished. It complicates this simple idea that temporary imbalance is not always a sign of injustice. The idea is, however, that insofar as it is possible, the balance ought to be maintained over each person's lifetime. The most frequently employed means of correction are compensation and punishment.

This idea, however, is too simple to be realistic. It rests on the mistaken assumption that benefits and harms can be measured by some common scale. If this were so, it would make sense to speak of adding or removing benefits and harms so as to achieve a balance. But it is not so because there is no common scale on which the multitude of possible benefits and harms could be compared and ranked. Whether the common scale is assumed to measure benefits and harms in terms of some objective unit, like money, or in terms of subjective judgments based on pairwise comparisons, makes no theoretical difference to the point that the assumption is false because different types of benefits and harms are often incommensurable. There are some undeserved harms for which no benefits could adequately compensate the victim and no harms could adequately punish the person causing them.

Consider compensation first. What could compensate people who were murdered by terrorists, who were mutilated in accidents for which they were not responsible, who were forced to spend the best years of their lives in concentration camps on trumped-up charges, or who contracted AIDS through blood transfusion? Take punishment next. What is the proportional punishment for mass murderers or torturers? There is no conceivable compensation or punishment that could redress such imbalances because no benefit or harm could be commensurate with what the victims have suffered. Disproportionality, therefore, unavoidably limits efforts at correction. As scarcity often makes it impossible to have a just system of distribution, so disproportionality frequently places correction beyond reach.

Contingency also affects the adjudicatory aspect of justice in the form of ubiquitous conflicts among incompatible values. The political life of most societies is a continuous effort to resolve the conflicts among such genuinely important values as freedom, justice, order, peace, rights, prosperity, security, privacy, autonomy, a healthy environment, civility, law abidingness, and so forth. The adjudicatory aspect of justice is supposed to resolve disagreements about what it is that people deserve. These disagreements arise out of disagreements about what the appropriate characteristics, relations, agreements, and conduct are that form the bases of desert. But these disagreements, in turn, reflect the different priorities that people in a society assign to values that they agree in recognizing as genuinely important. Reasonable and morally committed people can and do disagree whether, at a given time in a society, freedom is more important than order, prosperity than a healthy environment, privacy than security, autonomy than law abidingness, and so forth. And these disagreements unavoidably influence judgments about whether or not people deserve the benefits of freedom, privacy, wealth, autonomy, or whether they deserve the incompatible benefits of order, a healthy environment, security, or law abidingness, if they cannot have them both.

All societies must resolve such conflicts, and in most cases the reasonable resolution involves finding some compromise that mixes the conflicting values in some proportion. Such compromises, however, will have the inevitable consequence of leaving the parties who make them with the perfectly warranted sense that they have colluded in perpetrating an unjust political arrangement. For what they have done by making the compromise is to agree to an arrangement that is designed to provide more or less benefits or harms than what they regard as deserved. It is true that they have a good reason for overriding the claims of justice, namely, to avoid the deterioration of the disagreement into violence, but that does not change the fact that in their eyes—and in the eyes of their opponents—an injustice has been done. The adjudication of conflicts involving political compromises must be seen, therefore, as the management of injustice. Given the contingent facts of the plurality of conflicting values and the need for compromise, injustice will be a permanent, unavoidable, and frequent feature of political life.

One distinctive feature of conservatism is the acknowledgment of the imperfection of justice that results from scarcity, disproportionality, and conflict. The conservative response to this lamentable fact about the human condition is to reaffirm the ideal of justice. The ideal of justice is worth pursuing because good lives require it. That the ideal is shown on reflection to be unattainable does not mean that lives could not be made better by making society more just. The pursuit of perfect justice is doomed to failure. But the pursuit of justice, imperfect as it is bound to be, will make lives better, or at least less bad, because it is better to come closer to political arrangements that guarantee that people have what they deserve than to abandon the pursuit and thereby make injustice even more likely. The conservative acknowledgment of the imperfection of justice, therefore, is intended to free political thought of the false hope based on an illusory expectation that the ideal of justice can be achieved. The aim of justice is to reduce injustice. It is reason enough for the pursuit of justice that it will make lives better. And it is a bad reason for weakening the commitment to justice that what is gained from its pursuit is not as good as it might be if the human condition were different.

CHAPTER 9

The Basic Beliefs

The delicate and difficult art is to find, in each new turn of experience, the *via media* between two extremes: to be catholic without being characterless; to have and apply standards, and yet to be on guard against their desensitizing and stupefying influence, their tendency to blind us to the diversities of concrete situations and to previously unrecognized values; to know when to tolerate, when to embrace, and when to fight. And in that art, since no fixed and comprehensive rule can be laid down for it, we shall doubtless never acquire perfection.

— ARTHUR O. LOVEJOY, *The Great Chain of Being*

One of the advantages of the three-level structure of the political morality of conservatism is that it can accommodate the reasonable beliefs of rival moral and political outlooks without having to commit itself to the unreasonable beliefs that handicap them. Conservatives can readily acknowledge that some particular belief holds on one level and go on to deny without inconsistency that it holds on another level. Conservatives can proceed in this manner because the basic beliefs of conservatism—skepticism, pluralism, traditionalism, and pessimism—are intermediate positions between unreasonable extremes that nevertheless have some reasonable components. The strategy behind the basic conservative beliefs is to combine what is reasonable in the unreasonable extremes and to discard the rest. What is reasonable in them is the recognition that some particular belief is morally important; what is unreasonable in them is partly the inflation of the importance of that belief. By recognizing the importance of a particular belief on one level, conservatives do justice to what is reasonable in an extreme position, and by limiting the importance of that belief to a particular level, conservatives avoid its unreasonable inflation that vitiates the extreme position. This final chapter aims to show that this is indeed an advantage and that conservatism has it.

PLURALISM

It will be convenient to begin with pluralism. The rivals of pluralism are absolutism and relativism. Each has at its core a belief whose centrality any adequate political morality must recognize. The belief at the core of absolutism is that there are some moral truths that hold universally and objectively, regardless of what attitude any person, tradition, or society may have toward them. The denial of these truths is incompatible with morality because the aim of morality is to secure the conditions of good lives and these truths express some of the conditions. The defects of absolutism are that it supposes that the universal and objective conditions of all good lives are far more numerous than they are in fact and that it fails to recognize the rich diversity of societies, traditions, and conceptions of a good life that depend on a variety of conditions. The belief at the core of relativism is that there are many reasonable conceptions of a good life, they vary with individuals, traditions, and societies, with times and places, and that the contingencies of context and the character of historical periods and people leave an indelible mark on the way good lives are conceived. The defects of relativism are that it supposes that this diversity affects all conditions on which good lives depend and that it fails to recognize that the diversity of good human lives is a diversity of *human* lives whose requirements are in some respects the same.

Pluralism takes account of what is right in each of these beliefs and avoids what is wrong with them. Its strategy is to acknowledge that the beliefs hold on one level of political morality and to deny that they hold beyond that level. The absolutist belief holds on the universal level, and the relativist one on the social and the individual levels. Let us now see how this works out, first for absolutism and then for relativism

The moral truths absolutists rightly insist on concern primary values and required conventions. The primary values reflect universal and objective requirements that derive from basic physiological, psychological, and social needs whose satisfaction is dictated by human nature. Adequate nutrition, protection against arbitrary violence, treatment of ill-ness and injury, defense of property, some order and predictability in the interactions of people who are recognized as fellow members of a society are examples of primary values. Required conventions are devel-oped and maintained by a good society to protect the people belonging to it in their enjoyment of the primary values.

There may be some variations in the required conventions of good so-cieties, but the variations cannot be too great because if the minimum requirements of good lives, which these conventions protect, are lack-ing, then a society cannot be good. The minimum requirements, re-flected by primary values, define the core that required conventions must have and in respect to which they must be similar in different soci-eties insofar as they are good. Variations among required conventions occur in their periphery where questions arise about what exceptions to the required conventions could be justified, how exclusive or inclusive is membership within the society, and how conflicts among required con-ventions and among primary values are to be settled.

Required conventions are necessary for a good society, but their ne-cessity is prima facie, not unconditional. The required conventions of good societies must be similar because they protect universal primary values, but they may be dissimilar in the way they answer the question of what exceptions may justifiably be made in their applications. One an-swer is that a required convention protecting a particular primary value may be justifiably violated if the protection of some more important pri-mary value or values requires it. Which primary value may be more im-portant than another is often a contingent matter that depends on the circumstances that prevail in a particular society. That is one reason why there may be differences in the periphery of required conventions in different societies. These differences, however, do not change the moral necessity that the prima facie case for required conventions must be rec-ognized by all good societies. Indeed, their goodness partly depends on that recognition. The unjustified violation of required conventions is placed beyond toleration because it causes serious and unjustified harm, and thus it is evil. A society is justified in prohibiting such actions and in punishing their performance if the prohibitions are not heeded because they violate minimum requirements of good lives.

If absolutists merely held that human nature establishes some univer-sal requirements of all good lives and that these requirements are objective in that they hold regardless of what attitudes people have toward them, then pluralists would have no quarrel with them. But absolutists go far beyond this. They claim that there are universal and objective re quirements of good lives on the social and individual levels as well. It is this additional claim that pluralists, in agreement with relativists, reject because they think that human nature underdetermines the content of good lives and that the possibilities and limits that may be recognized on the social and individual levels are irreducibly plural.

The strength of relativism is precisely the insistence on this irre- ducible plurality. Relativists rightly emphasize the great diversity within and across societies of the traditions and conceptions of a good life that are regarded as morally acceptable. In this respect, there is no disagree- ment between pluralists and relativists. Relativists, however, go beyond this and assume that moral diversity cannot be justifiably limited. The fundamental reason they give for this assumption is that legitimate moral evaluation must be internal to particular societies. A society may evaluate the traditions and conceptions of a good life that exist within it, but any attempt to evaluate those of other societies is bound to be arbi- trary because there are no external standards to which moral evalua- tions across different societies could appeal. If standards of evaluation are internal to societies, then any attempt to evaluate the traditions or conceptions of a good life of another society involves appeal to stan- dards that are unacceptable to the society whose traditions and concep- tions of a good life are being evaluated. Different societies countenance different traditions and conceptions of a good life, they see human pos- sibilities and limits differently, and human lives are enriched by this di- versity. Political moralities should concern themselves with improving matters at home rather than meddling with what goes on elsewhere.

This way of thinking is popular, especially in Western societies where many people positively clamor to cultivate and spread guilt for past in- trusions into non-Western societies. It should give them pause, however, that other societies, such as China, Japan, Russia, India, and Islamic ones, have no such scruples. Furthermore, the traditions and concep- tions of a good life that exist elsewhere may involve not just benign rain dances, generous gift relationships, herbal cures, cute costumes and cus- toms, titillating sexual initiation ceremonies, or suggestive variations in patri- or matrilinear kinship, but torture, mutilation, female circumci- sion, child prostitution, vicious dictatorships, racism, gross exploitation, large-scale tribal, ethnic, and religious murder, extreme poverty and starvation caused by thieving native leaders, rampant disease, and the breakdown of order brought on by disloyal and corrupt elites. Those who bear in mind these widespread evils may be receptive to the claim that the imposition of limits on some possibilities that are regarded as acceptable in some societies may be justified. The question is whether the imposition of limits can be anything more than the arbitrary extension of standards internal to one society to another.

Pluralism leads conservatives to recognize two different kinds of legitimate—that is, non-arbitrary—justification for imposing limits on some possibilities of other societies. The first appeals to the external standard established by the minimum requirements of all good lives and formulated on the universal level of morality. The second appeals to standards internal to societies, but they are standards to which no good society can fail to conform.

The first kind of justification is simply a reminder directed toward relativists that the moral diversity of good societies presupposes that the minimum requirements of all good lives are met. There are great variations in what is regarded, for example, as acceptable or unacceptable forms of homicide, food, or sexual practice. But there can be no variation among good societies in recognizing that the lives of their members must be secure, that they must eat, and that they must reproduce and raise children. The diversity to which relativists point certainly exists, but it does not affect *that* human nature sets certain universal and objective requirements; it affects only *how* those requirements are met and *when* exceptions to them may be justifiable. The point relativists miss is that there is a basic universal level on which it is human similarities that matter, and that human diversity is possible only if the requirements derived from the similarities are generally recognized. A society may value human sacrifice, self-starving ascetics, and celibate priests or priestesses, but it cannot prescribe that a substantial number of people should adopt these practices unless it is bent on self-destruction.

There are thus external standards with reference to which societies can be compared and evaluated. There is nothing arbitrary about ascertaining which of two societies does better at protecting the lives, health, or security of its members. And there are excellent reasons for stating such plain truths as that a society that does not tolerate child prostitution, extreme poverty, female circumcision, the murder of minorities, or the torture of political dissenters is, in that respect, better than a society that encourages or tolerates these evils.

It is, however, also true that, these plain truths notwithstanding, the comparison and evaluation of different societies is difficult. The reasons for this are, first, that while one society may do better than another about protecting one primary value, the reverse may be true about another primary value. Second, societies have secondary values as well, and their comparison and evaluation is quite another matter. Third, societies also differ about when the prima facie case for their values may be justifiable overridden, and disagreements about that are notoriously difficult to settle. These complications, however, do not affect the point that tells against relativism: the minimum requirements of all good lives do provide external standards with reference to which different societies can be compared and evaluated without arbitrariness.

Relativists may grant this point, but continue to hold their position on the ground that the appeal to external standards thus conceived leaves intact much of the diversity that exists within and across societies. Their revised positions may be expressed as the claim that the moral diversity that prevails on the social and individual levels of different societies cannot be objectively evaluated because on these levels there are no external standards.

Pluralistic conservatives readily concede the absence of external standards on the social and individual levels, but deny that their absence makes all comparisons and evaluations arbitrary. This response rests on the second kind of justification mentioned above: non-arbitrary comparisons and evaluations based on standards internal to societies. This kind of justification concentrates on secondary values and variable conventions in respect to which moral diversity is not only recognized but insisted on by pluralistic conservatives.

Secondary values are social, variable, and optional. Societies, traditions, and conceptions of a good life differ partly because they are committed to different secondary values and/or different rankings of the same secondary values. There are many kinds of secondary values and many ways of ranking them. They may be moral, aesthetic, religious, athletic, scientific, commercial, pedagogic, and so forth; they may be connected with happiness, interests, duty, perfectibility, needs, virtues, honor, or dignity; they may be instrumental, intrinsic, or some mixture of the two; they may be the values of a few individuals, some institutions, particular traditions, or certain societies; they may be tied to physiological, psychological, or social requirements; they may be enduring or temporary, worth dying for or trivial, simple or complex, pleasurable or painful, capable of being appreciated by anyone or only by those trained to it; they may appeal to the intellect, the emotions, the imagination, the appetites, or the will; and so on and on.

Secondary values are as important for living a good life as primary ones. For, although primary values represent the minimum requirements, good lives require more than the minimum. If the basic physiological, psychological, and social needs created by human nature are satisfied, there is still the question of what individuals can do to make their lives good once the struggle for survival has been won and they have gained the luxury of choosing the manner in which they want to live. The question is answered in terms of secondary values.

Each society, tradition, and conception of a good life is characterized by a selection drawn from the available secondary values. For each, some set of secondary values comes to represent possibilities that are regarded as worth pursuing; and for each, limits must be imposed in order to protect individuals in their endeavors to realize the relevant possibilities. Variable conventions embody these secondary values and define the relevant possibilities and limits. The variable conventions of societies, traditions, and conceptions of a good life are, therefore, as different from each other as the secondary values that they represent and protect.

There is no disagreement between relativists and pluralists about the existence and desirability of this diversity, nor about its irreducibility, which results from secondary values being plural, and often incompatible and conflicting. The disagreement arises because relativists miss and pluralists stress the significance of the fact that no good society can do without some system of secondary values and variable conventions, even if the constituents of the system differ from society to society.

The prevailing system of secondary values and variable conventions of a society constitutes the evaluative background against which the people living in the society construct traditions and conceptions of a good life. This evaluative background is the repository of most of the possibilities and limits that individuals adopt and adapt for their own purposes. It is out of the possibilities that they select some as the goals of their self-direction, as the ways in which they endeavor to establish intimate relationships, and as the manner in which they relate in civil ways to those countless others of their fellow members whom they encounter in the impersonal transactions of everyday life. These are the possibilities that shape their ambitions and plans, inform their hopes and fears, provide the terms of their success and failure, establish the tenor of their daily lives, and set the common standards by which they evaluate themselves and others in the context of their society. These are the possibilities and limits that the variable conventions of a society protect.

Sharing such an evaluative background provides the moral identity of those whose lives are informed by the possibilities and limits. Their conceptions of a good life presuppose them and their attempt to live according to them is inseparable from the continued existence of this system of secondary values and variable conventions. Moral identity, understood in this sense, is thus as necessary to living a good life as is providing the minimum requirements expressed by primary values and protected by required conventions. And the need for it is as universal and objective as the need for the other.

Relativists miss the universality and objectivity of the need for moral identity for good lives because they are misled by the great diversity of the secondary values and variable conventions that constitute particular moral identities. What is universal and objective is the necessity of *having* a moral identity. The constituents that give content to various moral identities are dependent on the particular secondary values and variable conventions that hold in one society and may not hold in others. The *contents* of moral identities are therefore relative to societies, but the necessity of *having* a moral identity must be recognized in good societies because the good lives of the people who live in such societies depend on it.

The significance of the universal and objective necessity of having a moral identity for the disagreement between relativists and pluralists is that it provides a further non-arbitrary basis on which societies can be compared and evaluated. A society that protects its moral identity is morally preferable to one that does not. Because the protection is a matter of degree, and because moral identity involves such different areas of life as self-direction, intimacy, and civility, a society that offers more protection, extending to more areas of life, is morally preferable to one that offers less protection and of fewer areas. Such comparisons and evaluations can be made without prejudice to the content of the moral identities in question, provided only that the primary values and the required conventions protecting them are not violated.

The upshot is that the pluralism of conservatives can readily accommodate all the moral diversity that relativists insist on and still make it possible to offer reasoned criticism and justification of diverse societies, traditions, and conceptions of a good life. Pluralists are essentially committed to valuing diversity both within the moral identity that prevails in a particular society and in the differing moral identities of different societies. Pluralists recognize, however, that both kinds of diversity presuppose that particular societies protect the moral identity that prevails in them. Such protection is necessary and justified because traditions and conceptions of a good life depend on the possibilities and limits of which moral identity is the chief source.

None of this is incompatible with the acknowledgment that the moral identity of a society can be justifiably criticized, that it can, does, and often should change, and that some violations of its moral identity may be reasonable acts of moral protest which may subsequently be recognized as such. There is nevertheless always a presumption against the violations because most of them are not conscientious and justified acts of moral protest, but unreasonable acts that weaken the conditions on which depends everyone's chance in the society to live a good life. The presumption against any violation may be defeated, but only if there are good reasons for it. Pluralistic conservatives recognize the possibility of there being such reasons. Relativists, by contrast, cannot allow for there being justified violations of the prevailing standards because they regard the prevailing standards as the only standards of justification.

Considerable flexibility follows from the conservative commitment to pluralism. Conservatives agree with absolutists about there being universal and objective moral truths that all good societies, traditions, and conceptions of a good life must recognize. These truths are restricted to the universal level of morality, and absolutists are mistaken in assuming that they can be found also on the social and individual levels. Conservatives agree with relativists too about the desirability of having a generous diversity of values and conventions that enrich human lives, but this diversity is restricted to secondary values and variable conventions that occur on the social and individual levels of morality. Relativists, therefore, are mistaken in ignoring that the basic physiological, psychological, and social needs created by human nature establish universal and objective, al-

beit minimum, requirements for all good lives. Pluralism enables conservatives to combine the defensible aspects of absolutism and relativism
and to eschew the rest.

A further implication of conservatism is an approach to toleration.
There is hardly any political morality that does not claim to favor toleration. Avowing that commitment, however, is empty unless there goes
with it a principled account of how to think about what should and
should not be tolerated. Conservatives provide such an account. Toleration ought to be inversely proportional to the unjustified harm that an
action causes. The greater is the harm, the less the action that causes it
ought to be tolerated; and the less the harm, the more the action ought
to be tolerated. This, of course, cries out for a specification of how to determine whether harm is greater or lesser. The conservative specification is in terms of primary and secondary values. The violation of
primary values and required conventions normally causes serious unjustified harm, so on the universal level of morality there normally ought to
be no toleration. A good society will not normally countenance actions
that violate the minimum requirements of the good lives of its people.
The violation of specific secondary values and variable conventions usually causes less serious harm, so on the social and individual levels of
morality there ought to be as much toleration as possible. Lives and conduct that fail to conform to the prevailing traditions and conceptions of
a good life ought not to be interfered with unless they themselves interfere with the other prevailing traditions and conceptions of a good life.
Non-interference, however, should not be confused with respect. Lives
and conduct that fail to conform to the moral identity of a society ought
to be allowed, but not actually supported, especially if such support involves depriving people of scarce resources that enable them to live in
ways that reinforce the prevailing moral identity in order to bestow the
resources on others who undermine it.

SKEPTICISM

Rationalism and fideism, as they occur in political morality, are
at the opposite ends of a continuum, but they nevertheless share the
basic belief that the reasons for or against political arrangements must
be objective and that objectivity must be derived from factual considerations about the nature of the world. The facts may be transcendental,

aiming to find the reasons in a world beyond that which is open to commonsensical or scientific observation, or they may be natural, seeking reasons in whatever laws are supposed to regulate political affairs. Rationalists and fideists agree that unless factually supported objective reasons are found political arrangements cannot be reasonably evaluated. They disagree about whether such reasons can be found: rationalists think so, fideists do not. The rank of rationalists includes representatives from across the political spectrum, including some conservatives, and the same is true of fideists.

The strongest version of conservatism, however, is committed to skepticism, and it rejects both rationalism and fideism by rejecting their shared basic belief. Skeptics think that reasons for or against political arrangements can be found, but they do not think that these reasons must be factually based. Or, to put their view in terms of objectivity, the objective evaluation of political arrangements is possible, even though objectivity need not reflect factual truths about the nature of the world. It is crucial to understanding the position of skeptics that what they deny is *not* that reasons for or against political arrangements *may be* based on factual truths, but that they *must be* based on them. Skeptics recognize the possibility that there may be politically weighty reasons that are objective, without being based on factual truths about the nature of the world. The recognition of this possibility is perfectly compatible with there also being reasons that are based on factual truths about the world.

The implications of skepticism, therefore, are, first, that rationalists are right in believing that reasons for or against political arrangements can be found and fideists are wrong in denying it. Second, that fideists are right in denying and rationalists are wrong in believing that the reasons for many political arrangements are based on factual truths about the nature of the world, yet it does not follow that there are no reasons. The skepticism of conservatives thus once again represents an intermediate position that accepts what it regards as reasonable in two extreme positions and rejects what it takes to be unreasonable.

This flexibility is made possible by the conservative's three-level conception of political morality. For that conception allows skeptical conservatives to hold that on the universal level there are reasons based on factual truths about the nature of the world, whereas on the social and individual levels there are no such reasons. These reasons on the universal level are based on the basic physiological, psychological, and social needs created by human nature. The various satisfactions of these needs represent primary values whose protection is a minimum requirement of all good lives. Consequently, there are excellent reasons why the political arrangements of a society should include the enforcement of required conventions that protect primary values. And these reasons are based on objective truths derived from facts. On the universal level, therefore, rationalists are right and fideists are wrong. On the social and individual levels, however, fideists are right and rationalists wrong because on these levels there are no such reasons. Yet both of them are wrong on account of concluding from this that there are no reasons. According to skeptics, there are reasons for or against the political arrangements on the social and individual levels, but they are reasons of another kind.

These other kinds of reasons are evaluative, not factual. There is a sense in which these reasons are also based on the nature of the world, but they have to do with the evaluation of certain features of the world, rather than with the identity of those features. Such evaluations can be reasonable or unreasonable, objective or subjective, true or false, depending on the standards used in the evaluations. The evaluations concern political arrangements, and the standards used in them are the contributions of the arrangements to making good the society whose arrangements they are. How good a society is depends, in turn, on how good the lives of the people are who live in it. And how good those lives are is determined by the extent to which their requirements—the enjoyment of primary and appropriate secondary goods and the avoidance of primary and appropriate secondary evils—are met. The evaluations thus proceed from the human point of view; their standard is good lives for human beings; they are concerned with the effect various political arrangements have on human beings living good lives in the context of a particular society; and the political arrangements reflect features of the world, such as human nature, geography, economics, history, medicine, technology, and so forth.

On the universal level of morality, these evaluations, when they are reasonable, objective, and true, yield the sort of conclusions that rationalists seek. For the requirements of all good lives, the primary values, are, on that level, by and large the same. On the social and individual levels, however, this is not so. Because there is a plurality of societies, traditions, and conceptions of a good life, there is a plurality of ways in which the standard—good lives for human beings—can be applied. There is, therefore, a plurality of secondary values which can make societies, traditions, and individual lives good. On the social and individual levels, evaluations based on secondary values can be reasonable, objective, and true of a particular society, tradition, or life without the evaluations applying to other societies, traditions, and lives. The reason for this is that there is a plurality of secondary values that make societies, traditions, and lives good.

Another way of expressing the same point is that, on the universal level of morality, reason *requires* good societies, traditions, and lives to embody all the primary values. On the social and individual levels, reason requires good societies, traditions, and lives to embody some secondary values, but reason *allows* that the particular secondary values that they embody may differ from one good society, tradition, or life to another. This, of course, is not to say that on the social and individual levels anything goes. There still are standards that determine whether a particular political arrangement helps or hinders particular societies, traditions, or individuals in seeking particular secondary values and avoiding particular secondary evils.

Suppose, however, that, as is highly likely, there is disagreement in a particular society about some political arrangements because there is disagreement about the evaluation of a tradition or conception of a good life that the political arrangements foster or hinder. The parties to the disagreement agree in their description of the constellation of secondary values that a tradition or a conception of a good life embodies, but they disagree about its evaluation. Their disagreement is political. One asserts and the other denies that reason allows their society to have, say, a particular religious or sexual tradition or conception of a good life. Are such disagreements amenable to reasonable resolution, according to the skepticism of conservatism?

Generally speaking: yes, but it must be recognized that at a certain point reasons may come to an end. This point is distant and hard to reach, but it does exist because people may be divided by a deep disagreement that affects what they recognize as a reason. There is a great deal that can be achieved by reason, however, before that point is reached. Suppose, then, that there is a disagreement in a society about whether reason allows some secondary values of a particular religious or sexual tradition or conception of a good life to be regarded as such.

Skeptical conservatives approach this disagreement, in the first instance, by reflecting on the historical record of the tradition or conception whose secondary value is in question. If it has been in existence for a longish time, if it had and continues to have the allegiance of many people who claim that it enriches their lives, then the presumption is in its favor. For people's belief that a tradition or a conception makes their lives better counts as a reason for it. If others nevertheless reject these reasons, then they must explain why the reasons these people give are bad. Such explanations can be given. The strongest ones show that because of its secondary value the tradition or conception endangers the primary values protected by the political arrangements of the society and it is thus incompatible with the basic requirements of many other traditions and conceptions that command the allegiance of many other people in the society. If there is such an explanation, or a similar one, then reason disallows the secondary value of the tradition or conception that runs afoul of the primary values protected by the prevailing political arrangements. If there is no such, or similar, explanation, then reason allows the secondary value of the tradition or conception in that society. If, for example, the religious or sexual tradition or conception of a good life involves atheism or homosexuality among consenting adults, it violates no primary values, so reason allows it; if it involves human sacrifice or paedophilia, it does violate a primary value, so reason disallows it.

It may happen, however, that the disagreement is about the secondary value of a tradition or conception that is relatively new, and so there is no historical record from which reasons could be derived. Say that it has to do with a new religion that involves the habitual use of addictive drugs or it is sexual involving pornography on the Internet. The burden of argument then shifts, and it requires those who favor the constellation of secondary values of the new tradition or conception to explain why reason allows it. The strongest explanation is that it does not interfere with primary values, that its acceptance would enrich the available possibilities of life, and that there are some people who wish to make it their own. This explanation can also be defeated by showing that what it claims is false. If, however, it is not defeated by such arguments, then reason allows the addition of the new tradition or conception with its contested secondary value to those that already exist in that society.

Both of these cases are relatively easy. Hard cases are those in which a particular tradition or conception conflicts with another of the same society without violating the primary values protected by the prevailing political arrangements. The objection then is not that the other tradition or conception endangers primary values, but that its adherents regard some secondary goods as evil, or some secondary evils as good. In other words, people may find the secondary values of another tradition or conception morally objectionable. They want to change the prevailing political arrangements so as to prohibit the continued existence of the tradition or conception with the morally objectionable secondary values. Such conflicts may occur between those who regard homosexual marriage as always a secondary evil and those who think that it may be a secondary good; or between religious believers who hold that school prayer is a secondary good and atheists who believe that it is a secondary evil. Such cases are hard because the reasons to which their advocates appeal are based on secondary values that their opponents do not accept. The people who disagree, therefore, do not recognize as a reason what their opponents adduce as such.

Reason still has a foothold here because the parties to the conflict have a shared interest in maintaining the system of political arrangements that prevail in their society. They share that interest because their own traditions and conceptions are protected by those arrangements. They have a strong reason, therefore, to seek some compromise and not to allow their conflict to get out of hand to an extent that would threaten the conditions on which their own chances of living a good life depend. But what if the moral objection they have is so deep that they are unwilling to seek a *modus vivendi?* What if the secondary values of their traditions or conceptions embody absolute moral prohibitions, say against homosexual marriage or the denial of God, their opponents transgress them, and they think that upholding that moral prohibition is more important than their own chances of living a good life? Then reasons come to an end, and they have to fight.

For conservatives, this outcome is one of the worst things that can happen because it endangers the possibility of civilized life. It is much better to tolerate what one regards as immoral, if it concerns only specific secondary values, than to endanger the conditions that make good lives possible. Of course, it may be that the immorality is intolerable because it violates primary values and thus it already endangers those conditions. In that case, conservatives will fight. Their goal, however, will not be to stamp out what they regard as immoral, but to protect the political conditions of good lives. The two will come to one if the immorality involves the violation of primary values on which all good lives depend. The immorality, however, may be the violation of secondary values, which vary with societies, traditions, and conceptions of a good life. In that case, conservatives will fight to protect the conditions of good lives which are threatened by the uncompromising adherents of the secondary values of some society, tradition, or conception of a good life.

In sum, conservatives are skeptical because they reject the claim of rationalists that on the social and individual levels of political morality reason requires everyone to accept moral truths based on facts. The skepticism of conservatives derives from their pluralism regarding traditions and conceptions of a good life that foster good lives, and that pluralism, in turn, derives from their recognition, first, that the stock of secondary values is much greater than any reasonable tradition or conception of a good life could embody, and, second, that reason allows a large number of ways in which the relative importance of various secondary values could be judged. Reason requires traditions and conceptions of good life to embody some secondary values, but reason does not require that they should embody any specific secondary value. The skepticism of conservatives, however, is moderate, not extreme, because they believe that reason does require everyone to accept moral truths based on facts on the universal level of political morality. These truths concern primary values that are derived from the basic physiological, psychological, and social requirements of human nature, requirements that express the minimum conditions of all good lives, regardless of how they may come to differ as a result of being formed by the plurality of secondary values of the traditions and conceptions of a good life that people may come to adopt.

TRADITIONALISM

Traditionalism holds on the social and individual levels of political morality. It is a view about the political arrangements that would be most conducive to good lives in the context of a society where the primary values are on the whole protected by required conventions, so that the minimum requirements of good lives are met. Traditionalists defend the view that the political arrangements should foster the traditions that have stood the test of time in the history of a particular society. The significance of traditionalism emerges by understanding the reasons for favoring what it does and the reason for opposing what it opposes.

Traditionalists favor political arrangements that foster traditions that have continued to attract the allegiance of a significant number of people living in a society because participation in such traditions is an indispensable part of good lives. They oppose political arrangements that foster either social authority or individual autonomy at the expense of those that foster traditions. Their reason for this is not that there is something intrinsically wrong with social authority or individual autonomy. On the contrary, traditionalists regard both as important to living good lives, provided that they are kept in their appropriate places. The trouble with the political arrangements that traditionalists oppose is that they encourage social authority or individual autonomy in contexts where they have no legitimate place. Traditionalists think that the political arrangements that favor tried and true traditions are the best ways to assign appropriate importance to both social authority and individual autonomy and to defuse the tension between them.

Social authority is a society's power to enforce its political arrangements. This power may take the mild form of cultivating respect and loyalty for the prevailing arrangements. If that proves insufficient, then social authority may take the more severe form of using the threat or the actuality of force to ensure conformity. Social authority is thus the authority a society has over the individuals who live in it. If all goes well, this authority is exercised impartially and impersonally. It is perforce exercised by individuals over other individuals, those who exercise it do so, however, not as individuals, but as representatives of their society.

Social authority may or may not be justified. It is justified if the political arrangements it enforces protect the conditions of good lives of those who live in the society. These political arrangements are the required conventions that protect primary values on the universal level of political morality, and the system of variable conventions that protect the moral identity of a particular society on the social level. Social authority is unjustified if it goes beyond this level and aims to enforce some variable conventions of a tradition or a conception of a good life that forms part of the prevailing moral identity at the expense of others that are also part of it. In other words, social authority is justified if it is used to enforce the conditions of all good lives in the context of a society, and its use is unjustified if it involves forcing individuals to participate in particular traditions or to adopt particular conceptions of a good life rather than others. Social authority thus has no justified use on the individual level of political morality, its justified use on the social level is limited, and its use on the universal level may be fully justified.

Social authority must of course be distinguished from moral authority. Moral authority is exercised by individuals over other individuals, but those who exercise it act as individuals, not as representatives of their society. Moreover, they have moral authority because their lives and conduct testify to their qualifications, and they exercise their authority, not to enforce anything, but because they are invited to do so by those who turn to them for help in judging complex matters. More will be said about this below.

It may be thought that the moral space that is or ought to be left unoccupied by social authority should be filled by individual autonomy. This is a prevalent but nevertheless bad mistake with serious consequences that conservatives strive to avoid. It is true, not a mistake, that on the individual level of political morality individuals endeavor to make good lives for themselves; that good lives must be *made;* and that if the individuals whose lives they are do not do so, nobody will make it for them. And it is also true, not a mistake, that whether or not a life is good partly but necessarily depends on the judgment of the individual who lives it. For lives are good if they are satisfying to the agents and beneficial for others, and, while lives can be beneficial regardless of how their agents may judge them, they cannot be satisfying unless their agents judge them to be so. But it is not true that making a life good *must* involve the exercise of individual autonomy. A good life *may* be autonomous, or it may not be. There are many good lives in which autonomy plays only a negligible role.

The exercise of autonomy, it will be remembered, requires individuals to perform an action they choose from among several alternatives; the choice they make is not forced on them; and they favorably evaluate and understand the significance of the action they perform. The bad mistake conservatives strive to avoid is that of supposing that on the individual level of political morality the condition of good lives is that the preponderance of the agents' significant actions be autonomous. Conservatives thus deny that as the satisfaction of the minimum requirements is a condition of good lives on the universal level, and as the protection of the moral identity of a society is a like condition on the social level, so autonomy is a condition on the individual level. Conservatives accept that good lives may be autonomous, but they do not accept that a life cannot be good unless it is autonomous.

The fundamental reason conservatives have for rejecting the claim that autonomy is a necessary condition of all good lives is that it involves a grotesque misunderstanding of the way the vast majority of lives becomes good. The facts are that people are born into families; the families are parts of economic, ethnic, religious, racial, regional, and other communities; they learn to speak a particular language with a particular accent or dialect; they are educated in particular ways by schools, parents, and the clergy; they are influenced by what they read, the television programs they watch, the people they admire or detest; they are presented with a small number of ways in which they can earn their living, spend their leisure time, raise their children, have love affairs, or give shape to their ambitions; they learn from early childhood when to feel and how to express love, enmity, pride, self-respect, shame, guilt, fear, jealousy, anger, indignation, pity, sympathy, solidarity, and so forth; they learn what counts as success, failure, insult, recognition, prestige, or injustice; they learn when tears may be shed, when laughter is appropriate, what is funny, offensive, serious, or ridiculous, when, how, and what to eat, with whom they can and cannot make love, what to do in the face of illness and death; and they learn thousands of other like things.

None of these things do they learn autonomously. They learn them by participating in the various traditions that prevail in their contexts. They have choices, but the alternatives among which they can choose are small in number and set in advance. There is scope for their attempts to understand and evaluate their options, but they have not chosen, understood, or evaluated the standards to which these attempts appeal. If they are exceptional and they have questioned the standards, then it is their answers to those questions that they have accepted from one tradition or another. Yet the good lives that people make for themselves are made of these elements and their judgments about how good the lives are that they have made also depend on standards that they have not made but found in the traditions into which they were born and in which they were raised.

People, of course, can reject some of the traditions that have formed them, but only some. They are stuck with their families, mother tongue, education, and upbringing. And when they reject a tradition, they do not free themselves from traditions: they typically leave one tradition for another. Traditions are to human lives what countries are to the Earth. If you leave one, you enter another. There may be a few unallocated spots, but they are salty and wet, and it is absurd to suppose that good lives depend on finding and occupying them. Yet it is just that absurdity to which regarding autonomy as a condition of all good lives is committed.

As conservatives see it, the condition of good lives, on the individual level of political morality, is not the cultivation of autonomy, but participation in traditions that make good lives possible. Not all traditions do that and conservatives do not endorse all traditions indiscriminately. They favor only those that have stood the test of time. And they mean by that those traditions that continue to attract the allegiance of many people living in their society, form part of the prevailing moral identity, and protect the primary values and required conventions.

Traditionalism does not lead conservatives to deny that individuals must make good lives for themselves and that making them requires making choices and understanding and evaluating their significance. Conservatives think, however, that individuals do all this *by* participating in traditions because traditions provide the alternatives among which they choose, the standards of understanding and evaluation they employ, and the elements out of which they form their conception of what a good life would be.

Suppose, then, that the more modest claim is made on behalf of autonomy that it is a necessary condition, not of all good lives, but only of living according to a particular conception of it. This conception, has considerable importance because it is perhaps the most widely accepted one in contemporary Western societies. It may be conceded that participation in various traditions is an unavoidable condition of all good lives, but, the claim is, the conception of a good life as autonomous requires that participation be as autonomous as possible. The claim of this conception, then, is not that living according to it requires full autonomy, since that has been shown to be impossible, but that it requires increasing autonomy. The thought behind this more modest claim is that the conception of a good life it favors is one in which people have as much control over their lives as possible, that the more control they have, the more likely their lives are to be good, and that more control depends on greater autonomy. There will be few people living in contemporary Western societies who would not find this conception of a good life attractive. And it must be stressed that there is no reason why conservatives could not join those who wish to adopt this conception.

This, however, is not the end of the matter. Although the claim made on behalf of this conception is more modest than before, it is not modest enough. That it is not will emerge if it is considered how far increasing autonomy contributes to living a good life of this kind. There are two reasons for thinking that increasing autonomy in certain ways would make lives worse rather than better. The first has to do with the need for moral authorities and the second with the need to avoid evil.

The need for moral authorities arises when people are confronted with important alternatives among which they themselves realize that they cannot choose reasonably because they lack the experience and understanding to evaluate them. In such situations, increasing the agents' autonomy would merely compound the complexities. These are the situations in which the reasonable course of action is to appeal to moral authorities whose judgments rest on greater experience and understanding than the agents possess, and who can evaluate the agents' alternatives more reasonably than the agents can themselves.

This lack of experience and understanding presents a dilemma for those who conceive of good lives in terms of increasing autonomy. The increase of autonomy in complex situations is likely to make lives worse, not better, because it dooms the agents to having to make unreasonable choices, even though they could make more reasonable ones by following the advice of moral authorities. If, however, they turn to and heed moral authorities, then the unavoidable consequence of having been helped to choose more reasonably, and thus to make their lives better, is that their autonomy is decreased, not increased. For taking the advice of moral authorities means accepting their judgments, based on their experience, understanding, and evaluation, in place of the agents' own.

The second reason against the indiscriminate increase of autonomy derives from the need to avoid evil. That evil is prevalent and that good lives depend on making it less so will be acknowledged by all reasonable and decent people. It will perhaps also be acknowledged that the prevalence of evil is largely the result of human vices and the actions that follow from them. Insofar as vices and evil actions are autonomous, increasing autonomy will make evil more prevalent and good lives less likely. Insofar as vices and evil actions are non-autonomous, increasing autonomy may just make non-autonomous vices and evil actions into autonomous ones, and thus worsen the odds against good lives. In either case, increasing autonomy is likely to make lives worse, not better.

This conclusion may be denied by denying that increasing people's autonomy will give greater scope to their vices and evil actions. It may be thought that if people are autonomous, then they will understand and evaluate their actions correctly; they will see their actions for what they are; and then they will do what is good rather than what is evil. The assumption underlying this line of thought is that vices and evil actions are the results of interference with autonomy, and that occurs when bad political arrangements enrage, impoverish, humiliate, or discriminate against people. If these corrupting influences are removed, then people can function autonomously. Their judgments will be unclouded, they will know what the good is, and they will act accordingly.

The name for this pipe-dream is the Enlightenment Faith. It is the illusion of an epoch that stretches from Rousseau to contemporary liberalism. It is the secular equivalent of the religious faith of Christianity, which it is intended to replace. It is fueled by a groundless optimism that substitutes wishes for facts, refuses to face reality, ignores history, and radiates a moralistic fervor that leads the faithful to treat disagreement as a sign of immorality. The Enlightenment Faith deserves these harsh words for several reasons. It is rigged so as to allow no fact to count against it. Good actions are taken to confirm it because they are taken to reflect the autonomous goodness of their agents. Evil actions are also taken to confirm it because they are regarded as evidence of lack of autonomy that results from bad political arrangements that have corrupted their agents. Furthermore, defenders of the Faith do not ask the obvious question of why some political arrangements are bad. They refuse to see that political arrangements are often bad because the people who make them are wicked; that, since people are prior to the arrangements they make, sooner or later bad political arrangements must be taken as evidence for the evil propensities of those who make them, rather than the other way around as defenders of the Faith unreasonably suppose. They take no account of the fact that what they regard as an improvement of political arrangements, say the French or the Russian Revolution, often brings with it an increase rather than a decrease of evil; that there are people who remain uncorrupted by bad political arrangements; or that many people are corrupt, but not because of political arrangements. It is a Faith contrary to reason. It ought to have collapsed long ago under the weight of its own implausibility, but it has not because it sustains the naive optimism of those who hold it. The pessimism of conservatives is intended as a reasonable alternative to it.

The conclusion of this discussion of traditionalism is a combination of a critical and a constructive claim. The critical claim is directed against inflating the importance of social authority and individual autonomy. Social authority *is* important because it protects the primary values on the universal level and the moral identity of a society on the social level. But social authority has no legitimate place in interfering with individuals as they try on the individual level to decide for themselves which traditions they should participate in and what conceptions of a good they should adopt, provided that in doing so they do not violate the conditions of all good lives. Individual autonomy is also important because it is an essential feature of the particular conception of a good life that has been adopted by a large number of people in the contemporary Western world. But it is a mistake to suppose that individual autonomy is an essential feature of all conceptions of a good life. It is also a mistake to suppose that the more autonomy there is the more likely it is that lives will be better. Good lives also depend on moral authorities and on making evil less prevalent, and both require curtailing autonomy. Autonomy is good in its place, but from that it does not follow that more autonomy is better.

The constructive claim centers on the importance of traditions for living a good life. Traditions are repositories of the secondary values and variable conventions out of which people construct their conceptions of a good life, once the minimum requirements are met. The moral identity of a society is defined by the system of traditions that have endured in its history. They have endured because people have continued to participate in them, and they have done so because of their continuously confirmed belief that their participation makes their lives better than they would be otherwise. Traditions mediate between individuals and their society. Societies protect moral necessities, so they must be coercive. Traditions embody moral possibilities, so they provide opportunities without insisting that they be taken. Individuals would be lost without traditions because they would not know how to live once they are supplied with the necessities of life. Individuals learn from traditions about the possibilities of life, and the goodness of their lives depends on making some possibilities of some traditions their own. They make good lives for themselves *by* participating in traditions. That is why the political arrangements of a good society will recognize that participation in traditions is a condition of good lives, and that is why a good society will aim to protect not just the minimum requirements on the universal level and moral identity on the social level, but also traditions on the individual level of political morality.

PESSIMISM

The pessimism of conservatives is an attitude to the human condition. It is the *via media* between the optimism that rests on the belief in human perfectibility and the fatalism, despair, or cynicism that rests on the belief in irredeemable human corruption. In the modern world, the ultimate source of the belief in perfectibility is the Enlightenment Faith. That Faith is groundless because there is no reason to think and many reasons to doubt that bad societies are made bad merely by bad political arrangements. If that were so, the improvement of political arrangements would remove all the obstacles from the way of human perfectibility and all manner of things would thereby be made well. But it is not so because one rich source of bad political arrangements is the human propensity for evil. It stands in the way of improving political arrangements and it is a permanent obstacle to human perfectibility. From this, however, it does not follow that human beings are corrupt. There are many human propensities, and, although the one for evil is among them, another is the propensity for the good. And there are also propensities for reason, prudence, love, integrity, fellow feeling, loyalty, as well as propensities for the opposite. Human beings are neither basically good nor basically evil—they are basically ambivalent, and that renders illusory both the prospect of perfectibility and the prospect of corruption.

It will be asked: if that is so, then why is pessimism not similarly illusory? If optimism, on the one hand, and fatalism, despair, or cynicism, on the other, ultimately rest on indefensible simplifications, then why is the same not true of pessimism? Because of the coexistence of the undeniable facts of human vulnerability and the prevalence of evil. Evil is serious unjustified harm that human beings cause. No one can reasonably deny that evil is prevalent now and that it has been prevalent throughout human history, in the most various of circumstances, societies, and political arrangements. This would be just another fact in the natural history of humanity—on the same level of generality as the prevalence of religious belief, the hierarchical organization of societies, or the division of labor—if it were not for human vulnerability. The combination of the prevalence of evil and human vulnerability is a permanent threat to good lives. Pessimism is warranted because neither can be brought within human control to an extent sufficient to remove the threat. The threat can be greater or lesser, and it can be *made* greater or lesser by human effort. But such efforts cannot result in sufficient control to remove the threat because the efforts are themselves permeated with and thus unavoidably subject to the very threat that they aim to remove.

Insofar as the belief in human perfectibility denies the permanence of this threat and the belief in human corruption succumbs to hopelessness in the face of it, they are shallow views that respond to effects rather than to their cause. If the pessimism of conservatives were merely a reaction to the combination of the prevalence of evil and human vulnerability, it would be similarly shallow. The conservative attitude, however, goes deeper than this because it takes account of the underlying cause. That cause is the contingency that permeates the human condition, including human propensities and the efforts to control them.

Contingency is the name for the fact that humanity collectively and human beings individually are subject to causes that they cannot control, but which may influence them in ways that fundamentally affect the prospects of good lives. These causes may operate as external forces that threaten not just good lives, but life itself. They may be cosmic events, like the collision of a huge comet with Earth; microscopic happenings, such as the appearance of a deadly virus against which human beings have no immunity; or they may be mundane occurrences, like the exhaustion of necessary resources, volcanic eruptions, a new ice age, or a disease that disrupts photosynthesis.

The causes may also operate as internal forces that do not so much as impinge on human beings, but operate through them, making humanity itself the carrier of the threat to good lives. These internal forces may be the transmission of genetic traits incompatible with the maintenance of a good society; the persistence of emotional responses that once contributed to survival, but have become detrimental to it; or the insufficient resources of individuals to evaluate the information necessary for coping with the complexities of the organization of large, industrialized, computerized, highly productive societies that keep growing in population, in the rate of the consumption of scarce resources, in the intellectual and emotional demands they place on their members, in the gap between those who are trying to comprehend and cope and those who have given up hope and are filled with rage, self-loathing, resignation, passion for instant gratification, or with all of the above.

The image of human life that contingency suggests to those who are willing to face it is that of a ship afloat on vast and treacherous waters, with no land in sight, no maps available, no guarantee that the supplies needed to sustain those aboard will be replenished, no contact with other ships, and no known destination. The task at hand is to keep afloat, but the crew is unruly, discipline is poor, the command is forever changing hands, there is no safe haven, and the best that can be done is to cope with emergencies as they occur. In the face of this, optimism is quixotic; fatalism, despair, and cynicism are destructive; and pessimism is realistic.

The pessimism that is warranted, however, is not unrelieved because, to leave the image for hard facts, human efforts to achieve some control over contingency have been successful. If they had not been, humanity would have gone under long ago. These efforts are exerted in two directions: toward controlling the external causes to which humanity is subject and toward controlling the causes internal to human beings in order to approximate the good and to avoid evil. The means to the former are science and technology, and the means to the latter is morality.

Science and technology are, of course, the great successes of humanity. They have made human lives much better than they would have been without them. This said, it must be added immediately that there are two main reasons why their undoubted successes leave the threat of contingency diminished only a little. The first is that science and technology cannot alter the causes that threaten humanity. They can go some way toward understanding these causes and ameliorating some of their destructive effects. But they cannot prevent or change the course of cosmic events, they cannot overcome limitations intrinsic to humanity, and they cannot foresee and avert the untold number of adversities that may befall humanity. They can merely endeavor to cope with such matters as they arise. The going has so far been good, all things considered, but these are early days in human history and the odds for it continuing in the same manner are incalculable.

The second reason why science and technology have not seriously altered the threat of contingency is connected with their very successes. They have greatly increased human knowledge and control, even if that increase is small in comparison with what would be sufficient. The question about knowledge and control is how they are going to be used. They will be used either for good or for evil, and which it will be depends on the propensities of those who use them. On this score, no one who reflects on history can feel encouraged. The prevalence of evil is partly the result of the greatly increased power scientific and technological knowledge and control put at the disposal of wicked people and their followers. This familiar story need not be repeated again. Its familiarity, however, should not be allowed to obscure its moral, which is that the human effort to control contingency will reflect human propensities, that these propensities are for both good and evil, and that whether the good or the evil ones dominate is subject to that very contingency that they aim to control. This leads back to the second, internal, direction in which the efforts to control contingency need to be exerted: to the task of morality.

The aim of morality is to protect the conditions of good lives. The argument of this book has concentrated on the conditions that can be protected by political arrangements, but there are, of course, other conditions as well. Political arrangements are the arrangements of a particular society, and they are or ought to be intended for the benefit of the people who live in it. Their enjoyment of the benefits has the cost of having to live in conformity to the arrangements from which they benefit. In a good society, these arrangements will protect, first, the primary values and the required conventions that reflect the minimum requirements of all good lives on the universal level of political morality; second, the system of secondary values and variable conventions that form the moral identity of a society on the social level; and third, the traditions that provide the elements out of which individuals construct their conceptions of a good life on the individual level. The political morality of conservatives aims at this ideal. To understand yet another deep source of the pessimism of conservatives requires understanding both that the prevalence of evil and the unavoidable limitation of justice make the ideal unattainable and that the pursuit of the ideal is therefore more rather than less necessary.

One obstacle to the attainment of the ideal is the prevalence of evil. It is prevalent because human beings cause it, and they cause it largely because they have vices and they act in ways that reflect their vices. Vices may be acquired autonomously or non-autonomously. The vices of moral monsters, who cause evil knowingly and deliberately, because it is evil, and of amoral people, who knowingly and deliberately subordinate morality to other considerations, are autonomous. The vices of people who are habitually mistaken in their understanding and evaluation of the actions they freely choose to perform are non autonomous. But re gardless of whether the prevalence of evil results mainly from autonomous or non-autonomous vices, making it less prevalent requires placing and enforcing limits on the actions of agents who possess these vices. And this, of course, means prohibiting them from living according to their conceptions of a good life. If evil is prevalent, as it is, then the number of people in a society who will be prohibited from living according to their conceptions of a good life will be large. It is, therefore, a consequence of the prevalence of evil that in any society there will be a large number of people who will be forced to live in ways they do not want to live.

Such people will not feel the force of the argument that they ought to conform to the political arrangements of their society because it is a condition of the goodness of their own lives. They will not feel it because they will rightly believe that the political arrangements prohibit them from living as they think it would be good for them to live. They will thus form a permanent and substantial internal opposition to the prevailing political arrangements. A society must contain their opposition; it must force them to conform to the limits. The more successful a society is, the less prevalent evil will be in it. But the cost of success all is that the ideal of protecting the conditions of good lives for all people living in it will become unattainable. The very success of the society depends, not on protecting, but on removing the conditions of all the many conceptions of good lives that would make evil more prevalent. No wonder, then, that conservatives are pessimistic about the attainment of the ideal.

Another obstacle to the attainment of the ideal is the unavoidable limitation of justice. Justice is the human attempt to approximate the cosmic justice that would guarantee that in the long run the scales of morality will be balanced, that, when it is all said and done, the good will enjoy deserved benefits and the wicked will suffer deserved harms. Justice, then, is the human attempt to arrange society so that people in it will have what they deserve. The basis of what people deserve is some characteristic, relation, agreement, or conduct of theirs. These bases create claims that people should enjoy the benefits or suffer the harms appropriate to their bases. The system of justice of a society is intended to fulfill legitimate claims of desert and to correct failures to meet legitimate claims.

Justice conceived in this manner cannot be achieved because there is a non-culpable scarcity of resources that makes it impossible to satisfy all legitimate claims to security, health, education, good jobs, appropriate recognition, pleasant housing, enriching opportunities for leisure, and so forth. Nor is it possible to correct many recognized instances of injustice because some are the result of the contingency of life for which no one can be blamed, some harm people in ways that can neither be undone nor compensated for, and some people deserve benefits or harms that are disproportionately greater than what can be provided. Even if the political arrangements of a society did not fall short of the ideal on account of the prevalence of evil, they would still fall short because of the unavoidable limitation of justice. But of course evil is prevalent, and that makes the administration of justice suffer from avoidable limitations as well. These limitations will make evil more prevalent, which will limit justice further, which will add to evil, and so on and on. For those who face this, there is no reasonable alternative to pessimism.

If this conclusion is granted, it may still be asked how severe is the pessimism that is warranted by the combination of contingency, the prevalence of evil, and the limitation of justice. Conservatives deny that what is warranted is severe enough to result in hopelessness. The ideal of a good society that makes good lives possible for those who live in it is unattainable, but it can still be approximated. And for its approximation it is possible to call on moral resources that act as counterweight to contingency, evil, and injustice. These resources are political arrangements that have shown themselves historically to make lives better; the intrinsic attractions of living a satisfying and beneficial life; and the sense of justice that is outraged by the conspicuous discrepancy between what people have and what they deserve to have. These moral resources can be used to approximate the ideal, and in a society that aims to be good, they will be used. How effective they will be depends on the strength that the countervailing forces of contingency, evil, and injustice have in particular societies at particular times. The clash between these forces is one unavoidable feature of human lives. The outcome is never certain, and so it is always reasonable to do what can be done to favor the side that is—fallibly—regarded as good.

Notes

Introduction

[1] See Russell Kirk, *The Conservative Mind*, 6th rev. ed. (South Bend, Ind.: Gateway, 1978); Robert Nisbet, *Conservatism* (Minneapolis: University of Minnesota Press, 1986); Noel O'Sullivan, *Conservatism* (New York: St. Martin's Press, 1976); Anthony Quinton, *The Politics of Imperfection* (London: Faber and Faber, 1978); Clinton Rossiter, *Conservatism in America*, 2d rev. ed. (Cambridge: Harvard University Press, 1982); and Peter Viereck, *Conservatism Revisited* (New York: Scribner's, 1949).

[2] See Charles Covell, *The Redefinition of Conservatism* (London: Macmillan, 1986); Robert Devigne, *Recasting Conservatism* (New Haven: Yale University Press, 1994); Charles W. Dunn and J. David Woodard, *The Conservative Tradition in America* (Lanham, Md.: Rowman and Littlefield, 1993); John P. East, *The American Conservative Movement* (Chicago: Regnery, 1986); Russell G. Fryer, *Recent Conservative Political Thought* (Washington, D.C.: University Press of America, 1979); and George H. Nash, *The Conservative Intellectual Movement in America* (New York: Basic Books, 1976).

[3] See Quentin Hogg, *The Conservative Case*, rev. ed. (Harmondsworth: Penguin, 1959); Willmoore Kendall, *The Conservative Affirmation in America* (Chicago: Gateway, 1985); Torbjorn Tannsjo, *Conservatism for Our Time* (London: Routledge, 1990); and David Willets, *Modern Conservatism* (Harmondsworth: Penguin, 1992).

[4] See Hugh Cecil, *Conservatism* (London: Williams and Norgate, 1912); and Michael Oakeshott, "On Being Conservative," in *Rationalism in Politics*, ed. Timothy Fuller (Indianapolis: Liberty Press, 1991).

[5] See Bruce Frohnen, *Virtue and the Promise of Conservatism* (Lawrence: University Press of Kansas, 1993); William R. Harbour, *The Foundations of Conservative Thought* (Notre Dame: University of Notre Dame Press, 1982); and Francis Graham Wilson, *The Case for Conservatism* (Seattle: University of Washington Press, 1951).

See also the survey articles and bibliographies by Kenneth Minogue, "Conservatism," *Encyclopedia of Philosophy*, ed. Paul Edwards (New York: Macmillan, 1967); Anthony O'Hear, "Conservatism," *The Oxford Companion to Philosophy*, ed.

221

Ted Honderich (Oxford: Oxford University Press, 1995); Anthony Quinton, "Conservatism," *A Companion to Contemporary Political Philosophy,* ed. Robert E. Goodin and Philip Pettit (Oxford: Blackwell, 1993); and Rudolf Vierhaus, "Conservatism," *Dictionary of the History of Ideas,* ed. Philip P. Wiener (New York: Scribner's, 1968).

[6] See Robert N. Bellah et al., *Habits of the Heart* (Berkeley: University of California Press, 1985); Allan Bloom, *The Closing of the American Mind* (New York: Simon and Schuster, 1987); William F. Buckley, Jr., *The Jeweler's Eye* (New York: Putnam, 1968) and *The Governor Listeth* (New York: Putnam, 1970); Kenneth Minogue, ed., *Conservative Realism* (London: HarperCollins, 1996); and George F. Will, *Statecraft as Soulcraft* (New York: Simon and Schuster, 1983).

[7] The number of works that have a similar approach is small. See Lincoln Allison's *Right Principles* (Oxford: Blackwell, 1984); several of John Gray's essays in *Post-liberalism* (New York: Routledge, 1993) and *Beyond the New Right* (London: Routledge, 1993); Michael Oakeshott's *On Human Conduct* (Oxford: Clarendon, 1975), some of the essays in *Rationalism in Politics,* and *The Politics of Faith and the Politics of Scepticism,* ed. Timothy Fuller (New Haven: Yale University Press, 1996); and Roger Scruton's *The Meaning of Conservatism* (Harmondsworth: Penguin, 1980) share the approach but, it must be emphasized, not the basic assumptions and the substance of the present work.

Chapter 1: The Conservative Attitude

[1] For a distinction between conservatisms of enjoyment, fear, and reflection, see Walter Bagehot, "Intellectual Conservatism," in *The Collected Works of Walter Bagehot.* ed. Norman St. John Stevas (London: The Economist, 1986), vol. 6, pp. 95–98.

[2] Michael Oakeshott, "On Being Conservative," in *Rationalism in Politics,* ed. Timothy Fuller (Indianapolis: Liberty Press, 1991), p. 408.

[3] Czeslaw Milosz, *The Captive Mind,* trans. Jane Zielenko (Harmondsworth: Penguin, 1980), pp. 25–28.

[4] Elliott Mossman, ed., *The Correspondence of Boris Pasternak and Olga Friedenberg, 1910–1954,* trans. Elliott Mossman and Margaret Wettlin (New York: Harcourt Brace Jovanovich, 1981), pp. 303–4.

[5] Karl R. Popper, "Towards a Rational Theory of Tradition," in *Conjectures and Refutations* (New York: Harper and Row, 1968), p. 131.

[6] Edmund Burke, *Reflections on the Revolution in France,* ed. Conor Cruise O'Brien (Harmondsworth: Penguin, 1968), p. 181.

Chapter 2: What Is Conservatism?

It is odd but necessary to begin with a note about the Notes to this chapter. In several of the notes conservative views will be attributed to various people. This is not meant to imply that the people who hold these views are conservatives. They are conservative in respect to these views, but they also hold other views, and they may or may not be conservative. It is often very difficult to say whether or not a person is conservative, especially since few of the people referred to were concerned with formulating an explicit political morality.

¹ Reliable accounts of some of these disagreements may be found in Noel O'Sullivan, *Conservatism* (New York: St. Martin's Press, 1976) and Anthony Quinton, *The Politics of Imperfection* (London: Faber and Faber, 1978).

For general surveys and bibliographies of conservative ideas, see Kenneth Minogue, "Conservatism," *Encyclopedia of Philosophy,* ed. Paul Edwards (New York: Macmillan, 1967), Anthony O'Hear, "Conservatism," in *The Oxford Companion to Philosophy,* ed. Ted Honderich (Oxford: Oxford University Press, 1995); Anthony Quinton, "Conservatism," *A Companion to Contemporary Political Philosophy,* ed. Robert E. Goodin and Philip Pettit (Oxford: Blackwell, 1993); and Rudolf Vierhaus, "Conservatism," *Dictionary of the History of Ideas,* ed. Philip P. Wiener (New York: Scribner's, 1968).

Three useful anthologies of conservatives writings are Russell Kirk, ed., *Conservative Reader* (Harmondsworth: Penguin, 1982); Jerry Z. Muller, ed., *Conservatism* (Princeton: Princeton University Press, 1997); and Roger Scruton, ed., *Conservative Texts* (New York: St. Martin's Press, 1991).

Some of the classic works that have influenced the development of conservatism are Plato's *Republic,* Aristotle's *Politics, Nicomachean Ethics,* and *Rhetoric,* Machiavelli's *The Prince* and *Discourses,* Montaigne's *Essays,* Hobbes's *Leviathan,* Hume's *Treatise, Enquiries, Essays,* and *History of England,* Burke's *Reflections on the Revolution in France,* Tocqueville's *Democracy in America* and *The Old Regime and the French Revolution,* Hegel's *Philosophy of Right,* Stephen's *Liberty, Equality, Fraternity,* Bradley's *Ethical Studies,* Santayana's *Dominations and Powers,* Wittgenstein's *Philosophical Investigations* and *On Certainty,* and Oakeshott's *Rationalism in Politics* and *On Human Conduct.*

² Michael Oakeshott, "Scientific Politics" in *Religion, Politics and the Moral Life,* ed. Timothy Fuller (New Haven: Yale University Press, 1993), pp. 99–100.

³ This is the view of many religious conservatives mainly, but not exclusively, in the Catholic tradition. For surveys and bibliographies divided along national lines, see O'Sullivan, *Conservatism,* chap. 2 for France and chap. 3 for Germany; Klemens von Klemperer, *Germany's New Conservatism* (Princeton: Princeton University Press, 1957) for Germany; Quinton, *The Politics of Imperfection,* for England; Kirk, *The Conservative Mind,* for England and America; Charles W. Dunn and J. David Woodard, *The Conservative Tradition in America* (Lanham, Md.: Rowman and Littlefield, 1996); John P. East, *The American Conservative Movement* (Chicago: Regnery, 1986); George H. Nash, *The Conservative Intellectual Movement in America* (New York: Basic Books, 1976), and Clinton Rossiter, *Conservatism in America.* 2d rev. ed. (Cambridge: Harvard University Press, 1982), for America.

⁴ The roots of skeptical conservatism are to be found scattered in Montaigne's *Essays,* Hobbes's *Leviathan,* Hume's *Treatise, Enquiries, Essays,* and *History of England,* Burke's *Reflections on the Revolution in France,* Tocqueville's *Democracy in*

America and *The Old Regime and the French Revolution,* Santayana's *Dominations and Powers,* and Wittgenstein's *Philosophical Investigations* and *On Certainty.*

On Montaigne's conservatism, see John Kekes, *The Examined Life* (University Park: Penn State Press, 1992), chapter 4; on Hobbes's conservatism, see Michael Oakeshott, *Hobbes on Civil Association* (Oxford: Blackwell, 1974); on Hume's conservatism, see Shirley Robin Letwin, *The Pursuit of Certainty* (Cambridge: Cambridge University Press, 1965), part I; Donald W. Livingston, *Hume's Philosophy of Common Life* (Chicago: University of Chicago Press, 1984), chap. 12; and Sheldon S. Wolin, "Hume and Conservatism," *American Political Science Review* 98 (1954), pp. 999–1016; on Tocqueville's conservatism, see Roger Boesche, *The Strange Liberalism of Alexis de Tocqueville* (Ithaca: Cornell University Press, 1987); Frohnen, *Virtue and the Promise of Conservatism;* and Alan S. Kahan, *Aristocratic Liberalism* (New York: Oxford University Press, 1986); on Santayana's conservatism, see John Gray, "George Santayana and the Critique of Liberalism," *The World and I,* February 1989, pp. 593–607; on Wittgenstein's conservatism, see Charles Covell, *The Redefinition of Conservatism,* chap. 1; and J. C. Nyiri, "Wittgenstein's Later Work in Relation to Conservatism" in *Wittgenstein and His Times,* ed. Brian McGuinness (Oxford: Blackwell, 1982).

Some contemporary skeptical conservative works are Lincoln Allison, *Right Principles* (Oxford: Blackwell, 1984); John Gray, *Liberalisms* (London: Routledge, 1989), *Post-liberalism* (New York: Routledge, 1993), and *Beyond the New Right* (London: Routledge, 1993); Shirley Robin Letwin, *The Gentleman in Trollope* (Cambridge: Harvard University Press, 1982); Michael Oakeshott, *Rationalism in Politics, On Human Conduct* (Oxford: Clarendon, 1975) and *The Politics of Faith and the Politics of Scepticism,* ed. Timothy Fuller (New Haven: Yale University Press, 1996).

[5] For historical surveys of absolutist conservatism, see note 3 above. Some contemporary absolutist conservative works are John Finnis, *Natural Law and Natural Rights* (Oxford: Clarendon, 1980) and *Fundamentals of Ethics* (Oxford: Clarendon, 1983); Germain Grisez, *Beyond the New Morality* (Notre Dame: University of Notre Dame Press, 1988); Henry B. Veatch, *Human Rights* (Baton Rouge: Louisiana State University Press, 1985); and Eric Voegelin, *Order in History,* 5 vols. (Baton Rouge: Louisiana State University Press, 1954–87).

[6] The historical origins of relativistic conservatism are to be found in Giambattista Vico, *New Science,* trans. Thomas Goddard Bergin and Max Harold Frisch (Ithaca: Cornell University Press, 1970); Johann Gottfried von Herder, *Reflections on the Philosophy of the History of Mankind,* trans. T. O. Churchill (Chicago: University of Chicago Press, 1968); Wilhelm Dilthey, *Gesammelte Schriften,* 18 vols. (Stuttgart: B. G. Teubner, and Goøttingen: Vandenhoeck and Ruprecht, 1914–77); and, a step removed, in Edmund Burke, *Reflections on the Revolution in France,* ed. Conor Cruise O'Brien (Harmondsworth: Penguin, 1968). This tradition is most illuminatingly treated by Karl Mannheim, "Conservative Thought," in *Essays on Sociology and Social Psychology,* ed. Paul Kecskemeti (New York: Oxford University Press, 1953), and by Isaiah Berlin, "The Counter-Enlightenment," in *Against the Current,* ed. Henry Hardy (New York: Viking,

1980), and *Vico and Herder* (London: Hogarth, 1976). See also Michael Ear-marth, *Wilhelm Dilthey: The Critique of Historical Reason* (Chicago: University of Chicago Press, 1978).

[7] Contemporary works of pluralistic conservatism by and large coincide with those of skeptical conservatism, see note 4 above. For an account of pluralism in general, see John Kekes, *The Morality of Pluralism* (Princeton: Princeton University Press, 1993), and Nicholas Rescher, *Pluralism* (Oxford: Clarendon, 1993).

[8] For a general account of the political significance of human nature for politics, see Christopher J. Berry, *Human Nature* (London: Macmillan, 1986). For the specific connection between human nature and conservatism, see Christopher J. Berry, "Conservatism and Human Nature," *Politics and Human Nature*, ed. Ian Forbes and Steve Smith (London: Frances Pinter, 1983).

[9] Traditionalism is an expression that does not appear in any of the works listed below, but the position defended in them is very close to traditionalism so it is perhaps justified to claim affinity with them. See Francis Herbert Bradley, *Ethical Studies*, 2d ed. (Oxford: Clarendon, 1927), essays 5 and 6; John Kekes, *Moral Tradition and Individuality* (Princeton: Princeton University Press, 1989); Alasdair MacIntyre, *After Virtue* (Notre Dame: University of Notre Dame Press, 1981) and *Whose Justice? Which Rationality?* (Notre Dame: University of Notre Dame Press, 1988); Oakeshott, *On Human Conduct*, and Roger Scruton, *The Meaning of Conservatism* (Harmondsworth: Penguin, 1980).

[10] For an account of tradition in general, see Edward Shils, *Tradition* (Chicago: University of Chicago Press, 1981). See also John Casey, "Tradition and Authority," in *Conservative Essays*, ed. Maurice Cowling (London: Cassell, 1978); Thomas Stearns Eliot, "Tradition and the Individual Talent," *The Selected Prose of T.S. Eliot*, ed. Frank Kermode (New York: Farrar, Straus, and Giroux, 1975), and MacIntyre, *After Virtue*, chap. 15.

[11] By O'Sullivan, *Conservatism*, chap. 1 and Quinton, *The Politics of Imperfection*.

[12] This sort of pessimism may be found in the tragedies of Sophocles, especially in *Antigone*, Thucydides, *The Peloponnesian War*, Machiavelli, *The Prince* and *The Discourses*, Montaigne, *Essays*, Stephen, *Liberty, Equality, Fraternity*, Bradley, *Ethical Studies*, essay VII, and Santayana, *Dominations and Powers*. A recent statement of it is John Kekes, *Facing Evil* (Princeton: Princeton University Press, 1990).

Chapter 3: Approximating the Good

[1] For a much fuller account, see John Kekes, *Moral Wisdom and Good Lives* (Ithaca: Cornell University Press, 1995), especially chap. 2.

[2] For an illuminating account of the complexities of human nature as they bear on politics, see Christopher J. Berry, *Human Nature* (London: Macmillan, 1986). That any adequate political morality must recognize and protect primary goods is common ground among conservatives, liberals, Kantians, utilitarians, natural law theorists, and others. The list of primary goods is remarkably similar

in these views. See for instance Ronald Dworkin, "What is Equality?" *Philosophy and Public Affairs* 10 (1981), pp. 185–246 and 283–345; John Finnis, *Natural Law and Human Rights* (Oxford: Clarendon, 1980); James Griffin, *Well-Being* (Oxford: Clarendon, 1986); and John Rawls, *A Theory of Justice* (Cambridge: Harvard University Press, 1971).

Chapter 4: Avoiding Evil

[1] Georg F. W. Hegel, *Reason in History,* trans. by Robert S. Hartman (New York: Liberal Arts, 1953), p. 26.

[2] These complexities are discussed in Gerald Dworkin, *The Theory and Practice of Autonomy* (Cambridge: Cambridge University Press, 1988), especially chapters 1–3, and "Autonomy," in Robert E. Goodin and Philip Pettit, eds. *A Companion to Contemporary Political Philosophy* (Oxford: Blackwell, 1993). See also John Kekes, *Against Liberalism* (Ithaca: Cornell University Press, 1997).

[3] Hannah Arendt, *Eichmann in Jerusalem: A Report on the Banality of Evil* (New York: Viking, 1964).

[4] For a much fuller discussion of this question see Kekes, *Against Liberalism,* chapters 1, 7, and 9.

[5] John Rawls, *A Theory of Justice* (Cambridge: Harvard University Press, 1971), p. 245.

Chapter 5: The Enforcement of Morality

[1] Patrick Devlin, "Morals and the Criminal Law," in *The Enforcement of Morals* (London: Oxford University Press, 1968).

[2] Ronald Dworkin, "Liberty and Moralism," in *Taking Rights Seriously* (Cambridge: Harvard University Press, 1977); Herbert L. A. Hart, "Immorality and Treason," *The Listener,* July 1959, pp. 162–63, *Law, Liberty, and Morality* (Stanford: Stanford University Press, 1963), and "Social Solidarity and the Enforcement of Morals," in *Essays in Jurisprudence and Philosophy* (Oxford: Clarendon, 1983); Richard Wollheim, "Crime, Sin and Mr. Justice Devlin," *Encounter,* November 1959, pp. 34–40. For a survey of the controversy and a bibliography, see Basil Mitchell, *Law, Morality, and Religion in a Secular Society* (Oxford: Oxford University Press, 1970). See also Robert P. George, *Making Men Moral* (Oxford: Clarendon, 1993), chap. 2.

[3] Dworkin, "Liberty and Moralism," p. 246.

[4] Devlin, "Morals and the Criminal Law," pp. 13, 14, 15, 17.

[5] Hart, "Social Solidarity and the Enforcement of Morals," pp. 248–49.

[6] For another recent defense of the disintegration thesis, see George, *Making Men Moral.*

[7] For a discussion of disgust in general, see William Miller, *The Anatomy of Disgust* (Cambridge: Harvard University Press, 1996).

Chapter 6: Moral Tradition and Moral Identity

[1] Michael Oakeshott, *On Human Conduct* (Oxford: Clarendon, 1975), pp. 108–184.

[2] See Allan Gibbard, *Wise Choices, Apt Feelings* (Cambridge: Harvard University Press, 1990), chap. 4, for an illuminating discussion of the evolutionary significance of moral traditions.

[3] For similar lines of thought, see John Gray, "Agonistic Liberalism" in *Enlightenment's Wake* (London: Routledge, 1995), and Michael J. Sandel, *Liberalism and the Limits of Justice,* (Cambridge: Cambridge University Press, 1982), chap. 4.

[4] William David Ross, *The Right and the Good* (Oxford: Clarendon, 1930).

[5] Stuart Hampshire, "Two Theories of Morality" in *Morality and Conflict* (Cambridge: Harvard University Press, 1983), p. 14.

[6] Aristotle, *Nicomachean Ethics,* Book I.

[7] See George Sher, "Liberal Neutrality and the Value of Autonomy," *Social Philosophy and Policy* 12(1995), pp. 136–59, which reaches a similar conclusion by a different route.

[8] Irving Babbitt, *Rousseau and Romanticism* (New York: Meridian, 1955), pp. 157–58.

Chapter 7: Moral Authority

[1] E.g., Hannah Arendt, "What Is Authority?" in *Nomos I: Authority,* ed. by Carl J. Friedrich (Cambridge: Harvard University Press, 1958), and Carl J. Friedrich, *Tradition and Authority* (New York: Praeger, 1972).

[2] E.g., Robert P. Wolff, *In Defense of Anarchism* (New York: Harper and Row, 1970).

[3] E.g., Stanley I. Benn and Richard S. Peters, *Social Principles and the Democratic State* (London: Allen and Unwin, 1959), chap. 14; Richard E. Flathman, *The Practice of Political Authority* (Chicago: University of Chicago Press, 1980); Richard B. Friedman, "On the Concept of Authority in Political Philosophy," in *Concepts in Social and Political Philosophy,* ed. Richard E. Flathman (New York: Macmillan, 1973); and Joseph Raz, *The Morality of Freedom* (Oxford: Clarendon, 1986), chaps. 2–4.

[4] Wolff, *In Defense of Anarchism,* p. 18.

[5] Flathman, *The Practice of Political Authority,* p. 90.

[6] See Stanley I. Benn, "Authority," in *The Encyclopedia of Philosophy,* ed. Paul Edwards (New York: Macmillan, 1967); Steven Lukes, "Power and Authority" and "Perspectives on Authority" both in *Moral Conflicts and Politics* (Oxford:

Clarendon, 1991); Richard S. Peters, "Authority," *Proceedings of the Aristotelian Society,* supplementary volume 32(1958), pp. 207–20; Raz, *The Morality of Freedom,* chaps. 2–3.

[7] See Lukes, "Perspectives on Authority" and Peters, "Authority."

[8] Max Weber, *Economy and Society,* vols. 1–2, ed. and trans. by G. Roth and C. Willick (New York: Bedminster, 1968).

[9] See Lukes, "Power and Authority" and "Perspectives on Authority."

[10] Lukes, "Power and Authority," p. 92.

[11] See Friedrich, *Tradition and Authority.*

[12] One notable exception is Samuel Fleischacker, *The Ethics of Culture* (Ithaca: Cornell University Press, 1994). The present account is indebted to this work.

[13] The account is in Richard Wollheim, "The Sheep and the Ceremony" in *The Mind and Its Depths* (Cambridge: Harvard University Press, 1993), p. 1. Wollheim's account draws on Confucius, *Analects,* trans. with exegetical notes by James Legge (New York: Dover, 1971), bk. 3, chap. 17. It must be said that the text does not quite support Wollheim's interpretation, but that discrepancy may be ignored for the present purposes.

[14] For a fuller treatment, see John Kekes, *Moral Wisdom and Good Lives* (Ithaca: Cornell University Press, 1995).

[15] Peter F. Strawson, "Freedom and Resentment," in *Freedom and Resentment* (London: Methuen, 1974), p. 29.

[16] Plato, *The Republic* trans. by Robin Waterfield (Oxford: Oxford University Press, 1993), 514a-518c.

[17] Plato, *Republic,* 518a.

[18] See Peter Winch, "Authority," *Proceedings of the Aristotelian Society,* supplementary volume 32(1958), pp. 221–40.

[19] Gerald Dworkin, *The Theory and Practice of Autonomy* (Cambridge: Cambridge University Press, 1988), p. 32.

Chapter 8: The Ideal of Justice

[1] John Rawls, *A Theory of Justice* (Cambridge: Harvard University Press, 1971).

[2] Ibid., p. 5.

[3] Aristotle, *Nicomachean Ethics,* Book V.

[4] This account of desert draws on John Kekes, *Against Liberalism* (Ithaca: Cornell University Press, 1997), chap. 6, and it is indebted to Joel Feinberg, "Justice and Personal Desert," in *Nomos VI: Justice,* ed. by Carl J. Friedrich and John W. Chapman (New York: Atherton, 1963); William Galston, *Justice and the Human Good* (Chicago: University of Chicago Press, 1980); David Miller, *Social Justice* (Oxford: Clarendon, 1976); Michael J. Sandel, *Liberalism and the Limits of Justice* (Cambridge: Cambridge University Press, 1982); and especially to George Sher, *Desert* (Princeton: Princeton University Press, 1987).

[5] Rawls, *A Theory of Justice,* and *Political Liberalism* (New York: Columbia University Press, 1993).

6 See Kekes, *Against Liberalism,* chaps. 6–7.

7 Rawls, *A Theory of Justice,* pp. 310–11.

8 Rawls, *A Theory of Justice,* pp. 311–12.

9 Rawls, *A Theory of Justice,* pp. 100–102.

10 Rawls, *A Theory of Justice,* p. 27.

11 Rawls, *A Theory of Justice,* pp. 311–12.

12 Rawls, *A Theory of Justice,* pp. 100–101.

Works Cited

Allison, Lincoln. *Right Principles*. Oxford: Blackwell, 1984.

Arendt, Hannah. "What Is Authority?" In *Nomos I: Authority*. Edited by Carl J. Friedrich. Cambridge: Harvard University Press, 1958.

——. *Eichmann in Jerusalem: A Report on the Banality of Evil*. New York: Viking, 1964.

Aristotle. *Nicomachean Ethics*. Translated by W. D. Ross. In *The Complete Works of Aristotle*. Edited by Jonathan Barnes. Princeton: Princeton University Press, 1984.

——. *Politics*. Translated by Benjamin Jowett. In *The Complete Works of Aristotle*. Edited by Jonathan Barnes. Princeton: Princeton University Press, 1984.

——. *Rhetoric*. Translated by Rhys Roberts. In *The Complete Works of Aristotle*. Edited by Jonathan Barnes. Princeton: Princeton University Press, 1984.

Arrowsmith, William. "Introduction to *Hecuba*." In *The Complete Greek Tragedies: Euripides III*. Edited by David Grene and Richmond Lattimore. Chicago: University of Chicago Press, 1959.

Babbitt, Irving. *Rousseau and Romanticism*. New York: Meridian, 1955.

Bagehot, Walter. *The Collected Works of Walter Bagehot*. Edited by Norman St. John Stevas. London: The Economist, 1986.

Bellah, Robert, et al. *Habits of the Heart*. Berkeley: University of California Press, 1985.

Benn, Stanley I. "Authority." In *Encyclopedia of Philosophy*. Edited by Paul Edwards. New York: Macmillan, 1967.

Benn, Stanley I., and Richard S. Peters. *Social Principles and the Democratic State*. London: Allen and Unwin, 1959.

Berger, Peter L. *Facing Up to Modernity*. New York: Basic Books, 1977.

Berlin, Isaiah. *Vico and Herder*. London: Hogarth, 1976.

——. *Concepts and Categories*. Edited by Henry Hardy. London: Hogarth, 1978.

——. "The Counter-Enlightenment." In *Against the Current*. Edited by Henry Hardy. New York: Viking, 1980.

Berry, Christopher J. "Conservatism and Human Nature." In *Politics and Human Nature*. Edited by Ian Forbes and Steve Smith. London: Frances Pinter, 1983.

——. *Human Nature*. London: Macmillan, 1986.

231

Bloom, Allan. *The Closing of the American Mind.* New York: Simon and Schuster, 1987.

Boesche, Roger. *The Strange Liberalism of Alexis de Tocqueville.* Ithaca: Cornell University Press, 1987.

Bradley, Francis Herbert. *Ethical Studies.* 2d ed. Oxford: Clarendon, 1927.

Buckley, William F., Jr. *The Jeweler's Eye.* New York: Putnam, 1968.

——. *The Governor Listeth.* New York: Putnam 1970.

Burke, Edmund. *Reflections on the Revolution in France.* Edited by Conor Cruise O'Brien. Harmondsworth: Penguin, 1968.

Casey, John. "Tradition and Authority." In *Conservative Essays.* Edited by Maurice Cowling. London: Cassell, 1978.

Cecil, Hugh. *Conservatism.* London: Williams and Norgate, 1912.

Confucius. *The Analects.* Translated with exegetical notes by James Legge. New York: Dover, 1971.

Covell, Charles. *The Redefinition of Conservatism.* London: Macmillan, 1986.

Devigne, Robert. *Recasting Conservatism.* New Haven: Yale University Press, 1994.

Devlin, Patrick. "Morals and the Criminal Law." In *The Enforcement of Morals.* London: Oxford University Press, 1968.

Dilthey, Wilhelm. *Gesammelte Schriften.* 18 vols. Stuttgart: B. G. Teubner, and Gottingen: Vandenhoeck and Ruprecht, 1914–77.

Dunn, Charles W., and J. David Woodard. *The Conservative Tradition in America.* Lanham, Md.: Rowman and Littlefield, 1993.

Dworkin, Gerald. *The Theory and Practice of Autonomy.* Cambridge: Cambridge University Press, 1988.

——. "Autonomy." In *A Companion to Contemporary Political Philosophy.* Edited by Robert E. Goodin and Philip Pettit. Oxford: Blackwell, 1993.

Dworkin, Ronald. "Liberty and Moralism" in *Taking Rights Seriously.* Cambridge: Harvard University Press, 1977.

——. "What Is Equality?" *Philosophy and Public Affairs* 10 (1981), pp. 185–246 and 283–345.

Earmarth, Michael. *Wilhelm Dilthey: The Critique of Historical Reason.* Chicago: University of Chicago Press, 1978.

East, John P. *The American Conservative Movement.* Chicago: Regnery, 1986.

Eliot, Thomas Stearns. *The Complete Poems and Plays.* New York: Harcourt, Brace, 1971.

——. "Francis Herbert Bradley." *In The Selected Prose of T.S. Eliot .* Edited by Frank Kermode. New York: Farrar, Straus, and Giroux, 1975.

——. "Tradition and the Individual Talent." *In The Selected Prose of T. S. Eliot.*

Feinberg, Joel. "Justice and Personal Desert." In *Nomos VI: Justice.* Edited by Carl J. Friedrich and John W. Chapman. New York: Atherton, 1963.

Finnis, John. *Natural Law and Natural Rights.* Oxford: Clarendon, 1980.

——. *Fundamentals of Ethics.* Oxford: Clarendon, 1983.

Flathman, Richard E. *The Practice of Political Authority.* Chicago: University of Chicago Press, 1980.

Fleischacker, Samuel. *The Ethics of Culture*. Ithaca: Cornell University Press, 1994.

Friedman, Richard B. "On the Concept of Authority in Political Philosophy." In *Concepts in Social and Political Philosophy*. Edited by Richard E. Flathman. New York: Macmillan, 1973.

Friedrich, Carl J. *Tradition and Authority*. New York: Praeger, 1972.

Frohnen, Bruce. *Virtue and the Promise of Conservatism*. Lawrence: University Press of Kansas, 1993.

Fryer, Russell G. *Recent Conservative Political Thought*. Washington, D.C.: University Press of America, 1979.

Gadamer, Hans-Georg. *Truth and Method*. New York: Seabury, 1975.

Galston, William. *Justice and the Human Good*. Chicago: University of Chicago Press, 1980.

George, Robert P. *Making Men Moral*. Oxford: Clarendon, 1993.

Gibbard, Allan. *Wise Choices, Apt Feelings*. Cambridge: Harvard University Press, 1990.

Gray, John. *Liberalisms*. London: Routledge, 1989.

———. "George Santayana and the Critique of Liberalism." *The World and I*, February 1989, pp. 593–607.

———. *Post-liberalism*. New York: Routledge, 1993.

———. *Beyond the New Right*. London: Routledge, 1993.

———. "Agonistic Liberalism." In *Enlightenment's Wake*. London: Routledge, 1995.

Griffin, James. *Well-Being*. Oxford: Clarendon, 1986.

Grisez, Germain. *Beyond the New Morality*. Notre Dame: University of Notre Dame Press, 1988.

Hampshire, Stuart. *Morality and Conflict*. Cambridge: Harvard University Press, 1983.

———. *Innocence and Experience*. Cambridge: Harvard University Press, 1989.

Harbour, William R. *The Foundations of Conservative Thought*. Notre Dame: University of Notre Dame Press, 1982.

Hart, Herbert L. A. "Immorality and Treason." *The Listener*, July 1959, pp. 162–63.

———. *Law, Liberty, and Morality*. Stanford: Stanford University Press, 1963.

———. Social Solidarity and the Enforcement of Morals." In *Essays in Jurisprudence and Philosophy*. Oxford: Clarendon, 1983.

Hayek, Friedrich A. *The Constitution of Liberty*. Chicago: Regnery, 1960.

Hegel, Georg W. F. *The Philosophy of Right*. Translated by T. M. Knox. Oxford: Oxford University Press, 1952.

———. *Reason in History*. Translated by Robert S. Hartman. New York: Liberal Arts, 1953.

Herder, Johann Gottfried von. *Reflections on the Philosophy of History of Mankind*. Translated by T. O. Churchill. Chicago: University of Chicago Press, 1968.

Hobbes, Thomas. *Leviathan*. London: Dent, 1962.

Hogg, Quentin. *The Conservative Case*. Rev. ed. Harmondsworth: Penguin, 1959.

Holmes, Stephen. *The Anatomy of Antiliberalism*. Cambridge: Harvard University Press, 1993.

Honderich, Ted. *Conservatism*. Boulder, Colo.: Westview Press, 1990.

Hume, David. *A Treatise of Human Nature.* Edited by L. A. Selby-Bigge. Oxford: Clarendon Press, 1960.

——. *An Enquiry Concerning the Principles of Morals.* Edited by L. A. Selby-Bigge. Oxford: Clarendon Press, 1961.

——. *The History of England,* 6 vol. Indianapolis: Liberty Press, 1983.

——. *Essays Moral, Political, and Literary.* Edited by Eugene F. Miller. Indianapolis: Liberty Press, 1985.

Kahan, Alan S. *Aristocratic Liberalism.* New York: Oxford University Press, 1986.

Kekes, John. *Moral Tradition and Individuality.* Princeton: Princeton University Press, 1989.

——. *Facing Evil.* Princeton: Princeton University Press, 1990.

——. *The Examined Life.* University Park: Penn State Press, 1992.

——. *The Morality of Pluralism.* Princeton: Princeton University Press, 1993.

——. *Moral Wisdom and Good Lives.* Ithaca: Cornell University Press, 1995.

——. *Against Liberalism.* Ithaca: Cornell University Press, 1997.

Kendall, Willmoore. *The Conservative Affirmation in America.* Chicago: Gateway, 1985.

Kirk, Russell. *The Conservative Mind.* 6th rev. ed. South Bend, Ind.: Gateway, 1978.

——, ed. *The Conservative Reader.* Harmondsworth: Penguin, 1982.

Kissinger, Henry. *A World Restored.* Boston: Houghton Mifflin, 1957.

Klemperer, Klemens von. *Germany's New Conservatism.* Princeton: Princeton University Press, 1957.

Larmore, Charles E. *Patterns of Moral Complexity.* Cambridge: Cambridge University Press, 1987.

Letwin, Shirley Robin. *The Pursuit of Certainty.* Cambridge: Cambridge University Press, 1965.

——. *The Gentleman in Trollope.* Cambridge: Harvard University Press, 1982.

Livingston, Donald W. *Hume's Philosophy of Common Life.* Chicago: University of Chicago Press, 1984.

Lovejoy, Arthur O. *The Great Chain of Being.* New York: Harper and Row, 1960.

Lukes, Steven. *Moral Conflicts and Politics.* Oxford: Clarendon, 1991.

Machiavelli, Niccolo. *The Discourses.* Translated by Leslie J. Walker, revised by Brian Richardson. Harmondsworth: Penguin, 1970.

——. *The Prince.* In *Selected Political Writings.* Edited and translated by David Wootten. Indianapolis: Hackett, 1994.

MacIntyre, Alasdair. *After Virtue.* Notre Dame: University of Notre Dame Press, 1981.

——. *Whose Justice? Which Rationality?* Notre Dame: University of Notre Dame Press, 1988.

Mannheim, Karl. "Conservative Thought" in *Essays on Sociology and Social Psychology.* Edited by Paul Kecskemeti. New York: Oxford University Press, 1953.

Miller, David. *Social Justice.* Oxford: Clarendon, 1976.

Miller, William. *The Anatomy of Disgust.* Cambridge: Harvard University Press, 1996.

Milosz, Czeslaw. *The Captive Mind*. Translated by Jane Zielonko. Harmondsworth: Penguin, 1980.

Minogue, Kenneth. "Conservatism." In *Encyclopedia of Philosophy*. Edited by Paul Edwards. New York: Macmillan, 1967.

——, ed. *Conservative Realism*. London: HarperCollins, 1996.

Mitchell, Basil. *Law, Morality and Religion in a Secular Society*. Oxford: Oxford University Press, 1970.

Montaigne, Michel de. *Essays*. In *The Complete Works of Montaigne*. Translated by Donald M. Frame. Stanford: Stanford University Press, 1958.

Muller, Jerry Z., ed. *Conservatism*. Princeton: Princeton University Press, 1997.

Nash, George H. *The Conservative Intellectual Movement in America*. New York: Basic Books, 1976.

Nisbet, Robert. *Conservatism*. Minneapolis: University of Minnesota Press, 1986.

Nyiri, J. C. "Wittgenstein's Later Work in Relation to Conservatism." In *Wittgenstein and His Times*. Edited by Brian McGuinness. Oxford: Blackwell, 1982.

Oakeshott, Michael. *Hobbes on Civil Association*. Oxford: Blackwell, 1974.

——. *On Human Conduct*. Oxford: Clarendon, 1975.

——. *Rationalism in Politics*. Edited by Timothy Fuller. Indianapolis: Liberty Press, 1991.

——. *Religion, Politics and the Moral Life*. Edited by Timothy Fuller. New Haven: Yale University Press, 1993.

——. *The Politics of Faith and the Politics of Scepticism*. Edited by Timothy Fuller. New Haven: Yale University Press, 1996.

O'Hear, Anthony. "Conservatism." In *The Oxford Companion to Philosophy*. Edited by Ted Honderich. Oxford: Oxford University Press, 1995.

O'Sullivan, Noel. *Conservatism*. New York: St. Martin's Press, 1976.

Peters, Richard S. "Authority." *Proceedings of the Aristotelian Society,* Supplementary volume 32(1958), pp. 207–20.

Plato. *The Republic*. Translated by Robin Waterfield. Oxford: Oxford University Press, 1993.

Quinton, Anthony. *The Politics of Imperfection*. London: Faber and Faber, 1978.

——. "Conservatism." In *A Companion to Contemporary Political Philosophy*. Edited by Robert E. Goodin and Philip Pettit. Oxford: Blackwell, 1993.

Rawls, John. *A Theory of Justice*. Cambridge: Harvard University Press, 1971.

——. *Political Liberalism*. New York: Columbia University Press, 1993.

Raz, Joseph. *The Morality of Freedom*. Oxford: Clarendon, 1986.

Rescher, Nicholas. *Pluralism*. Oxford: Clarendon, 1993.

Ross, William David. *The Right and the Good*. Oxford: Clarendon, 1930.

Rossiter, Clinton. *Conservatism in America*. 2d rev. ed. Cambridge: Harvard University Press, 1982.

Sandel, Michael. *Liberalism and the Limits of Justice*. Cambridge: Harvard University Press, 1982.

Santayana, George. *Dominations and Powers*. New York: Scribner's, 1951.

Scruton, Roger. *The Meaning of Conservatism*. Harmondsworth: Penguin, 1980.

———, ed. *Conservative Texts*. New York: St. Martin's Press, 1991.

Sher, George. *Desert*. Princeton: Princeton University Press, 1987.

———. "Liberal Neutrality and the Value of Autonomy." *Social Philosophy and Policy* 12(1995), pp. 136–59.

Shils, Edward. *Tradition*. Chicago: University of Chicago Press, 1981.

Sophocles. *The Complete Greek Tragedies: Sophocles I-II*. Edited by David Grene and Richmond Lattimore. Chicago: University of Chicago Press, 1969.

Stephen, James Fitzjames. *Liberty, Equality, Fraternity*. Cambridge: Cambridge University Press, 1967.

Strawson, Peter F. *Freedom and Resentment*. London: Methuen, 1974.

Tannsjo, Torbjorn. *Conservatism for Our Time*. London: Routledge, 1990.

Thucydides. *The Peloponnesian War*. Translated by Rex Warner. Harmondsworth: Penguin, 1954.

Tocqueville, Alexis de. *The Old Regime and the French Revolution*. Translated by Stuart Gilbert. New York: Doubleday, 1955.

———. *Democracy in America*. Translated by Henry Reeve. New York: Schocken, 1970.

Veatch, Henry. *Human Rights*. Baton Rouge: Louisana State University Press, 1985.

Vico, Giambattista. *New Science*. Translated by Thomas Goddard Bergin and Max Harold Fisch. Ithaca: Cornell University Press, 1970.

Viereck, Peter. *Conservatism Revisited*. New York: Scribner's, 1949.

Vierhaus, Rudolf. "Conservatism." In *Dictionary of the History of Ideas*. Edited by Philip P. Wiener. New York: Scribner's, 1968.

Voegelin, Eric. *Order in History*. 5 vols. Baton Rouge: Louisiana State University Press, 1954–87.

Weber, Max. *Economy and Society*. Volumes 1–2. Edited and translated by G. Roth and C. Willich. New York: Bedminster, 1968.

Will, George F. *Statecraft as Soulcraft*. New York: Simon and Schuster, 1983.

Willets, David. *Modern Conservatism*. Harmondsworth: Penguin, 1992.

Wilson, Francis Graham. *The Case for Conservatism*. Seattle: University of Washington Press, 1951.

Winch, Peter. "Authority," *Proceedings of the Aristotelian Society*, Supplementary volume 32 (1958), pp. 221–40.

Wittgenstein, Ludwig. *Philosophical Investigations*. Translated by G. E. M. Anscombe. Oxford: Blackwell, 1968.

———*On Certainty*. Translated by Dennis Paul and G. E. M. Anscombe. Oxford: Blackwell, 1969.

Wolff, Robert. *In Defense of Anarchism*. New York: Harper and Row, 1970.

Wolin, Sheldon S. "Hume and Conservatism." *American Political Science Review* 98 (1954), pp. 999–1016.

Wollheim, Richard. "Crime, Sin and Mr. Justice Devlin." *Encounter*, November 1959, pp. 34–40.

———. *The Mind and Its Depths*. Cambridge: Harvard University Press, 1993.

Index

237